EMBRACING SEXUALITY

Over the past few decades our experience and understanding of human sexuality has changed remarkably. The women's movement, the gay rights movement, and a growing social tolerance for diverse lifestyles - the landscape in which we view human sexuality - has been greatly altered. Cohabitation, experimental relationships, and remarriage after divorce are all practices that scandalize our grandparents but seem normal to our children. Yet, the mainstream Christian Churches appear to have been little more than bystanders in the midst of this revolution. Roman Catholic teaching on sexual and marital morality has not substantially changed since 1968, the date of Paul VI's encyclical on contraception, *Humanae Vitae*.

This book represents an attempt to initiate a meaningful conversation between the institutional Church and the laity about some of the fundamental and concrete issues involving human sexuality and relationships. Drawing upon both their professional expertise and their personal experience, eleven authors invite the hierarchy and the whole community of the Church to reconsider their understanding and appreciation for this vital dimension of human existence. The first part of the book suggests three different ways to approach the understanding of human sexuality, in terms of relationship, spirituality and our bodily existence. Part two examines three critical but frequently neglected experiences of sexuality, that of women, of young persons and of the homosexual community. Part three takes account of how human sexuality has been evaluated in the eyes of the Christian Churches; and part four considers how the Churches might 'embrace' human sexuality in a manner that speaks to contemporary women and men in the context of their lived experience.

Embracing Sexuality

Authority and experience in the Catholic Church

Edited by
JOSEPH A. SELLING
Katholieke Universiteit Leuven

Routledge
Taylor & Francis Group
LONDON AND NEW YORK

First published 2001 by Ashgate Publishing

Reissued 2018 by Routledge
2 Park Square, Milton Park, Abingdon, Oxon OX14 4RN
711 Third Avenue, New York, NY 10017, USA

Routledge is an imprint of the Taylor & Francis Group, an informa business

Publisher's Note
The publisher has gone to great lengths to ensure the quality of this reprint but points out that some imperfections in the original copies may be apparent.

Disclaimer
The publisher has made every effort to trace copyright holders and welcomes correspondence from those they have been unable to contact.

A Library of Congress record exists under LC control number: 2001087675

ISBN 13: 978-1-138-70473-2 (hbk)
ISBN 13: 978-1-315-20254-9 (ebk)

Contents

PART IV: EMBRACING SEXUALITY

Foreword

This collection of essays had its origin in two seminars that took place at Sarum College, Salisbury, in December 1999 and March 2000. The Sarum Seminars came into being as part of a larger project in Great Britain dedicated to "Authority and Governance in the Church". That project began in 1997 under the auspices of the Research Centre of The Queens Foundation for Ecumenical Theological Education in Birmingham. The theme of this undertaking was to move "from confrontation to conversation" and represented an attempt at open dialogue between representatives of the governing structures of the Church and the faithful on a wide range of issues.

After the renewal of the Second Vatican Council, many people felt that an openness had been created within which a new style of collaboration would take place and all the members of the faithful would be able to participate. Within a relatively short time after the council, however, many felt that the hopes for a new sense of collaboration and consultation were not being realised. An increasing number of issues appeared to be dealt with in a manner that resembled the pre-conciliar period. Not a few observers have speculated that this course of events began in 1968, with the promulgation of Paul VI's encyclical on the regulation of fertility, *Humanae Vitae*.

In the time since the council, however, many more issues have surfaced in just about every area of social and private life. Two factors seem to have played an important role in this, namely, the accelerating advances made in the sciences, especially medicine and communications, and the rapidly changing customs and mores which, at least in part, have been the result of those advances. Although a number of important issues facing the Church today are of an explicitly ethical nature, many more issues have surfaced, ranging from disciplinary practices to policy positions, all of which would appear to benefit from the input, the experience and the expertise of the ordinary members of the community. And yet, most of the faithful feel that they rarely if ever have an opportunity to collaborate in the decision and policy-making processes of the Church to which they belong.

The parent project on "Authority and Governance" stimulated a number of sub-projects, one of which was dedicated to exploring the areas of human relationships and human sexuality in regard to Church teaching. A group of laypersons, including representatives of the sponsoring organisations and experts in the field of inquiry, came together in February 1999 to discuss the possibilities for the sub-project. The authorities at Sarum College graciously offered the use of their facilities for this and the subsequent meetings of the seminars.

The first task of the preparatory group was to determine the goal of the seminars and to outline a procedural and topical approach. In the spirit of moving from "confrontation to conversation", it was felt that it was best to avoid any polemics or direct dispute with well known positions of the magisterium of the Church on issues related to relational and sexual morality. For that reason, there would be no systematic presentations of those current positions. It was also felt that the current teachings of the magisterium were well enough known not to need repetition. In many ways, it was the generally widespread knowledge of these positions that formed the basis for the need for a "conversation" in the first place. For these positions had been formulated in such a way that they did not adequately reflect the experience and understanding of the issues on the part of the faithful.

The members of the preparatory group shared the conviction that while most adult Christians accept sexuality as a "normal" part of life, most of the traditional teaching of the Church seemed to be based upon an exaggerated sense of danger, even fear, with respect to sexual matters. They believed that the greatest single step forward that could be made in renewing relational and sexual morality would be simply to approach these aspects of human life in a positive manner, as primarily in service to human relationships. Human sexuality, in and of itself, needed to be accepted, appreciated and celebrated by the Church as a gift of God and an occasion of grace.

If Vatican II could describe marriage as an occasion for mutual sanctification, then sexual relations should be characterised as participating in that sanctification. If all human relations can in one way or another be characterised as "sexual", because all human persons participate in the experience of being-a-woman or being-a-man in the world with others, then sexuality itself is not simply something good, it is an intimate part of what it means to be a human person and must therefore be attended to in all our relations.

Because the traditional view of human sexuality in the Church was largely negative and suspect, it was suggested that the way forward in this area would need to be positive and appreciative. The Church needs not only to "accept" human sexuality but actively to "embrace" it. To accomplish this, more and perhaps "new" information is needed in order to construct an alternative perception. In the spirit of "conversation", then, the Sarum seminars were aimed at bringing together people who might be able and willing to bring forth this information, based upon their knowledge and experience of human (sexual) relationships.

The essays in this book have been arranged thematically into four parts. In the first part an attempt is made to review our understanding of human sexuality from various perspectives. Jack Dominian brings more than forty years of his psychiatric experience working with couples and individuals to the fore in order to describe the role of sexuality in interpersonal encounter. Philip Sheldrake investigates the relation between spirituality and sexuality, while Maaike de Haardt offers a reflection upon the renewed appreciation for the corporeal dimensions of sacramentality which naturally has a bearing upon our understanding of sexuality as well.

Part two takes up what many feel have been three largely neglected areas of the experience of sexuality, especially in regard to the Church's understanding and teaching. Mary Grey introduces us to the female experience of sexuality and Anna Roper attempts to lead us through a young person's experience, against the background of contemporary Western culture. Elizabeth Stuart sets out an understanding of homosexual experience viewed in the context of friendship.

The third part of this collection then turns to the issue of speaking ethically about human sexuality, specifically from a Christian point of view. James O'Connell first gives an overview of the problems involved in formulating a policy of sexual ethics against the background of the Church's more comprehensive understanding of "freedom and the law" in the light of the Gospel's call for a "law of love". Adrian Thatcher presents a synopsis of teaching about human sexuality in the Protestant tradition by using the example of three Church governing bodies attempting to issue statements about the topic. Joseph Selling looks to the future and suggests a way forward in the renewal of our sexual ethics.

Part four of the collection goes slightly beyond the presentations given at Sarum, first by including Lisa Sowle Cahill's response to the papers presented. Having read all the papers and responses, she provides us not only with a general reflection but also with an American perspective on contemporary sexual mores. Marcella Sires, who presented a workshop at Sarum on communication, concentrates her written reflections upon the problem of how any "conversation" at all might be carried on between an institution and the members of that institution. Finally, Mary Grey and Joseph Selling present an overview of the discussions that took place at Sarum and the subsequent report that was made to the parent project on "Authority and Governance".

J. Selling
September, 2000

Contributors

Lisa Sowle Cahill is J. Donald Monan Professor of Theology at Boston College, Chestnut Hill MA. She is past president of the Catholic Theological Society of America and the author of several monographs and articles, including *Sex, Gender & Christian Ethics* (Cambridge University Press, 1996) and *Family: A Christian Social Perspective* (Fortress, 2000).

Jack Dominian is a Catholic Christian psychiatrist who has worked, studied, lectured and written extensively on marital relationships, for more than forty years. He is founder of One Plus One, a marriage and partnership research institute located in London. His books include *Passionate and Compassionate* (Darton, Longman & Todd, 1991), *Proposals for a New Sexual Ethic* (Darton, Longman & Todd, 1977), and *Let's Make Love* (to be published in 2001).

Mary Grey is Scholar-in-residence at Sarum College, Salisbury and D.J. James Professor of Pastoral Theology, University of Wales, Lampeter. Her publications include: *Redeeming the Dream* (SPCK, 1989), *Prophecy and Mysticism: The Heart of the Postmodern Church* (T. & T. Clarke, 1997) and *The Outrageous Pursuit of Hope* (Darton, Longman and Todd, 2000). She and her husband, Dr Nicholas Grey, are co-founders of the NGO Wells for India, working with desert communities in Rajasthan.

Maaike de Haardt is Catharina Halkes Professor for Feminism and Christianity at the Catholic University of Nijmegen and senior lecturer in Women Studies in Theology at the Catholic University of Brabant. Her publications include *Dichter bij de dood* (1993, *Nearer to Death. Toward a Feminist Theology of Death*) and a co-edited monograph, *Begin with the Body. Corporeality, Religion and Gender* (Peeters, 1998).

James O'Connell is emeritus Professor of Peace Studies at the University of Bradford. He has taught politics and philosophy in Britain, Nigeria and the U.S.A. He has written on African politics, ethnic conflict and conflict resolution as well as on philosophy and theology.

Anna Roper graduated in Social and Political Science from Cambridge and holds an M.A. in Pastoral Studies (Theology) from Heythrop College. She has worked as a teacher in regular as well as special education and has experience as a lay chaplain and director of pastoral care.

Joseph Selling is Professor of Moral Theology at the Katholieke Universiteit Leuven, Belgium. An American citizen, he has been living in Belgium since 1972. His interests and principal areas of publication are in fundamental Christian ethics and sexual and conjugal morality.

Philip Sheldrake is Vice-Principal and Academic Director at Sarum College, Salisbury and Honorary Professor in the Department of Theology and Religious Studies at the University of Wales, Lampeter. He was the Hulsean Lecturer at the University of Cambridge during 1999-2000 and is regularly a Visiting Professor at the University of Notre Dame. Philip Sheldrake has written widely on spirituality both from the standpoint of academic theology and for a more general readership.

Marcella Sires is a sexologist and a psychotherapist specialising in systems therapy and communication techniques. She holds degrees in Philosophy as well as in Family and Sexual sciences. Besides working as a counsellor for an international university, she has a private practice in Brussels, and does consulting work for several multinational corporations.

Elizabeth Stuart is Professor of Christian Theology and Director of the Centre for the Study of Theology and Religion at King Alfred's College, Winchester. She is executive editor of the academic journal *Theology and Sexuality* and author of a number of books on sexuality written from a lesbian and gay perspective including *Just Good Friends: Towards a Theology of Lesbian and Gay Relationships* (Mowbray, 1995) and *Religion is a Queer Thing* (Cassell, 1998).

Adrian Thatcher has been Professor of Applied Theology at The College of St. Mark and St. John, Plymouth, since 1995. Ordained a Baptist minister, he has been a theology teacher since 1974. He became an Anglican in 1988. His most recent book is *Marriage After Modernity: Christian Marriage in Postmodern Times* (Sheffield Academic Press, 1999).

PART I

UNDERSTANDING SEXUALITY

Chapter One

Sexuality and Interpersonal Relationships

Jack Dominian

Nowadays we associate sexual intercourse with love and understand it as an expression of love. What we take for granted today has a long and tortuous history in which love was not emphasised. Rather up to our own day it was procreation that was considered its primary purpose and the Church agonised over its pleasurable aspects. The long story of how Christianity found its way from understanding sexual intercourse as procreation to love deserves a book, but at the beginning of this article I will attempt a brief history of its development.

A Short History of Christianity and Sexuality

We trace this history from the first two chapters in *Genesis* where we find two accounts of creation. The second one, known as the Yahwistic, is the older of the two, dating from about the tenth century BC.

> Yahweh God said, "It is not right that the man should be alone. I shall make him a helper." So from the soil Yahweh God fashioned all the wild animals and all the birds of heaven. These he brought to the man to see what he would call them; each one was to bear the name the man would give it. The man gave names to all the cattle, all the birds of heaven and all the wild animals. But no helper suitable for the man was found for him. Then, Yahweh God made the man fall into a deep sleep. And, while he was asleep, he took one of his ribs and closed the flesh up again forthwith. Yahweh God fashioned the rib he had taken from the man into a woman, and brought her to the man. And the man said: "This one at last is bone of my bones and flesh of my flesh! She is to be called Woman, because she was taken from the Man." This is why a man leaves his father and mother and becomes attached to his wife and they become one flesh. Now, both of them were naked, the man and his wife, but they felt no shame before each other. (Gen 2:18-25)

There are several points to be made about this passage. First, the earliest commentary about creation points to the relational nature of the communion between man and woman. Secondly, the man and woman are treated as equals. Thirdly, in his extensive treatment of this passage, the present pope, John Paul II, refers to the nuptial nature of the body. It was created for sexual communion.[1] Fourthly, in its pristine created state the couple were naked and unashamed of their nakedness. Fifthly, sexual intercourse or being one flesh were situated within marriage. The modern emphasis on sexual intercourse as being the heart of the relationship of the married couple is based on a theologically sound basis, emanating from the scriptures.

The first passage of Genesis, which is actually the later of the two emphasises the procreational element of sexual intercourse.

> God said, "Let the earth produce every kind of living creature in its own species: cattle, creeping things and wild animals of all kinds." And so it was. God made wild animals in their own species, and cattle in theirs, and every creature that crawls along the earth in its own species. God saw that it was good.
>
> God said, "Let us make man in our own image, in the likeness of ourselves and let them be masters of the fish of the sea, the birds of heaven, the cattle, all the wild animals and all the creatures that creep along the ground." God created man in the image of himself, in the image of God he created him, male and female he created them.
>
> God blessed them, saying to them, "Be fruitful, multiply, fill the earth and subdue it, be masters of the fish of the sea, the birds of heaven and all the living creatures that move on earth." God also said, "Look, to you I give all the seed-bearing plants everywhere on the surface of the earth, and all the trees with seed-bearing fruit; this will be your food. And to all the wild animals, all the birds of heaven and all the living creatures that creep along the ground, I give all the foliage of the plants as their food." And so it was. God saw all he had made, and indeed it was very good. (Gen 1:26-31)

In this passage the emphasis is on procreation, an interpretation of sexual intercourse which was to assume its prominent meaning until our day. What is often forgotten is that in this passage we find the concept that God found good all that he had made, indeed, not only good but "very good". The centuries of pessimism about the value of sexual intercourse are really neutralised by this fundamental understanding of the goodness of coitus.

The New Testament has very little to say directly about sexual intercourse. Indirectly, we note the virginity of the mother of Jesus (Lk 1:27), his own, single state and the new idea of the goodness of the single state dedicated to God (Mt 19:10-12). Although Jesus remained single, he was clearly in favour of marriage, as he carried out his first miracle at the feast of Cana (Jn 2:1-12). The fullest account of sexual teaching is to be found in Paul, in his first letter to the Corinthians. Here he supports marriage and sexual intercourse between spouses, but he clearly identified himself with the single state (1 Cor 7:1-40).

Thus, we open the Christian era with the Judaic tradition in which marriage and sexual intercourse are firmly established and valued. This is in no way altered by Jesus or Paul. However, the fact that they both put forth the single state dedicated to God as an ideal has had a lasting effect on Christianity. Henceforth, Christianity would witness to an acceptance of marriage goodness of sex for procreative purposes, but it would also demonstrate a proclivity for the single state.

From the Greek world surrounding it, Christianity was also influenced by a Stoic philosophy which considered that what was best for the body was a strict control of the emotions which led to *apatheia*. In Stoicism the mature person had all his or her emotions under strict control and was indifferent to them. Stoic thought undoubtedly influenced the early Fathers of the Church. The next five centuries saw some of the giants of Christianity. The Greek and Latin Fathers exhibit negative interpretations of sexuality and sexual intercourse in particular.[2]

We start with Tertullian, who, in the second century, proclaimed that continence brings down the gift of the Holy Spirit. If sanctity was not be obtained through martyrdom, then continence was the next best thing. Tertullian appears to be the first to make this important statement, which had long influence in the Latin world, namely that abstinence from sex was the most effective way to achieve clarity of the soul. Tertullian and the other fathers enunciated the theology. The practice was taken up by the members of several Christian communities who renounced married life.

Clement of Alexandria did not preach the renunciation of intercourse but was a wholehearted supporter of Stoicism with its strict control over the emotions. He also believed in a strict control over sexuality, which meant the avoidance of frequent intercourse or the use of various positions which would maximise pleasure.

Origen, in the beginning of the third century, considered sexuality as a mere passing phase. He put his belief into practice and castrated himself. For him, virginity stood for the original state and reflected the purity of the soul. Sexual intercourse coarsened the spirit.

By 303 AD, the Council of Elvira declared: "bishops, priests, deacons and all members of the clergy connected with the liturgy must abstain from their wives and must not beget sons".[3]

John Chrystostom, the most gifted preacher of his age, believed that marriage was a superfluity rendered necessary only by the fall of Adam. For Ambrose, the body was a peril that might engulf the soul. Every human being bore an ugly scar and that scar was sexuality. He saw continence as the answer. During the same fourth century, we encounter Jerome, who was an ardent apostle of virginity. Jerome was the heir of Origen and he communicated vividly the awareness of the sexual dangers of the body.

The last father to be considered is Augustine, the greatest of them all.[4] Augustine knew from extensive personal experience that sexual intercourse had a deep connection with pleasure. He was a very sexual person and in the famous words written in his *Confessions* he says, "Lord, give me chastity and continence, but not now".[5] Augustine held a contemporary minority view in believing that there would have been sexual intercourse between Adam and Eve. But his preoccupation centred around original sin. He believed that original sin lead to the loss of an effective ordering of man's passions, leading to concupiscence. He associated concupiscence with sexual intercourse and the transmission of original sin with coitus. Thus, sexual intercourse was always accompanied by sin. If the motivation was procreation, the sinfulness was removed. But for any other purpose, intercourse remained at least venially sinful.

With Augustine we reach the pinnacle of early Christian pessimism about sexuality. The Church was not to follow Augustine in his sexual theology absolutely, although he had a powerful effect on the theology of marriage. The devaluation of one of God's most precious gifts started in the early Christian centuries and produced a massive distortion of the goodness of sex. Although in subsequent centuries modifications were made, the pessimism remained.

The middle ages saw a mixture of the rigorism of Augustine with a softening of attitudes. Thomas Aquinas proposed that the primary end of intercourse is procreation and he admitted that pleasure was attached to this act. Although at the height of this pleasure the man lost control of his will, the right motivation toward procreation made the pleasure legitimate. Nevertheless, Aquinas remained ambivalent about the act, which he considered as inferior matter.[6]

Noonan writes that a new theory of sexuality emerged with Martin le Maitre in the fifteenth century at the University of Paris. Le Maitre swept away the Augustinian understanding of sexual intercourse and asserted that coitus is legitimate for repayment of the marital debt, or for the avoidance of fornication. This constituted a new approach, seeking bodily health and the calming of the mind. He advanced the totally new position that sexual pleasure can be experienced firstly for its own sake and secondly to avoid tedium and the ache of melancholy. These views were radical for their period and consequently have had to wait until modern times to find wide acceptance.

The Reformation produced a major change when Luther and other reformers allowed the marriage of the clergy. Nevertheless Luther was steeped in Augustinian thought on sexuality and saw human beings ravaged by concupiscence. For him, marriage was a hospital for the sick. Although Luther permitted the marriage of clergy, this was a pragmatic step, a concession to human needs. It was not the result of a detailed analysis of the experience of sexual intercourse which remained surrounded with question marks.[7] The reformers denied the sacramental nature of marriage, and the Council of Trent reaffirmed it. This Council expressed for the first time the teaching that husbands are to love their wives as Christ loved the Church, echoing Paul, but there was no connection between this love and sexual intercourse.

For the next three centuries there was no great advance in the theology of marriage or of sexual intercourse. At the beginning of the seventeenth century Frances of Sales advanced the idea of the goodness and holiness of sexual intercourse in his *Introduction to the Devout Life* for married couples.[8]

The eighteenth and nineteenth centuries saw the development of medical science. In the nineteenth century, the graffian follicle in the ovary was identified and the crucial role of the woman in fertilisation was finally understood. This closed a long chapter in which life was believed to be transmitted by the male seed alone.

Inevitably, with the improvement of medical care, the rate of infant mortality was reduced and the question of family size came into focus. As far as the Catholic Church was concerned, this was associated with the use of contraception. Noonan's book deals with the history of contraception in the Catholic Church quite extensively.

In modern times, Leo XIII, in his encyclical *Arcanum Divinae* in 1880, emphasised that marriage is not only for children but also for the welfare of the spouses. Since this encyclical, the importance of the spouses has come into prominence, but there is no advance in the understanding or evaluation of sexual intercourse.

Then, in 1930, the Anglican Church approved artificial contraception. This received an immediate reply in *Casti Connubii* which reasserted the condemnation of contraception. Pius XI, continuing the trend of Leo XIII, emphasised the importance of love in the interior formation of husband and wife.

In the 1940's and 1950's the Catholic Church was preoccupied with the arguments whether marriage could be defined in terms of primary and secondary ends as stated in the canon law of 1917/18, or whether there was something bigger which characterised the sacrament. I traced this debate in my first book on marriage[9] and included in that documentation the important view of H. Doms.[10] For Doms, marriage was the "fulfilment of love in the community of life of two persons who make one person". "This inner meaning of marriage includes the performance of the sexual act, although it has no conscious interest in procreation..."

Finally, the Second Vatican Council jettisoned the language of primary and secondary ends and characterised marriage and the family a "community of love".[11] After nearly 2000 years, the Church came to see marriage as a community of love. The few pages of the documents of Vatican II on marriage and the family have an unprecedented richness which have yet to be explored.

More specifically on sexual intercourse, the Council states, "this love is uniquely expressed and perfected through the marital act. The actions within marriage by which the couple are united intimately and chastely are noble and worthy ones. Expressed in a manner which is truly human, these actions signify and promote mutual self giving by which spouses enrich each other with a joyful and a thankful will".[12]

After the council, Paul VI promulgated the encyclical *Humanae vitae* in 1968, in which the ban on contraception was reiterated and every act of intercourse was said to have a procreative and a unitive meaning. I do not wish to examine the controversy surrounding this encyclical.[13] What is absolutely certain, however, is that the controversy over *Humanae vitae* and the fear of disagreeing with the official teaching of the church have led to a silence of exploring the meaning of sexual intercourse and the riches that were opened by the second Vatican Council but remain unexplored.

Over the last 30 years I have been exploring the meaning of love and sexual intercourse in my research[14] and in this article I would like to outline briefly my findings.

The Biology and Psychology of Sexual Intercourse

I shall begin by outlining the biology and psychology of sexual intercourse. Before coitus takes place, there is sexual attraction and sexual desire. Generations of Catholics were haunted by the belief that sexual thoughts were sinful and, in the days when confession was fashionable, much of the content of confession was taken up with sexual matters. Nowadays, we appreciate that we are sexual beings and that sexual thoughts are the natural product of that state. It is normal and moral to have sexual feelings. But it is more than that. It is part of God's design for humanity. Sexuality is a human channel for the divine and we find this in the Hebrew scriptures in the *Song of Songs*. These few pages describe in poetic form the sexual and love feelings of a man and woman. They anticipate by thousands of years the erotic literature of our day.

> Beloved: "Let him kiss me with the kisses of his mouth, / for your love-making is sweeter than wine; / delicate is the fragrance of your perfume, / your name is an oil poured out, / and that is why girls love you." (1:1-3)

> Duo: "As a lily among the thistles / so is my beloved among girls." (2:2)
>
> Beloved: "On my bed at night I sought / the man who is my sweetheart." (3:1)
>
> Lover: "How beautiful you are, my beloved / How beautiful you are!/ Your eyes are doves, / behind your veil; / your hair is like a flock of goats / surging down Mount Gilead... / your lips are scarlet thread / and your words enchanting. / Your cheeks, behind your veil / are halves of pomegranate... / Your breasts are two fawns, / twins of a gazelle, that feed among the lilies." (4:1-5)
>
> Beloved: "My love is fresh and ruddy, / to be known among ten thousand. / His head is golden, purest gold, / his locks are palm fronds / and black as the raven. / His eyes are like doves... / His cheeks are beds of spices... / His lips are lilies / distilling pure myrrh. / His hands are golden, rounded, / set with jewels of Tarshish." (5:10-14)

Here is unashamed celebration of physical beauty, both male and female, which is the basis of sexual attraction. What is depicted here three thousand years ago is the basis of sexual arousal, the prelude of sexual communion, and within this state is to be found the divine, God's approval of the glory of his creation. The scene is now set for sexual intercourse. Because it is part of common human experience, I shall outline the phases of sexual union which Masters & Johnson describe in their well known book *Human Sexual Response.*[15] Despite the fact that it was full of medical, technical jargon, the book became a world-wide success.

Our understanding of sexual intercourse includes a description of the four phases of coitus. Phase one is called the excitement phase. The first sign in the man in this phase is, of course, the erection of the penis, which is a clearly observable fact and is due to vaso-congestion, that is, the pouring of blood in the penile tissues which engorge. The modern drug Viagra works by effecting this vaso congestion for men who are impotent. In the woman there is a moistening of the vagina, enlargement of the breasts and muscular tension, with quickening of the breathing and heart rate.

The excitement phase gives way to the plateau phase, with the entry of the penis into the vagina and further quickening of the heart and breathing, while a flush appears on the bodies of the couple. This is experienced as mounting erotic pleasure which reaches the third phase of the climax, the peak of excitation, with discharge of semen by the man and a number of orgasmic muscular spasms in the woman. The orgasm is the moment anticipated in every act of intercourse and is accompanied by intense pleasure and ecstasy.

Finally, there is a resolution phase in which the muscular tension subsides, respiration and blood pressure return to normal and the couple relax.

Throughout human history sexual intercourse, which may last from a minute to half an hour, has been pursued for its intense pleasurable content. This pleasure has been the source of much anxiety and criticism in Christian history and in order to make it acceptable it has been posited that it is the reward for the possibility of procreation. Thus, procreation has come to play a vital role in understanding the meaning of coitus.

Although procreation is undoubtedly an important component in sexual intercourse, it is clear in our day that, with the size of the family being reduced to an average of two children and sexual intercourse continuing well into later life, the main purpose is not procreation but relational. We only need a few acts of sexual intercourse to produce the desired family. But from the pattern of nature, from the design that God has placed in humanity, we can see that the woman is only fertile about three days every monthly cycle, so that the overwhelming number of days that the couple have sex are not open to procreation, whereas every act is open to its relational purposes. But before we consider what the relational purposes can be, let us consider a few more psycho-biological phenomena.

One of the worries of the early Christian Fathers and the theologians of the Middle Ages was the position that couples adopted for having sex. Preoccupied as they were with fulfilling its primary end of procreation, theologians specified that only one position was morally acceptable, namely the man above and the woman below, for this was considered the best position for fertilisation.

We now know that any position will lead to fertilisation and that the primary concern of the couple is the enjoyment of the act. The "missionary position", with man on top, is acceptable to some couples and not to others. With women's emancipation being a prominent issue and the power conflict in intercourse a subject of much speculation, particularly in women's journals, the position of the woman above the man has become widely acceptable. Indeed, the primary consideration of intercourse is erotic pleasure and any position which satisfies the couple is licit, morally and psychologically. It has been very hard for theology to appreciate that the main preoccupation of the couple is not procreation, except when a child is planned, and that at all other times the intention is to maximise pleasure. With pleasure having a question mark placed after it for such a long time, theology and the psychology of sexual intercourse spoke different languages. It is only now that there is a confluence of understanding, with a theology that appreciates that pleasure is part of God's plan of creation.

Given that pleasure is such an important component of intercourse, we next examine its frequency. There is a copious amount of American and British data on the frequency of sexual intercourse. James found that the frequency of sex in the first month of marriage was seventeen times, but by the end of the first year it had been reduced to eight times per month.[16] The same research suggested that while the rate is reduced by one half in the first year, it then takes another twenty years for it to halve again.

Other studies show that on average for the younger married couple intercourse takes place about twice a week. Kinsey,[17] Hunt[18] and Blumstein & Schwartz[19] show a decline in frequency with age. The reasons for the fall in frequency are the arrival of children, work, commuting, housework, financial worries, fatigue and a certain familiarity.

Although ageing has an effect on the sexual frequency of coitus, the two sexes respond differently. Kinsey concluded that for the male, from the early to the middle years the decline in sexual activity is remarkably steady and there is no point at which old age suddenly enters the picture. For the female, the author painted a somewhat different picture. There is little evidence of steady decline in sexual response for the female until late in life. In a study by Brecher, among the over 70's, some 60% of the couples were having sex.[20]

A particular point of reference for women is the cessation of menstruation experienced as menopause. Traditionally, the menopause ushered in the end of procreation and therefore should, in theological theory, signal the end of sexual activity. Of course it does not, because the couple continue to enjoy each other's presence. But there is some evidence that there is a decline in sexual desire for women post-menopausally.[21] This decline is variable and other research has concluded that, in the overall reduction of sexual activity with age, the effect of menopause is small.

Theologians and the Church have praised childbearing and connected it with sexual intercourse. There is evidence that childbirth is a time when there may be tension between couples. This tension may be the result of the wife becoming depressed after the birth of her child, irritability and loss of interest in sexual intercourse up to a year after the delivery. When these manifestations persist they may be the basis of marital difficulties.

To summarise, we observe that sexual intercourse is intimately linked with falling in love and, when the course is courtship and direct entry into marriage, coitus takes place at high frequency in the first year and then drops to an average of about twice a week. The obvious manifestation of intercourse is its intense sexual pleasure, culminating in the orgasm. Although this is its predominant characteristic, sexual intercourse is an encounter between persons and its meaning is inter-personal. In the section that follows I shall explore this meaning in terms of a language in which the couple are speaking to each other with their bodies. This is a communication of love. But what are they saying to each other? It is a language which shifts the individual from egoism to a mutuality of sharing with each other. It is a shift from the technology of pleasure to mutual commitment. Finally, it is a shift from potentially meaningless pleasure to meaningful interaction. This meaning depends entirely on what the partners are conveying to one another. The physical becomes the channel of communication of the personal. This personal communication develops with time as the couple moves from being in love to loving. As this loving changes with time, sexual intercourse speaks a different language.

Sexual Intercourse as Personal Communication

Through coitus a couple encounter each other. This encounter is pictured in literature and poetry, but in fact it leaves a train of feelings that can be described psychologically in at least six different ways.

Affirmation of Identity

Every time a couple make love, they have the potential of saying to each other, "I recognise you, I appreciate you, I want you". It is an exchange which first of all says that, of all the infinite possibilities of choice, the spouse has been recognised as the most important person in the world. When something happens to us, it is common to ask the question "Why me?" In sexual intercourse, the body answers that question. Nobody else is being selected. Week after week, there is recognition that the spouse matters above all others. Although repetition may dull the message, it is a message of extreme importance. Hence, one understands all the associated consternation surrounding jealousy and episodes of adultery. We get accustomed to being recognised above everybody else and being chosen as such. Of course it is the relationship that makes the selection but it is intercourse that gives it its unique significance.

This repetitive singular recognition extends its meaning to say that the choice is one of appreciation. The spouse one makes love to may have faults, may be imperfect, may have caused pain, may have disappointed, but, despite all his or her limitations, is appreciated for what he or she is. Intercourse is an act of faith in what the person is and what they hopefully may become. Intercourse at the beginning of marriage is an expression of the idealisation with which we hold our spouse. At the beginning, he or she is felt to be perfect and intercourse is an expression of that feeling. With the passage of time, flaws appear in the personality. These flaws are recognised and idealisation is reduced. There remains a solid experience of the goodness of the partner and a measure of this recognition is translated into coitus. What intercourse is saying is, "You may not be perfect, but you are good enough". This appreciation goes on until death or until the relationship breaks up.

With the passage of time, the initial idealisation fades but new depths of goodness and meaning are found and intercourse verifies the new discoveries. It is the act that communicates and reinforces the continuing discovery of each other. Finally, in this personal exchange intercourse is saying that the spouses want each other. Every act of sexual intercourse is a renewal of the marital vows. It is saying that, despite the passage of time, the couple need and want one another. The expectations may have become diluted, the disappointments undoubtedly grow, but, as long as the act continues, it signifies that there is a mutual fulfilment, however limited it may be.

Sexual intercourse signifies a powerful attestation of affirming identity. Just as the parents are the persons who give us our identity, so spouses continue to affirm each other. In the next section we shall see that in Christianity we believe that God is the author of our identity. This identity is transmitted in an ambassadorial fashion through our parents when we are children and by our spouses when we are adults.

Sexual Identity

We come to each other in life as sexual persons. Sociology defines gender as concerned with the femininity and masculinity of the person. It takes into consideration the way we dress, talk and act, the things we do, the roles we assume. In sexual intercourse we summarise and express all these characteristics in and through our bodies. In receiving each other's bodies we receive the talents we cherish in each other. Through intercourse, we make available the strengths and weakness of our masculinity and femininity and, genitally, we are saying to each other what sort of person we are in our gender.

Part of the gender manifestation is the whole exchange of action in intercourse. Who takes the initiative to suggest intercourse? In what way is this initiative made? Through a look, a touch, a word? This liturgy of exchange is a private code of sexual communication. It this part of the exchange of sexual signalling between the couple. They are speaking to each other through sexual desire and, as we have seen, it is a divine language.

It is here that there is an exchange of personal power between the couple. Who has the confidence and the temerity to ask? Who has the confidence and the temerity to suggest a particular sexual position for intercourse? In this sexual exchange, the couple are testing initiative, confidence, certainty and are drawing out the fears of rejection, guilt and uncertainty.

Beyond the drama of erotic invitation, there is actually the celebration of the body itself. The man makes the woman feel fully sexual and vice versa. In the course of ordinary life she is aware of her breasts, thighs, face, and so forth but now, as her husband delights in her presence, she delights in her sexuality. Her sexuality comes to life in and through her body, through her breasts, belly, and thighs she rejoices in her sexual identity. This is what the *Song of Songs* celebrates. The same occurs vice versa and the woman awakens the sexual identity of the man. Thus sexual intercourse gives two verifications of the personality. The personal and the sexual. With the passage of time, the couple give to each other an awareness of their personality. In intercourse and through these two parameters, the individual changes from being an object of impersonal admiration and lust to being a person subjective to awareness and love. The partners mutually endow each other with personal meaning. It takes years and decades to convert the initial idealisation to an enduring personal meaning, and sexual intercourse pays a central role in this transformation.

Self Esteem

Modern psychology has made us aware that at the heart of our personality is the way we feel about ourselves. There is a world of difference between feeling good and not feeling good about who we are and what we can do. It is no exaggeration that self esteem supports courage, initiative, perseverance and achievement in our life. The alternative is doubt, uncertainty, fear, anxiety and self depreciation. We gain our self esteem from two sources, the feeling of being loveable and the worth of our achievement. Our parents give us a mixture of acceptance, vindication of ourselves and uncertainty. Psychoanalysis has argued convincingly that our adult self esteem has its roots in our childhood. The genetic contribution also plays a part, but upbringing is crucial.

As already indicated, spouses take over where parents leave off. Spouses have two main levers with which to achieve their ends, first in the quality of the relationship and secondly in sexual intercourse. Sexual intercourse is a continuing thread in establishing the spouses' lovability and goodness. In a space of a few minutes, the loved one emerges from intercourse with a feeling of well-being. He or she is really loved.

The actual exchange of the act itself is another. Did the couple really express fully their body's potential? Did touch conjoined with erotic feeling convey fully the genital consummation? This is the world of sexual feelings and pathology. Over time couples acquire the art of how to please one another. They learn that a combination of touch, stroking, massaging, thrusting and positioning give full expression to sexual pleasure, the culmination of which in turn assists the goodness and self esteem of each other. This self esteem draws its strength from the relationship of the couple, culminating in intercourse, which expresses physical erotic accomplishment and personal affirmation.

Relief of Distress

Couples enter their bedroom to make love, full of the realities of daily life. They may be tired, depressed, anxious, concerned, worried about their work, the children, their relations and their personal traumas. They start intercourse burdened with these worries. But intercourse has a variety of relaxing experiences. It is par excellence a psychosomatic event in which the *psyche* influences the *soma*. There is a widespread myth of the wife who does not want sexual intercourse, who complains of a headache. There is very little description of the aftermath of intercourse as a shooting, relieving and relaxing physical experience in which physical discomfort is relieved. Here the language of intercourse is almost medicinal. It is the relief of distress.

This distress is both physical and psychological. In our time, depression and anxiety are very common. The features of depression are mood changes, tiredness, irritability, lack of concentration and lack of well being. There is no doubt that successful sexual intercourse can lift the mood. I remember well one of my patients who was getting nowhere with his medication declaring that the best remedy for depression was a good "shag".

Reconciliation

The intimacy in marital couples inevitably leads to quarrels, conflict and pain. This is an inevitable aspect of interpersonal closeness. Most of these conflicts are resolved, forgiven and forgotten quickly. But some are more severe and the pain is more persistent. The pain and withdrawal may last days, weeks or even longer periods. During this time the partners feel offended or hurt and avoid each other. They may find apologies difficult or insufficient. It may take time for the pain to subside. Finally, it does subside and they make love. Sexual intercourse is now a language of forgiveness and reconciliation. It is the moment when they return to entrance each other as lovers. Hurt subsides. There is a real examination of the conflict and, after intercourse verbal communication may be restored and further healing take place.

Thanksgiving

How do couples celebrate their mutuality? They may give presents to each other, they may take out each other for a meal, they may say verbally "thank you". But sexual intercourse can be the most powerful way of saying "thank you" to each other. Through intercourse, their complete availability to each other, they express thanks for being together, yesterday, today and hopefully tomorrow. It is their recurrent act of the eucharistic experience.

The above six dimensions of personal encounter may be actualised by sexual intercourse at any time in the course of the marriage. But with the passage of time the couple find a deeper personal meaning in their sexual encounter. These six meanings stand out but are not exhaustive. In the theology of *Humanae vitae*, there is only mention of a unitive and a procreative element. The above description has attempted to enlarge the understanding of these meanings to reflect the experience of loving couples.

From Falling in Love to Loving

We have seen that the couple fall in love and that sexual intercourse is an expression of that intense feeling between the partners. The frequency of coitus, which may be daily for the first few months, shows the desire of the couple to be one. With the passage of time the relationship changes from falling in love to loving. The state of loving describes most marriages. Loving fluctuates, but, on the basis of my experience dealing with couples, I would suggest that there are three features which encapsulate its characteristics. These features are *sustaining, healing* and *growth*.

By *sustaining*, I mean five features which communicate love to the couple through different behaviour characteristics. My choice of these five are availability, communication, demonstration of affection, affirmation and resolution of conflict. They are not arbitrary choices. They express the transfer of affection from childhood to adulthood and can be demonstrated through empirical qualitative experiences.

Availability

The child is sustained by the availability of parents and in their presence finds the anchor for its security. The same applies to the couple. When the couple are physically together, the company of each other gives them the feeling of being recognised, wanted and appreciated. A walk together, a meal, spending time together are ways in which they take in each other through vision, sound, smell and touch. After being together for some time, their awareness of each other is enhanced and they want to consummate this through sexual intercourse.

We appreciate the longing for each other that separation and absence brings and, after a period away from each other, the first thing that couples want to do is to make love to renew their togetherness. The same applies to the time they spend together. Intercourse seals their physical awareness of each other.

Communication

Physical presence defines one characteristic of love. Verbal communication defines another. It is through words that partners reveal to each other their inner world. They reveal who they are, what they think and feel and what they think and feel about each other. In modern marriage, communication has become a key dimension of love. When the relationship deteriorates, so does communication. Words reveal the inner world of a person and the consequent awareness of that world wishes to find concrete expression. Sexual intercourse becomes that channel. Coitus after communication is a sign of understanding and accepting what has been said and at the same time indicating that the couple are ready to receive further revelations about each other. Sexual intercourse after verbal communication is a form of assent that the communication has been received. The body affirms the word and, through sex, there is a total communication of the whole person.

Demonstration of Affection

As a child, especially a young child, kisses and caresses convey the affective dimension of love. Couples continue to demonstrate their affection for one another through touch, kisses and caresses. This dimension is one of the clearest indications of loving. There are two strands to demonstrating affection. The first is as a preliminary to sexual intercourse. The second is in the course of everyday life, when the gestures are detached from sexual intercourse. Both are powerful ways of saying "I love you" and are intimately connected with sexual intercourse.

Affirmation

Childhood is a time of development. One of the most powerful sources of this development is the affirmation the child receives from its parents, teachers and others. This affirmation is also needed in adult life. When we do something well we want to be appreciated. Spouses are ever present to appreciate each other. After appreciation, a glow enters our being. This glow wants celebration, and that celebration may be found in sexual intercourse. Not only is sexual intercourse a sign of affirmation, but it is also a sign of encouragement and hope for the future.

Resolution of Conflict

Reference has also been made to the proximity of conflict to intimacy. Conflict is an inevitable part of intimacy, but out of conflict stems growth. Sexual intercourse plays a vital role in the process of reconciliation aftermath.

In these five dimensions there is an interpersonal exchange between loving and sexual intercourse. As with the personal exchanges, other parameters can be added but the five mentioned here provide a prominent basis.

Beyond sustaining there is *healing*. We emerge from childhood as wounded people. The wounds in childhood are part of the first intimate experience of life. Marriage is the second intimate experience of life which provides an opportunity for healing. Psychologists have described the forms in which this healing takes place. There are basically three forms of healing. The first is physical. In Western Society there are few childhood diseases which leave their impact on adulthood.

The second is psychological and this is the most common wound experienced in the West today. Men and women suffer from lack of self esteem, lack of confidence, insecurity, doubts about themselves, bouts of depression and anxiety, rejection, guilt, uncertainty, fear and the accompanying varieties of phobias.

When these conditions are severe they need expert attention. In their lesser forms, they are extremely common, indeed universal. Spouses can be agents of healing to each other. Couples give to each other a second opportunity to receive love, security, reassurance, trust and acceptance. Over time, healing takes place and this healing can be reinforced by sexual intercourse.

Thirdly, there is the possibility of sexual healing. We have now come to realise how widespread is sexual abuse in childhood. As a result of traumatic sexual experiences, some adults associate their sexuality with fear, mistrust, anxiety and guilt. It is here that gentle, reassuring, loving sexual intercourse can give the person the feeling that sex can be a wholesome, good experience, surrounded by trust against mistrust, relaxation against tension and fear, the ability to enjoy against feeling guilty and, finally, to feel like sexual persons without shame or distress.

We are accustomed to read accounts of marital breakdown and the conflict surrounding divorce. What we read nowhere is the account of healing which takes place slowly, over time, in millions of marriages. There is little doubt that a good marriage achieves more healing than all the therapy that takes place in various forms of psychotherapy.

Finally, beyond sustaining and healing we have *growth*. Over time a couple develop socially and psychologically. This goes on imperceptibly and is not always visible to the couple. But those who see them after a period of time can see the difference. We grow in a whole variety of ways, some of which may be illustrated in the following.

There is a growing awareness of self. The most noticeable dimension is the shift from dependence to independence and finally to interdependence. At the beginning of a marriage we tend to rely on our partner to make decisions, take the initiative, tell us what to do. Little by little we find our confidence and assume more responsibility for ourselves. We grow into independence. We become more creative. Beyond assertiveness, we develop two characteristics. Slowly, and sometimes very slowly, we become less egoistic. We grow much more aware of the other person. We get in touch with their feelings, needs, their ways. We move from egoism to sharing and even to becoming altruistic and generous. As our basic needs are met, so we can go beyond them to become aware of what our spouse needs and to give it to them. We not only become more altruistic but also more sensitive to each other, that is to say more empathetic. We are able to read the inner word of our partner more accurately. We assess their mood more accurately, and respond to it sensitively.

Another feature of growth is our creativity. With the passage of time we develop skills, initiatives, ideas to create. The creation may be a recipe or a book, a new way of decorating the home. We are insecure whether we shall succeed and the reassurance of our partner is vital. In the sexual field we give expression to all these changes by making love with a new awareness of ourselves. Although coitus may appear to be the same, we are now different people carrying it out. More narrowly over sexual intercourse itself, we may get the confidence to tell our partner about hidden erotic wishes which we can communicate without fear of being rejected. We may have more confidence to display our sexual feelings without diffidence and so not only do we engage in intercourse as different people, but we also engage in intercourse itself with a deeper and wider meaning.

We can see that sexual intercourse is much more than an orgasm. The physical pleasure accompanying intercourse both initiates and leads to personal appreciation and interpersonal loving communication. Sexual intercourse is not an isolated experience. It is an essential component of the ongoing interaction of the couple. Physical pleasure is a language which speaks to the couple of their marriage and love for each other. The implications of this are that the morality of sexual intercourse should be concerned with the understanding of it that safeguards its continuity, reliability and predictability. What sexual intercourse needs for the expression of its integrity is to be placed in an environment which allows the free expression of its multiple meanings. This environment needs exclusiveness, faithfulness, commitment and permanency. It is only with these characteristics that it can do justice to the multiple expressions of sexual encounter.

Traditionally, we used to place sex within marriage to safeguard the potential birth of a child and its subsequent nurturing. We can see now that the conditions of marriage, namely exclusiveness, faithfulness, commitment and permanency not only serve procreation but are an essential safeguard for the very essence of sexual intercourse, guaranteeing over time its various expressions. Thus it is not that sex is only legitimate within marriage but that marriage with its specific characteristics of permanency, exclusiveness, faithfulness and commitment safeguards the character of sexual intercourse. We can see now that the temporary, occasional, transient, promiscuous act of intercourse allows physical pleasure but none of its various personal meanings, and its wrongness is not that all these acts take place outside marriage but that these settings deny the full richness of what intercourse means. So we now recognise that personal, interpersonal and moral dimension to sexual intercourse.

The Spiritual Dimension of Sexual Intercourse

I would like to conclude with a short consideration of the spiritual dimension of coitus.

We accept God as a creator who gives identity to the world he created through his love. He hands over this creation to human beings and we continue his work through marriage, in which the chief feature is sexual intercourse, a profound expression of love. For the married, the chief demonstration of God's love is sexual intercourse. It is the central and recurrent act of prayer in the couple's life. The carnal becomes the manifestation of divine love. Thus the body, far from being a source of suspicion, fear and anxiety, becomes the main instrument of conveying the continuing will of God in creating, redeeming and transforming human nature. Embodiment is the channel of the divine. The embodiment is expressed in the nakedness of the couple who now find their original state of innocence.

More specifically when we come to sexual intercourse, it reflects the inner world of Trinity in that the Trinity expresses the relationships of persons, the Father and Son, whose fruit is the Spirit of love, and who are essentially one but are completely separate persons. We find in sexual intercourse an interpersonal union of love in which, at the moment of consummation, the spouses are one and yet at the same time they are separate persons. Thus God as love, God as Trinity, God as creativity are all to be found in the expression of sexual intercourse and, since sexual intercourse in marriage is the undertaking of the overwhelming majority of people, the understanding, safeguarding and appreciation of it is a major part of evangelisation.

Notes

1 John Paul II, *The Theology of the Body* (Boston: Daughters of St. Paul, 1997).
2 One of the best books that explores this period is Peter Brown's *The Body and Society: Men, Women and Sexual Renunciation in Early Christianity* (London: Faber and Faber, 1988).
3 Council of Elvira, Canon 33, E.J. Jonkers (ed.).
4 See, P. Brown, *The Body and Society*; K. Power, *Veiled Desire* (London: Darton, Longman & Todd, 1995); J.T Noonan, *Contraception* (Harvard: Harvard University Press, 1967).
5 *Confessions*, 8, 7, 17.
6 *Summa Theologiae*, Suppl. q. 41, art. 3, ad. 2.
7 M. Porter, *Sex, Marriage and the Church* (Victoria, Australia: Dove, 1996).
8 Francis de Sales, *Introduction to the Devout Life* (London: Burns & Oates, 1962).
9 Jack Dominian, *Christian Marriage* (London: Darnton, Longman & Todd, 1967).
10 See H. Doms, *The Meaning of Marriage* (London: Sheed & Ward, 1939).
11 *Pastoral Constitution of the Church in the Modern Word*, Part II, Chap. 1, para. 47.
12 *Ibid*, para. 49.
13 For a recent, non-controversial assessment see J.A. Selling, "The 'Meanings' of Human Sexuality", *Louvain Studies* 23 (1998) 22–37.
14 *Marriage, Faith & Love* (London: Darton, Longman & Todd, 1981); *Sexual Integrity* (London: Darton, Longman & Todd, 1987); *Passionate and Compassionate Love* (London: Darton, Longman & Todd, 1991).
15 W.H. Masters and V.E. Johnson, *Human Sexual Response* (Boston: Little, Brown & Co., 1966).
16 W.H. James, "The Honeymoon Effect on Marital Coitus", *Journal of Sex Research* 17 (1981) 114.
17 A.C. Kinsey, W.B. Pomeroy and C.E. Martin, *Sexual Behaviour in the Human Male* (Philadelphia: Saunders, 1948) and *Sexual Behaviour in the Human Female* (Philadelphia:

Saunders, 1953).
18 M. Hunt, *Sexual Behaviour in the 1970's* (Chicago: Playboy Press, 1974).
19 P. Blumenstein and P. Schwartz, *American Couples* (New York: William Morrow, 1983).
20 E.M. Brecher, *Love, Sex & Aging: A Consumer's Union Report* (Boston: Little Brown, 1984).
21 See, T. Hallstrom, *Mental Disorders & Sexuality in the Climacteric* (Gothenburg: Scandinavian University Books, 1973).

Chapter Two

Spirituality and Sexuality

Philip Sheldrake

Clearly any attempt to describe a relationship between spirituality and sexuality demands that we take seriously our own embodiment, the erotic and a definition of the "self" that places relationships in the "outer" world at the heart of human identity.

To begin with, however, it seems useful to summarise my underlying understanding of spirituality. Spirituality is a word that is sometimes difficult to pin down. There have been attempts to offer generic definitions that transcend the assumptions of specific religious traditions. However, a number of writers question the validity and coherence of this process.[1] In Christian terms, a working definition might be that spirituality describes how individuals and groups appropriate traditional Christian beliefs about God, the human person, creation, and their interrelationship, and express these in worship, fundamental values and in the practice of everyday life. Thus, spirituality is the whole of life viewed in terms of a fundamental relationship with God, in Jesus Christ, through the indwelling of the Spirit and within the community of believers.

Such a definition calls into question the classical dichotomies that have characterised conceptions of spirituality in the past and which make it difficult to understand sexuality as a spiritual issue in any deep sense. I understand spirituality to be concerned with all dimensions of human existence, rather than with some kind of spiritual plane that can be distinguished from material existence. Spirituality is also concerned with action in the external world as much as with interiority. It is an ecclesial and social matter rather than something that is purely individual. Finally, spirituality should not be thought of essentially as *experience* but rather as *practice* – not in the sense of special devotional or spiritual practices alone but as the *practice* of everyday life.

Understanding Sexuality

For the sake of clarity, I also need to summarise briefly what I understand by sexuality. It is a word we use to describe our very way of *being* as humans and also our way of relating – both to ourselves and to what is other than ourselves.

Sexuality is not limited to explicit sexual expression or activity of any kind although it obviously includes these. For this reason, in a very important sense, we cannot renounce *sexuality* even though we may renounce certain forms of *sexual expression*.

The Christian spiritual tradition has often used erotic language as a way of talking about the relationship between God and humanity. However, this has rarely translated itself into serious attention to human sexuality as spiritual experience or practice. The problem is that, from quite an early stage of its history, Christianity tended to treat sexuality and "the erotic" as particularly symptomatic of a world that was fallen away from God. For classical Christianity, it was human sexual *language* that was useable in terms of human encounters with God rather than human sexual *experience*. The result was an uncomfortable paradox. While *eros* transformed into spiritual energy might be fine, there was, at the same time, a separation between holiness and sexual activity.

The historical origins of Christianity's traditional problems with the body, passion and sexuality are complex. Perhaps the most elegantly written, comprehensive and balanced account in English is Peter Brown's *The Body and Society* which charts the rise of sexual renunciation in early Christianity.[2] Many factors played their part. There was, first of all, a certain inheritance from Stoic philosophy. Spiritual significance was accorded to the repudiation of pleasure and to the avoidance of uncontrolled passion. Then there were late imperial Roman attitudes toward masculinity as the measure of what it was to be human. This involved the need to maintain male integrity by means of detachment, self-sufficiency, autonomy and the avoidance of softness. Detachment and self-sufficiency were the hallmarks of the true man. This later received powerful reinforcement from such medieval theologians as Jean Gerson who accused women of being determined seducers threatening male autonomy.[3] Ambrose, the fourth-century Bishop of Milan, explored male detachment in explicitly Christian terms by linking it to the virtue of integrity. This involved two things. First, one should maintain *boundaries*. "To surrender any boundary line was to court the ancient shame of the Roman male – it was to 'become soft', to be 'effeminated'."[4] Secondly, it was "the precious ability to keep what was one's own untarnished by alien intrusion".[5] For Ambrose, virginity perfectly expressed integrity because it guaranteed a body and soul kept whole and entire. Significantly, integrity was a *male* virtue partly, one supposes, because women's *physical* integrity was consistently marred by their menstrual cycle.

These cultural values were reinforced by the theological link that was gradually forged between the wholeness that was our presumed destiny in heaven, involving resurrection of the body, and the desire to anticipate this through the bodily intactness of virginity in the here and now. So, "integrity" later coalesced with a medieval fear of fragmentation and belief "that wholeness – non-partibility and non-passibility – is God's ultimate promise to humankind". Wholeness is crucial to salvation.[6] Medieval thinkers, like the Franciscan Roger Bacon, suggested that people should prepare for the eternal integrity of bodily resurrection by striving for moral and physical intactness in the present age.[7]

Human non-passibility related to the way that God was increasingly seen, after the Patristic period, as radically impassible. Late Roman Stoic philosophy replaced the more scriptural image of a God of desire with a God distanced from the uncertainties of passion.[8] This suggested a new goal for Christian leadership – priesthood "in the image of a passionless God". It was through detachment that the priest revealed God. "The celibate leader becomes a spiritual *paterfamilias*, continuing the Roman secular tradition of masculine domination and distance."[9]

If we move forward beyond the Reformation, we see that the creation of semi-monastic seminaries to train Roman Catholic clergy helped to ensure the primacy not only of a spirituality of celibacy but also of a *culture* of celibacy, which is a much more complex matter. Seminaries, from the late sixteenth century to the 1960s, also set out to inculcate in students the attitudes and behaviour patterns of a spirituality of separation, of a priestly caste spiritually superior to the laity and to the married "ministers" of the Churches of the Reformation.

There is a particularly disturbing expression of disgust with human conception and women's bodies to be found in a late-seventeenth-century collection of meditations for English Roman Catholic seminarians. The language is historically conditioned but there can be no doubt that negative attitudes such as these to women, sexuality and the human body have had a long and damaging effect on spirituality in the Roman Catholic context.

> ...For the manner of thy begetting is so foule that the name, nay the lightest thought of it, defileth the purest minde, so that our B. Sauiour refused none of our miseries, but onely that; and the matter so horrid, so foule, that all other dung is pleasant and gratefull in respect of it; nay we dare not in discourse giue it a name, for our owne shame & others offence....
>
> I cannot imagine any prison so darke, so straight, so loathsome, as the wombe of a woman, in which the child is inclosed, & enwrapped in most foule, bloudy and matterous skinnes or membranes, for no lesse, then nine whole moneths; so straighned and pressed, that neither hand nor foot can he stirre or moue: his food, the filthy menstrous bloud of his mother, a thing so nasty, and poisonous, as that what soever it toucheth, it infecteth, like the plague or lepry....[10]

Celibate Culture, Power and Spirituality

I do not wish to labour the point unnecessarily, but the development of a "celibate culture" stands for much more than sexuality. The historical process within which spiritualities emerge and develop inevitably creates groups who predominate and others who are subordinate. It is not unfair to reflect upon the Christian tradition in terms of those who seek to control, produce and then dispense spirituality at any given time and those who are made into recipients of spiritual bequests that originate with others. This is an issue of power: who has it, how it is used (consciously or not), and what are the effects, in different contexts, on those who are structured, at different times, as a spiritually dependent underclass?[11]

Criticisms of the mandatory rule of celibacy for the Western Catholic priesthood (as opposed to a freely chosen way of life) have generally concentrated on sexuality, women or the body rather than addressed the equally important issue of power itself. What we confront at the moment, it seems to me, is a crisis of meaning for an ecclesiastical *culture* that has depended on a complexity of symbols (including mandatory celibacy) and on a particular theory of hierarchy, separation and spiritual superiority. I use "culture" in the sense generally understood by anthropologists. In this case it implies an interrelated set of attitudes, values and ways of behaving that are specific to a male clerical world rather than to celibates *per se*. These both govern the lifestyle of ordained leaders and constitute a framework that affects all elements of the Church's life and mission including male attitudes to women and their own self-understanding. Celibate culture encompasses a total world view.[12]

Celibate culture faces an apparent contradiction. Having developed a more positive theology of marriage in recent years, how do we avoid implying, by *mandatory* celibacy, that committed relationships are still second-class ways of serving God? The 1990 Roman Synod stated that celibacy consecrated priests in "an intimate union with Christ the bridegroom, who so loved his bride, the Church, that he gave up his life for her". This was perceived by many thoughtful married people as denigrating their own lives for it is in these same terms that the *married* state has often been described since Vatican II. Equally, the use of a marriage metaphor to describe the relationship of a priest to Jesus or to the Church can be spiritually deceptive.

The crisis of celibate culture today is partly related to positive changes in attitudes concerning male-female relations and relatedness in general. The superstructure of celibate culture was built on the premise that human intimacy distracted our attention from God. However, "sexuality-as-lust" has been replaced by "sexuality-as-relatedness". There is also a crisis of "the masculine" linked to shifts in gender roles, an erosion of a patriarchal understanding of the family and serious questions about our one-sided imaging of God. Sexuality is no longer interpreted in terms of purely male experience. Therefore, women should not be seen as *objects* of male desire and, by extension, as dangers to male integrity. A view of sexuality that focused on the naturally lustful male, plagued by the need to relieve his sexual tensions, encouraged an over-emphasis on the male libido. There is now a quite different understanding of sexual expression at the service of equal human relationships. Desire and pleasure are increasingly seen as having spiritual potential rather than as threats to higher ideals.[13] As we have seen, the partial connection between the origins of Christian teaching on virginity and Stoic philosophy led to the spiritual significance of a repudiation of pleasure.[14]

The values of relatedness and collaboration are also increasingly experienced as central to the nature of the Church and its message. They offer the possibility of a healthier theory and practice of leadership, authority and ministry. In summary, human sexual needs have been transformed both in the way they are understood and in terms of the wider context within which they come to consciousness.

Another way of understanding a spirituality of detachment and separation is that if celibacy, in a male perspective, preserves bodily integrity, this relates to a search for *reliability*. Because of its eschatological dimension, Christian spirituality has frequently been tempted to escape from all that is perceived as unreliable. Because the flesh and human intimacy are affected by decay and uncertainty they are patently not reliable. Celibate culture images the Church as "sacred space" and, because everything sacred has been associated with eternity, what is connected with the Church must be characterised by imperishability. The supposed superiority of a celibate life lies partly in the fact that it is perceived as uniquely able to represent this understanding of the Church. Images of the impassible, predictable God safely removes the sacred from all that is impermanent. How difficult, then, to seek and find God in the provisionality of human relationships.

The French philosopher and historian of spirituality, the late Michael de Certeau, questioned sharply the notion that Christian identity can be described in terms of some definitive theoretical construct. Indeed, Christian spirituality, rooted in the image of an empty tomb, should question the temptation to seek excessive stability, power and completed systems.

> The temptation of the "spiritual" is to constitute the act of difference as a site, to transform the conversion into an establishment, to replace the "poem" [of Christ] which states the hyperbole with the strength to make history or to be the truth which takes history's place, or, lastly, as in evangelical transfiguration (a metaphoric movement), to take the "vision" as a "tent" and the

> word as a new land. In its countless writings along many different trajectories, Christian spirituality offers a huge inventory of difference, and ceaselessly criticises this trap; it has insisted particularly on the impossibility for the believer of stopping on the "moment" of the break – a practice, a departure, a work, an ecstasy – and of identifying faith with a site.[15]

We need to beware of appearing to critique the choice of celibacy when we critique the culture. However, celibate culture currently is a dimension of the kind of spiritual temptation that de Certeau criticises in the Church.

In summary, for much of the Christian era the perceived precondition of a profound spirituality has been the absence of sexual activity and this has become associated with spirituality as a power system built on a theology of hierarchy and exclusions.

The Self

Such a summary of the problem of relating sexuality to spirituality seems necessary. However, I want to concentrate attention now on exploring some positive ways of re-envisioning spirituality in relationship to human sexuality, including its active expression, as a path to holiness and to God.

First of all, we need to ask how we fundamentally understand "the self". This involves a number of different issues and I have chosen to select only one. One of the most critical issues in attempting to think together sexuality and spirituality is our concept of human personhood or the self. There is no room to do justice to this complex theme. What follows is a very modest summary of some important pointers.

It has been argued that modern Western culture suffers from a divide between interiority and exteriority. "It is a divide between subjective experience and worldly experience, self and city."[16] According to the historian Richard Sennett, this divide is based on an unacknowledged fear of exposure. Exposure has the connotation of threat rather than enhancement of life. Sennett blames elements of the Christian theological tradition for this classic inward-outward divide.

Essentially, Augustine is seen to lie at the heart of the problem. It is possible to interpret his *City of God* as a classic expression of the triumph of the inner "city of God" in search of eternal fulfilment over the world of particular places and human history. In that Christians continue to have to live in a material world, this external world of social relationships is to be viewed with suspicion. To be fair, such a clear cut distinction between inner and outer worlds may have less to do with Augustine himself than with later interpretations of him and applications of his thought in both Catholic and Protestant circles.

Some modern theologians have also attacked Augustine for individualism in his approach to the Trinity. Despite the evidence that may be gathered from an immediate study of his *De Trinitate* this judgement may be unfair. For one thing it is unlikely that Augustine would have understood the notion of "individual" in our modern sense. In terms of Augustine's intellectual world, "individuals" did not reflect the life of God in some self-contained way. On the contrary, it is humanity, a plurality of persons, which is in the image of God. Interestingly, Augustine's commentary on Genesis is quite clear that privacy or self-enclosure is the most insidious form of this-worldly pride which would not be reflected in the Heavenly City. This was precisely because such an attitude goes against what is public, shared, and common.[17]

Theology and spirituality, not least in the Roman Catholic tradition, have also been permeated by Enlightenment assumptions about the self, especially Cartesian assumptions about the knowing subject.[18] For Descartes, the bedrock of the self was not in the outer world of relationships, society, the practice of everyday life or action, but in a state of *pure mind* which is, it seems to me, another version of "soul" as a self-enclosed and protected interiority.[19] Notions of society or community are important because, for Christians, religious experience is never simply the product or possession of an individual person who is isolated from a community of faith or from an inherited religious tradition. Overall, the "modern" Enlightenment idea of the human self tended to emphasise our essentially rational and autonomous qualities.

Post-modern thought at its best exposes the illusory quality of this understanding of human identity. "That self-grounding, self-present modern subject is dead: killed by its own pretensions to grounding all reality in itself. Thanks to the post-moderns, that subject should be unmourned by all."[20] In contrast, the post-modern image of the self is not isolated or disengaged from the social world but is in some sense brought into existence by it. Because the self exists in a complex and mobile network of relationships, there cannot be said to be such a thing as a complete or completed self. On the face of it, this view may appear merely as another version of post-modern fragmentation. However, the Christian dynamic implied by the doctrine of redemption also requires that we see that

> the self at any given moment is a *made* self: it is not a solid, independent machine for deciding and acting efficiently or rationally in response to stimuli, but is itself a process, fluid and elusive, whose present range of possible responses is part of a developing story.[21]

Post-modernism may encourage spirituality to reject the individualism that has frequently characterised previous perspectives. Our identities are constituted by being in relationship.

In Christian terms this offers significant connections between our understanding of human identity and the doctrine of the Trinity. "Relatedness is not something simply external to the divine reality but is something internal to the divine life as well."[22] Any version of Christian spirituality that is individualistic in tone fails to reflect the communion of equal relationships that is God-in-Trinity. It is not surprising that the nature of the Christian life was always an issue in the debates about the doctrine of God. To think of God as Trinity is fundamentally to assert, among other things, that within God there is society or relationship. To affirm that human beings are created in the image of God implies that they are called to share more and more in the deep communion that is divine life itself. The crucial issue is the intimate link between the fundamental nature of God and God as revealed through creation and salvation.[23]

Spiritualities that are disengaged from the world rather than committed to it, and to its transformation, fail to reflect the irrevocable commitment of God to the world in Jesus Christ. This is what the doctrine of the Incarnation seeks to express. Belief in the Incarnation also invites people to adopt a balanced approach to human nature and especially to its material dimension, the body. This should be neither radically pessimistic nor naively optimistic. The Incarnation is more than a defence of the reality and importance of the human nature of Jesus Christ. It is a governing principle of Christian living; of God's way of relating to creation and our way of response. This means that the Christian vision of God, and God's self-disclosure, forces spirituality to accord a fundamental importance to material existence and human relationships.

To affirm God as Trinity touches every aspect of Christian belief, attitudes and living.[24] The concept of "relationality" has become a popular focus for contemporary reflections on the Trinity. The problem is that such a concept is capable of being reduced to a rather simplistic equation that goes something like this. "God is social therefore human life is social." Despite the dangers of reductionism, the concepts of relationship and community do seem to offer especially fruitful connections between doctrine and spirituality. This shift is understandable as relatedness stands in sharp contrast to inherited images of God as essentially distinct from the world, free from the limitations imposed by change and by time and disengaged from the impact of human events. In terms of spirituality, this view tended to reinforce individualistic, disengaged and anti-material attitudes. According to a relational model, the doctrine of the Trinity reveals a quite different understanding both of the nature of God and of human personhood in the image of God. The fundamental truth of our existence is that human beings and God are both rooted in mutual self-giving love. To exist consists of being-in-relationship.

Eros in God

I now wish to suggest five themes to bring together an appreciation of spirituality and sexuality: recovering the spiritual quality of the erotic; the human call to intimacy; liberation from our private will and overcoming our divided hearts; our understanding of union – with God and with other humans; and finally, the question of stepping outside our enclosed selves in a non-abusive crossing of boundaries. These themes represent no more than one person's (indeed, one *man's*) experience and thinking. The invitation through these themes is simply for all of us to reflect on two questions. How does the practice of sexuality make spiritual sense? How does the practice of spirituality make sexual sense?

It is clearly important to express the inclusive nature of God's love and that God has no favourites, in the notion of *agape* (or universal love). But we also need to redeem the notion of *eros* in God. God also loves specifically, longingly and in a particular way and this, essentially, is what *eros*-love implies. Pseudo-Dionysius actually defines God as *eros* or longing.

> And we may be so bold as to claim...that the Cause of all things loves all things in the superabundance of his goodness, that because of this goodness he makes all things, brings all things to perfection, holds all things together, returns all things. The divine longing [*eros*] is Good seeking good for the sake of the Good.[25]

For Pseudo-Dionysius, this divine longing causes God's movement out of self in an "ecstasy" of creation. God desires both to outpour and, at the same time, to draw all creation back into the divine life. So, ecstasy becomes reciprocal. God ecstatically goes out of self into the diversity of creation, including human beings. At the same time, each person is drawn out of fragmentation and dispersion into union, into the "singleness" of life in God. The power that describes both of these ecstasies is "eros".

To say that there is *eros* as well as *agape* in God expresses something important both about the love of God or human desire for God and about the "erotic" in human relations. We have inherited a distinction between *agape* love (disinterested or universal) and *eros* love (passionate and particular) that makes them two different kinds of love. Our commitment to "the particular", whether place or people, often struggles spiritually in a losing battle with what is presumed to be the higher value of "detachment" from all purely human loyalties. The Christian community is frequently tempted to retreat from real, down-to-earth human history into a condition of timelessness and into the myth of being perfect, self-contained and complete.

A radical separation of *agape* love and *eros* love not only does not square with biblical images of God but also does not correspond to human experience.

It is possible to see *agape*, a more universal love, as something we always need to grow into rather than something we automatically possess. We inevitably experience our capacity to love initially as always specific and exclusive. Yet, human love is continually called to move beyond its instinctive limitations. There are sharp reminders that God has no favourites (Acts 10: 34 and Romans 2: 11) and that "there can be neither Jew nor Greek, there can be neither slave nor free, there can be neither male nor female – for you are all one in Christ Jesus" (Galatians 3: 28). However, truly disinterested love is not *impersonal.* It is deeply engaged and yet free from self-seeking. We can only learn how love can become disinterested *agape* in and through the passionate commitment of *eros.* We cannot bypass committed, particular love in the search for self-transcending love. *Agape* and *eros* are not two loves but two qualities in the one human love just as they are complementary aspects of Love itself or God.

If we can recover the unity between *agape* and *eros* we may be able to resacralise "the erotic" which has too often been reduced to a superficial titillation of the senses. The relationship between the different forms of love should not be seen as opposition or choice. In the end, *eros* just as much as *agape* (*caritas*, charity) is expressive of the same drive towards union with the One. Christianity's tendency to steer clear of the erotic has often set the spiritual over against human culture and experience. Spiritual passion for God has a close, positive relationship to other seemingly more ordinary forms of desire. In important respects, the latter are doorways into the former. In other words, our relationship with God is expressed, "embodied" perhaps, in and through rather than despite all our human and material commitments.

Another danger in ignoring the spiritual significance of *eros* love is that this may actually undermine rather than enhance the possibility of a mystical experience of God. Combating the anti-mystical tendencies of his own classical Protestant tradition, the Lutheran theologian Paul Tillich actually defined *eros* as "the mystical quality of love" in his *Systematic Theology.*[26] Religion without *eros* will tend to be reduced to moral values and dutiful rituals. "If the eros quality of love with respect to God is rejected, the consequence of this rejection is that love toward God becomes an impossible concept...replaced by mere obedience to God."[27]

Eros in God also makes it possible to come to know the divine in the experience of human sexual relations. Indeed, human relations provide our primary image of God in everyday terms. It is not so much that God needs to be brought into human loving in order to redeem its essentially profane nature but rather that true eroticism, is always an experience "in God". God *is* erotic power properly understood. God is our capacity to love revealing itself in the matrix of all human relations. For Pseudo-Dionysius, God is both what all created reality yearns for and also the very yearning itself as experienced in different ways at different levels of creation:

> Why is it...that theologians sometimes refer to God as Yearning and Love and sometimes as the yearned-for and the Beloved? On the one hand he causes, produces, and generates what is being referred to, and, on the other hand, he is the thing itself....[28]

As Paul Tillich put it more directly: "In every moment of genuine love we are dwelling in God and God in us."[29]

Our desire, therefore, may be understood as a metaphor for embodying God. There is desire and an anguish of longing in us precisely because there is desire in God in whose image we are created. Clearly, the desires that are significant for following the path of the gospel are those that, directly or indirectly, have to do with God. However, this does not necessarily imply a direct connection with personal prayer or worship. In principle, any event or set of circumstances may become a setting that stirs our deepest longings. Christianity, founded on the belief of God's incarnation in the human person Jesus, exists to embody God. One of my students once powerfully wrote: "Our bodies are God's body language." This implies that what we do to and with our bodies, to other people's bodies and to all the embodiments that make up created reality, we do, as it were, to God.

The Human Erotic

Eros love is applicable to deeply intimate but not genital friendships between single people whose sexuality is mature. Eros-love does transcend purely physical desire but it does not bypass it. When directed towards another human being, eros love includes the physical but is not oriented *primarily or exclusively* to pleasure or to the release of physical tension. Eros-love strives ultimately for union with whatever we perceive to be the source of value for us. In Christian terms, this is not some impersonal force but is God-in-me, God-in-the-other and God-as-the-love-between-us. This move towards union involves a process of transcending our sense of fragmentation and separation. In an alienated or dysfunctional culture, eros-love may actually be in conflict with the prevailing misshapen attitudes to sex. A true eros-love views "the other", our partner, as a subject with which we seek to be united rather than an object to be used for pleasure, release or breeding.

There is an important difference between false eroticism and true eros-love. The first is an uncontrolled desire to draw other people into oneself. It therefore tends to be invasive and possessive. Ultimately if we are prone to false eroticism we want to be gratified. We do not truly want other people for themselves. In contrast, eros-love is a unitive power bringing together elements that really belong to each other. In terms of human sexual encounter, true desire is always a desire for union with the other mediated through bodies. Spiritually, the human body is the sacrament of a person. A true erotic desire recognises the sacrament for what it is – something that points beyond itself to a profound unity between persons.

In our experiences of sexual desire, love is not primarily universal even if it is ultimately open to universality. Sexual desire is particular, passionate and embodied. In the same way, God, incarnate in the man Jesus, is revealed as passionately engaged with the particular circumstances of our world and with all people in particular. Sexual desire, if it runs deep, is similarly self-giving and committed. Yet the idea that the body language of human love is a concrete articulation of the love of God revealed in Jesus Christ seems pretty daring to some people. How can we compare the love of God with the urgent, painful and sometimes wounding experiences of human longing and passion? And so, it has been commonplace to separate sex from the Incarnation. Is it not the case that many people think that Jesus was like us in all things but...*sex*? God becomes human in a physical, and therefore sexual, person who experienced pleasure, pain and need.

We need to move beyond a tendency to underestimate the erotic and reduce it to the fulfilment of social needs. Sexuality is about more than cementing stable families and reproducing the human race. It is this kind of reductionism, at least as much as a fear of bodily powers, that led sexual renunciation rather than sexual experience to become *the* way of spiritual growth and, therefore, the privileged icon of God's self-gift in Jesus. Spiritual elites "reproduced" through attracting vocations rather than through sexual interaction. As a result, sexual union became the province of the secular, if not the profane, rather than of truly spiritual people. It is only in more recent times that a committed sexual relationship was capable of being understood as vocational.

Intimacy

> Here we are, you and I, and I hope a third, Christ is in our midst.....
>
> God is friendship.......But still what is true of charity, I surely do not hesitate to grant to friendship, since "he that abides in friendship, abides in God, and God in him".[30]

These words of Aelred, the twelfth-century Yorkshire Cistercian, in his book on friendship, remind us that it is important not to reduce our understanding of sexuality to genital activity as if this one area provides the whole meaning of intimacy. Sexuality in its broadest sense covers the whole experience of embodiment. Affective sexuality involves a huge area of feelings and emotions that move people towards others. It is, if you like, what enables people to express tenderness, closeness and compassion. It follows that intimacy is not reserved to certain categories of people and unavailable to others. Single people, including those committed for various reasons to celibacy, are equally called to intimacy with other humans. Those who are within committed relationships need to discover how to become appropriately intimate, in a non-genital way, with people who are not their partners.

The call to intimacy is an invitation to take risks. For all human love comes to an end, may deceive, is partial, is not totally and finally reliable. Yet, the human capacity and need for intimacy is a call to find *within* this risk the love of God that is constant and faithful. Deep human friendship is a powerful contribution to a loving union with God. The call to intimacy also involves a realisation that however much two people love each other they never possess or own each other nor ever fully know each other. There is always an area of inalienable strangeness in the other person.

The Christian insights about eros-love and agape-love remind us that to become fully human we are called to seek the integration of particular and universal love. Only within experiences of intimacy with other people do humans learn a way of being fully present both to themselves and to others rather than being superficial and remote in their emotional lives. The risk of intimacy, rather than the apparent security of emotional detachment, reveals the truth of human identity, teaches about availability, educates in truthful self-disclosure and of all human experiences is the one most likely to provoke real change.

The search for love also reveals the need for a balance between solitude and intimacy. What we find in human relationships we also find in relationships with God. To say that solitude and intimacy need to remain in balance is to affirm two things. First, humans need a sufficient degree of rootedness in themselves before they can move outwards to others in a non-abusive way. "Solitude" describes that necessary place and time of waiting where people learn how to receive – themselves, God and other people – in disinterested love. The ability to receive in such a self-transcending way does not come easily. To learn to wait and then to learn the fruitful communication of intimacy is always painful for it involves a stripping away of unreal expectations and selfish demands and yet, at the same time, a deepening and sharpening of true desire.

Secondly, an intimacy that is spiritually healthy always allows the other person to remain securely in their own space. The German poet Rainer Rilke, in *Letters to a Young Poet*, suggested that real love does not consist in merging but means "that two solitudes protect and border and salute each other".[31] That seems an excellent description not only of human intimacy but of God's intimacy with humankind revealed in and through human loving.

Liberation from Private Will

The desert ascetics of the early Christian centuries understood well the greatest human emotional battle: how to overcome our divided hearts. In concrete terms this is the struggle in daily experience to be liberated from a false and destructive individuality – the tyranny of private will. Paradoxically, abstinence from sexual relations was seen to be important by early Christians only because of the role it played in this greater struggle. The conflicts we all experience with the "desires of the flesh" simply reveal the more deeply-rooted, essential flaws of the heart. The early ascetics sensed an absolute quality in the choice of sexual abstinence that made it a powerful symbol of the boundary between the spiritual innocence they desired and complicity with things of this world. They were considered to be heroes not so much because they had risen totally above the needs of the flesh but because their bodily discipline gained them hearts that were all of a piece.

When we allow ourselves to become aware of sexual desire we gain important indicators of the deeper and more complex levels of our existence. This awareness offers the possibility of growing into maturity not only psychologically but also spiritually. For example, our experience of sexual arousal tends to be seen primarily as instinctual. However it is also a matter of personal choice and discernment. In other words, we may be frequently aroused but we make options as to whether to act upon those feelings. Cultivating awareness of what comes into play as we are aroused, and as we choose to act or not act, is a vital experience. Gradually, we learn to respond not with compulsive behaviour but by considering options based on self-awareness and the awareness of other people. This, in the best sense, is the moral dimension of sexuality. It is essentially linked to the inner life in the Spirit rather than simply to abstract norms.

Equality, mutuality and reciprocity are the hallmarks of mature, free, non-possessive, non-abusive love. The depths of intimacy, including sexual union, are profoundly kenotic or self-giving in their direction. We are moved towards a shedding of our inauthentic selves and come to live and act more and more from within the truth of our deepest identity. We grow in our capacity to be available, to be appropriately disclosed, to be strong yet vulnerable, deeply moved to change rather than to stand stubbornly and fearfully in the safe and known.

To give and to receive sexually has a sacramental quality as long as it truly aspires to be a gift of *self* and a joyful receiving of another person, rather than merely an exchange of bodily stimulations. Spirit touches spirit. We might borrow the old Catechism language about sacraments, "it is an outward sign of inward grace", of a deeper inner reality. Appropriate sexual body language is a sacrament of "real presence" – both the true and unashamed presence of one person to another and, within that and cementing that self-disclosure, the "real presence" of the indwelling God. We may recognise God in the breaking open of self, for each other.

Sexual intimacy is eucharistic, a liturgy that may heal and restore loving partners to a spiritual centredness. Those who freely unite themselves to another come to know themselves at the same time as profoundly self-possessed, rather than invaded. Here, desire becomes more than a physical urge and is discovered to be that power within us that enables us to overcome our fears of absorption. The acceptance of my body by another and my acceptance of theirs, in intimate touch and mutual delight, is ultimately transformed into a deepening sense of the wholesomeness of my *person*. As we truly come into possession of our self, and learn to dwell in the self, we are also led into a movement beyond self to the other. And as, in turn, we come truly to dwell in the particular and personal love of the other person we are led even further by that same movement of openness. This does not occur without pain and struggle. By deep intimacy we move slowly towards the horizon of non-exclusive, universal love where, as in God, *eros* and *agape* are found ultimately to be one.

Sexual Union and Union with God

There is a beautiful account of spiritual communion in sexual intimacy in the extraordinary diary for the years 1941-43 of the Dutch Jew, Etty Hillesum.

> Perhaps that is the only real way of kissing a man. Not just out of sensuality but also from a desire to breathe for one moment through a single mouth. So that a single breath passes through both....
>
> And then for a short hour we had shared one breath as I had been wanting to do for many, many weeks. And I had rested so confidently and with so much surrender in his arms and yet full of sensual tension. But above everything else there was that shared breath. And in that short hour so much strength flowed into me that I believed I could live on it my whole life long.[32]

One of the spiritual books that had an early effect upon me when I first read it in the 1970's was the profound and beautifully written *Yes to God* by the late Alan Ecclestone. Amongst other things, it daringly (or so I thought at the time) had a chapter on "Spirituality and Sexual Love". Perhaps that simple fact was, in the long term, more important than the content of Ecclestone's words, but a number of his phrases and images remain powerful. First, sexuality represents our passion to become engaged. Secondly, it is "a great hunger", "a perception of beauty", "an intense pleasure". Yet it is ordered in such a way that "it challenges those divided by it to seek and find at another level a unity of being". Most powerfully of all, Ecclestone concluded that,

> The primitive impulse to deify sexual love was not wholly misguided; it has all the features of great mystical experience, abandon, ecstasy, polarity, dying, rebirth and perfect union.... It prompts between human beings those features characteristic of prayer; a noticing, a paying attention, a form of address, a yearning to communicate at ever deeper levels of being, an attempt to reach a certain communion with the other.[33]

If much mystical literature had traditionally used the language of sexual intimacy to describe our relationship with God, Ecclestone turned this, as it were, on its head. He used the language and experience of mysticism and prayer to express with great power the fullest potential of sexual union.

When sexual union is the consummation of deep, exclusive and faithful love between two people, it may be a sacrament of a union with God, and in God with all that is, for which God has created and redeemed humankind. Shared sexual joy, as a step towards God rather than as a substitute for it, is a genuine act of worship. Etty Hillesum learned a great deal about this from her close friend and lover Julius Spier.

> To him everything is of a piece, he does not separate the physical from the spiritual and feels so close and familiar to me precisely because his life is so much more coherent than mine.[34]

Of course, there are other kinds of human communion and communication that have something of the same possibility, but sexual intimacy between faithful lovers involves an intensity, a risky self-abandonment that makes this potentially a most powerful symbol.

In his unusual attempt to reintegrate sexuality with religious mysticism (*The Meaning of Love*), the controversial Russian theologian Vladimir Solovyev pointed out that human love pays little attention to pure multiplication of the species. Solovyev suggested that what he called "sex love" figured more strongly wherever the feeling of love for a unique person took on an unconditional importance – unconditional, not least, as to their capacity to be a good procreator! The desirability of the other is not dependent on her or his "usefulness".[35]

The ecstatic reading of sexual intimacy has historically found more acceptance in parts of the Jewish community than in Christianity. In Hasidic mysticism, the Song of Songs, while still associated with Passover time as symbolic of the mutual love between God and Israel, was also granted an explicitly interpersonal interpretation. Thus, it was sometimes read on the

Sabbath evening as a reminder that the beginning of the Sabbath saw the arrival of a "Bride" who was to be welcomed. Sexual intercourse between partners was also encouraged on the Sabbath night. To make love out of the fullness, relaxation and joy of Sabbath was the earthly counterpart of the holy union that occurred on the Sabbath evening between the *shechinah* (the indwelling presence of God, sometimes seen as the feminine aspect) and the masculine aspect of God.

To draw a parallel between sexual union and mystical union with God, as some Jewish traditions, Solovyev and Ecclestone do, should not appear blasphemous. If there is a blasphemy it lies, rather, in the fact that sexual union has been so downgraded that we find the parallel disconcerting. Union with a human partner is no longer naturally associated with our calling in Christ to be drawn into the life of God. Nor does union suggest the possibility of a participation by loving partners in the ecstatic, creative outpouring of God. This is far more than simply being procreators in a purely biological sense.

It seems to me that the contemporary criticism of patriarchy opens up the possibility of a more positive evaluation of sexuality and its conscious re-integration into the sacred. A patriarchal way of seeing tends to give sacred significance mainly to the biological aspects of sex. Thus, particular emphasis has been placed, at least implicitly, on the active male fertilisation of passive matter provided by a female incubator. The mystical-sacred dimension of sexual union is effectively diminished in such an unequal understanding of sexuality. Instead of stepping back in awe at the mystery of sexuality, we have also tended to prescribe how it should be conducted and thus to atomise it. This diminishment of sex is true both of pornography (sex is only for pleasure) and, sadly, of too much Christian moral teaching (sex is only to make babies). When compared to a richer vision, both views are revealed as reductionist and functional.

A Crossing of Boundaries

Sexual relations may at times be a major source of ecstasy in its proper sense of stepping outside the enclosed "self". However, we have been conditioned not to encroach on the domain of the sacred that traditionally was presumed to lie beyond such profane things. There has also been a tendency in Christian mystical theory to limit the ecstatic to a very narrow band of extraordinary experiences given to few, rather strange, people. There is a contrary movement today, accepted albeit with caution even by more conservative writers, to understand mysticism as a more everyday reality than has traditionally been appreciated.

Whether interpreted broadly or more narrowly, ecstasy may best be understood precisely as an experience of the temporary dissolution of the normal boundaries of perception and living. The Jewish diarist, Etty Hillesum, at times experienced intimacy in a similar way.

> He leant against the wall of Dicky's room and I leant gently and lightly against him, just as I had done on countless similar occasions in the past, but this time it suddenly felt as if the sky had fallen as in a Greek tragedy. For a moment my senses were totally confused and I felt as though I was standing with him in the centre of infinite space – pervaded by threats but also filled with eternity. In that moment a great change took place within us, for ever.[36]

Ecstasy is a moment in which some otherwise distant reality is glimpsed as here and now and at one with oneself. Whether in the context of contemplation or sexual intimacy, it is something that it is dangerous and damaging to grasp for its own sake. It is after all possible to become addicted to such heightened experiences. Certain depth experiences have their place in any fully human life and are *not* to be viewed with suspicion. But in contemplative mysticism particular experiences have no meaning in themselves. Their value is merely as a means towards the transformation of life as a whole. So, the temporary dissolution of boundaries involved with sexual intimacy serves the more general transformation of two people and their growing together into union on every level of their being. In other words, the unitive "glimpses" that sexual intimacy provides serve to deepen human identity and our perceptions of the way reality is.

We need to maintain a certain delicacy here. As with God's relationship with us, human intimacy involves holding in proper balance an appropriate dissolution of personal boundaries and yet the continued respect for personal space. It is an unfortunate fact, of which we are being made increasingly aware these days, that the sexual crossing of boundaries has often been violent and abusive. At the heart of most cases of sexual abuse, including rape, lies the desire to gain power over another human being. Sexual violation of boundaries seems to be used to meet a number of needs that have little to do with real sexual desire, let alone with love.

True human desire, just like God's desire for us, is respectfully attuned both to the self and to the partner. Each person may be lost in the other but individual boundaries are not abused or invaded. Each person freely allows them to be crossed in a way that enhances each partner rather than destroys his or her identity.

Conclusion

It is easy to spend a great deal of time lamenting how institutions, such as the Church, inhibit us from developing a *transformed practice* either of spirituality, or sexuality or both in relation to each other. Michel de Certeau, in his provocative writings on the human city, may offer a useful paradigm for thinking about these things differently.[37] He suggests that it is not only those who stand on top of high buildings, with an overview of the city grid, who are capable of saying "*this* is the city – this is what the city *means*". He points to the "subversive, resistant practice" of those who simply walk the streets and thus make the city "something else" that is not available to mere observers on high buildings. In determining what the city is, we need to turn our attention away from the producers (city planners) or the product (a theoretical city plan) and towards the consumers (the pedestrians). Such a paradigm suggests an interesting path towards re-envisioning the spiritual qualities of sexuality. In the end it is not the "producers", those in the role of authority, or the "product", the theoretical constructs, that alone determine what sexuality means. We also need to listen attentively to the voices of pedestrians – those who "walk the streets of everyday living and wrestle spiritual and sexual meaning out of their contexts and personal circumstances".

Notes

1 For example, see, Jon Alexander, "What do recent writers mean by spirituality?" *Spirituality Today* 32 (1980) 247-256. See also Philip Sheldrake, *Spirituality and Theology: Christian Living and The Doctrine of God* (London: Darton, Longman & Todd, 1998/New York: Orbis Books, 1999) 33 ff and 58-59.

2 Peter Brown, *The Body and Society: Men, Women and Sexual Renunciation in Early Christianity* (London: Faber & Faber, 1991).

3 The whole of Brown, Chapter 1, concerns classical Roman attitudes to masculinity and to relations with women. On Gerson, see Caroline Walker Bynum, *Jesus as Mother: Studies in the Spirituality of the High Middle Ages* (Berkeley: Univ. Pr., 1982) 135-136. For some other classic examples of medieval male celibate's fear of women, see, R.W. Southern, *Western Society and the Church in the Middle Ages* (London: Hodder and Stoughton, 1970) 314-315.

4 Peter Brown, *The Body and Society*, p 347; see the reference to Ambrose's, *De Officii*, n. 30.

5 Brown summarises Ambrose's understanding of integrity on p 354.

6 Caroline Walker Bynum, *Fragmentation and Redemption: Essays on Gender and the Human Body in Medieval Religion* (New York: Zone Books, 1991) 12.

7 Cited in Bynum, *Fragmentation*, p 269.

8 On the influence of Stoic philosophy on the early Church, see Peter Brown, *The Body and Society*, chapter 1 and pp 128-30.

9 James and Evelyn Whitehead, "Re-imagining the Masculine", *The Way* 32 (1992) 113-122, p 121.

10 *Meditations Collected and Ordered for the Use of the English College of Lisbo By the Superiors of the Same College* (2nd ed.; Douai: Baltazar Bellere, 1663), from the First Part,

"Meditations for Beginners or for the Purgatiue way", The First Chapter, The First Meditation ("What man is according to his body"), pp 2-3. I am grateful to Peter Harris of Allen Hall, London for this reference.

11 I have sought to address these issues throughout my *Spirituality and History* (2nd ed.; London: SPCK, 1995/New York: Orbis Books, 1998).

12 I am particularly grateful for the comments of Catherine Ryan OSM who is involved in a research project on the organisational analysis and behaviour of religious groups.

13 See, for example, Joan H. Timmerman, *Sexuality and Spiritual Growth* (New York: Crossroad, 1992).

14 See Peter Brown, *The Body and Society*, Chapter 1; and Jacques Le Goff, *The Medieval Imagination* (trans. by Arthur Goldhammer; Chicago: Univ. Pr., 1988) 93-103, "The repudiation of pleasure".

15 Michael de Certeau, "The Weakness of Believing: From the Body to Writing, A Christian Transit", in Graham Ward (ed.), *The Certeau Reader* (Oxford: Blackwell, 2000) p. 236.

16 Richard Sennett, *The Conscience of the Eye: The Design and Social Life of Cities* (London: Faber & Faber, 1993) xii.

17 See Robert Markus, *The End of Ancient Christianity* (Cambridge: Univ. Pr., 1990) 78.

18 For an important, if controversial, critique of theology's dependence on the Cartesian view of the self, see, Fergus Kerr, *Theology after Wittgenstein* (2nd ed.; London: SPCK, 1997).

19 René Descartes, "Meditations" in *The Philosophical Writings*, Vol 2 (Cambridge: Cambridge Univ. Pr., 1985) 18.

20 David Tracy, *On Naming the Present: Reflections on God, Hermeneutics and Church* (Maryknoll, N.Y.: Orbis, 1995) 16.

21 Rowan Williams, *Resurrection: Interpreting the Easter Gospel* (London: Darton, Longman & Todd, 1982) 29.

22 Theodore Jennings, "Making Sense of God", in Peter Byrne and Leslie Houlden (eds.), *Companion Encyclopedia of Theology* (London/New York: Routledge, 1995) p. 911.

23 See, for example, Anthony Meredith, "Patristic Spirituality", *Ibid.*, 536-557.

24 There are a number of useful surveys of contemporary Trinitarian writing. See, for example, David S. Cunningham, "Trinitarian Theology since 1990", *Reviews in Religion and Theology* 2 (1995) 8-16; Christoph Schwöbel, "Introduction: The Renaissance of Trinitarian Theology: Reasons, Problems and Tasks" in Christoph Schwöbel (ed.), *Trinitarian Theology Today: Essays on Divine Being and Art* (Edinburgh: T. & T. Clark, 1995); also Colin Gunton, "The Trinity in Modern Theology", in Byrne & Houlden, *Companion Encyclopedia*, 937-957.

25 Pseudo Dionysius, *The Divine Names*, 4.10, in *Pseudo-Dionysius: The Complete Works* (trans. Colm Luibheid; New York: Paulist Press, 1987).

26 Paul Tillich, *Systematic Theology* (Chicago: Univ. Pr., 1963) Vol. 3, *passim.*

27 Paul Tillich, *Love, Power and Justice* (New York: Oxford Univ. Pr., 1954) p. 30.

28 Pseudo Dionysius, *The Divine Names*, 4.14.

29 Paul Tillich, *The New Being* (New York: Scribner, 1955) p. 29.

30 Aelred of Rievaulx, *Spiritual Friendship* (trans Mark F. Williams; London/Toronto: Associated University Presses, 1994), Book 1: sections 1, 69 & 70.

31 Rainer Maria Rilke, *Letters to a Young Poet* (New York: W.W. Norton & Co., 1954) p. 59.

32 Etty Hillesum, *An Interrupted Life* (New York: Washington Square Press, 1985) p. 117.

33 Alan Ecclestone, *Yes to God* (London: Darton, Longman & Todd, 1975) p. 88.

34 Etty Hillesum, *An Interrupted Life*, p. 111.

35 See Vladimir Solovyev, *The Meaning of Love* (London: The Centenary Press, 1945).

36 Etty Hillesum, *An Interrupted Life*, pp. 172-173.

37 Michel de Certeau, *The Practice of Everyday Life* (Berkeley: Univ. of California Pr., 1988), Part III "Spatial Practices", Chapter VII, "Walking in the City".

Chapter Three

Bodiliness and Sacramentality

Maaike de Haardt

In this paper I wish to reflect on the meaning of embodiment, or the meaning of the body in relation to our understanding of sacramentality. These days it is not a novelty when theologians or philosophers focus on the body or embodiment, and it is difficult to gain a comprehensive view of the literature which covers not only the theological and philosophical disciplines, but many sociological and historical studies as well.[1] My central perspective in discussing bodiliness and sacramentality emanates from the ambivalence and ambiguity that surrounds the way we deal with both the body and sacramentality. This applies to the sciences, the churches and the way we deal with our bodies and sacramentality on a daily basis.

The Constructed, Living Body

As far as the body is concerned, it is not only the recognition of the genderedness of the body that brings a good deal of (healthy) confusion into our frequently abstract and universalistic way of thinking. The same holds true for the growing recognition of the constructionist character of our beliefs or opinions on the gendered body, and the many forms these constructions can take. Moreover, the body plays an important role as an object of and a vehicle for the construction of social, cultural and, above all, religious reality. The body is sign and site of all imagination.[2] As anthropologists and historians convincingly demonstrate, every culture naturalises a certain view of the human body to carry social meanings; body symbolism is always subservient to social intentions; certain social stratifications bring forth corresponding symbolic expressions of the body. For instance, hierarchy treats the body as a hierarchy; sects treat it as a closed system, individualism treats the body as pervasive energy. Consequently, it is impossible to speak of universal meanings of the body.[3]

The growing insights into the cultural, constructed, contextual, artificial, symbolic and epistemological dimensions of contemporary reflection on the body, make it almost impossible to speak of the body in an unambiguous, univocal and therefore obvious way. Even the "material basis" of these reflections, the body as a so-called "solid state of matter" is not as solid as we would like to think. And yet, when we refer to our bodies, or to our embodied way of being, we do so in an obvious way. It seems that we have no alternative. After all, the factual embodied existence, as complex and ambiguous as it is, is the only "thing" we have. And perhaps for that reason it is the only "matter" that ultimately can transcend the contemporary, sophisticated, philosophical and theological post-modern reflection on the fragmented, nomadic, performative, multi-layered and de-stabilised concepts of bodily identity and body-symbols. Perhaps it is only because of our concrete, however ambiguous, bodies, that in the end we can say, "I am" even without knowing "who" I am; even out of the awareness that the "who" is constantly changing, as is the body; and even knowing that the "I" is not identical with the body.

However, from a liberation and feminist theological perspective, and without minimalising the relevance of the aforementioned reflections, I would state that in the end bodies – concrete, living, dying, suffering, oppressed, laughing, crying, singing, eating, loving bodies – are the only matter that really matters: socially, politically and theologically.

Renewed Interest in Sacramentality

Contemporary reflections on sacramentality may be less elaborate and less multi-disciplinary than those on the body, we can nevertheless find a renewed interest in this subject, and not only among theologians. Part of this renewed interest and the corresponding research involves reflections on the so called "secular society" and the recognition of its "invisible religion", as sociologist of religion Thomas Luckmann calls it.[4] The strict division Western society, that is its sciences and churches, has made between the secular and the religious seems to lose its validity.[5] This should not only be interpreted as a consequence of the increasingly multi-religious character of Western society or of the effects of globalisation. The loss of the validity of the rigorous distinction between the secular and the sacred is primarily the result of the fact that, as empirical research has shown, many people even though they left the churches, consider themselves neither non-religious nor non-Christian.[6] For theologians, philosophers of religion, sociologists and anthropologists this development is "food for thought" because it criticises and undermines the conventional, scholarly diagnoses of religion and its definitions of what counts as religious.

Therefore, it is no coincidence that a renewed reflection on the meaning of religion, on religious sensibilities and on the point of reference regarding sacramentality, appear on the scene of theology and religious studies, although I must add that these insights and influences are still marginal. We encounter these efforts in the field of ritual studies, in (religious and spiritual) life histories, in studies on the religiosity of everyday life, and we find traces of it in the field of sacramental theology. The aim of this beginning cooperation of anthropologists, social scientists, religious studies scholars and theologians is to gain insight in the diversity of ways ordinarily people construct their lives in and through their way of living.[7]

Besides these developments, there is also a stream of renewal from within theology and Christianity, that is, where the traditional definitions and concepts are heavily criticised and newly interpreted by liberation theologians, feminists and/or non-Western theologians. Here one finds the limits, the exclusive and oppressive character of much of traditional, Western theology. We realise that we need new methods and new contents of theological thinking. In line with the aforementioned developments, I have in mind particularly the works of Asa Maria Isasi-Diaz, Delores Williams and Mary Mclintock-Fulkerston, although they use very different methods as well as genres of theological discourse.[8] These authors each try to open up the emancipatory or liberating potential of the Christian tradition by emphasising and exploring the shifting cultural functions, served by religious beliefs, in different Christian communities. These authors are also fully aware of the differences gender, race, and class make in the construction of cultures. The next step would be to integrate the results of these explorations in systematic theology so that the "anthropological turn" in theology has actual influence on the interpretation of the Christian tradition and its theological concepts.

Thus it becomes more and more important to examine "how" people believe, whether they call themselves Christian or not, instead of "what" they believe.[9] It is at this point that the concept of sacramentality enters the reflection. Sacramentality is always related to a praxis of experiences of transcendence or the sacred.

The Dangerous Potential of Sacramentality

Sacramentality is generally interpreted as the inherent possibility of the material world to be a manifestation of the sacred. But the acknowledgement of a reality as sacred is always an interpretation of a sensory, perceived reality. There are no inherently sacred objects nor is any object, event or person sacred "as such". And with this the first ambivalent and ambiguous element of sacramentality is given, a point to which we will return. Things are made sacred by a special context, mediated by sensory perception and recognised by the surrounding culture. This sacramentality is not a specifically Christian invention or characteristic. Anthropologists and religious studies scholars have shown that every culture has its own sacred spaces, persons and events. In our experience, most of the time the usual, recognised context of the sacred, at least in the Western Christian world, is a Christian and an institutional one. The churches hold, so to speak, the monopoly on sacramentality. A monopoly which historically and according to the internal order of the churches, is mainly restricted to the sacraments, whether seven, two or three.

Formally speaking, "sacraments are highly focused action-words within a larger liturgical context".[10] However, the Catholic tradition also holds an older, more general view on sacramentality that is broader than the sacraments or the sacrament-related so-called "sacramentalia".[11] Here we find the above mentioned general meaning of sacramentality in an explicitly Christian context and interpretation. This is considered to be a specific Catholic characteristic, called the sacramental principle, according to which "everything is, in principle, capable of embodying and communicating the divine".[12] This theologically highly valued principle that would be recognised by most Catholics as part of their spontaneous way of viewing the world, is nevertheless not very influential in reforming actual church practices. In a way this is understandable, since the implications of this fundamental principle are far-reaching, as I will demonstrate. It can be used, and in fact is used, by feminist and other theologians from all over the world to contradict contemporary dominant, oppressing and exclusive theological and ecclesiological concepts, images, attitudes and praxis, whilst at the same time we can refer to a venerable theological tradition.[13] And in this case I am not only thinking of Catholics. Potentially sacramentality could – at least in principle – endanger the status quo. Susan Ross even asserts that because of this "hidden" or "implicit" sacramentality of the Roman Catholic tradition, people, especially women, in spite of all their problems with the church, in the end do not leave their church.[14] This would imply that sacramentality, that is the concrete and lived experiences of divine presence, creates its own forms of (spiritual) power and praxis, more or less independent of the authorised sacramental praxis.

The meaning of the sacramental principle is, first of all, the recognition or the insight that all creation is sacred: all of being – human, animal, vegetable, mineral – is potentially revelatory of the divine and is to be treated as such. A second implication concerns the deep conviction, implied in the sacramental principle, that traces of God have to be found in the world, not by denying or leaving the world. A sense of God's presence is only approached in and through the material world. This is not to say that God and the world are identical, but that creation participates in God's reality. Thirdly, sacramentality is not only a general principle but is itself constitutive of revelation. In a way we find here an analogy to the "natural law" (understood not in a restricted or narrow-minded sense): "there is not only a logic and order in creation but a revelatory dimension to nature that goes beyond logic to an encounter with the source of life. In nature and in historical existence, one can find God".[15]

Sacramentality presupposes a continuity between the natural and the supernatural. From a Christian perspective, sacramentality, embedded in creation, emphasises the human capability to recognise the sacred, to recognise God's presence in every aspect and dimension of life.[16] Actually, it implies a positive view of humanity and an optimistic anthropology. In my opinion, sacramentality, can be interpreted as a strong force against all historical and contemporary (religious) movements that have looked upon material reality as intrinsically evil; that have neglected to care for all of the material world, nature as well as humans; that have neglected the integrity of creation. In this sense the apparent primarily aesthetic interpretation of sacramentality should not be restricted to an aesthetic appreciation, nor should it lead to aestheticism. There is an ethical dimension to sacramentality on a fundamental level.[17] Furthermore, from the perspective of sacramentality all Christian "otherworldliness", or body/matter/life-denying spirituality, can – again, in principle – be criticised.

An Ambiguous History: Body and Sacramentality

However, it is more complicated than that. One of the reasons of the complexity is that the Roman Catholic tradition itself ignored, contradicted, or as some would say even frustrated, her sacramental principle by, among other things, proclaiming a world-denying asceticism and a suspicion of the body, notably the female body. In the course of history, body, nature, sexuality and women became icons of evil. Women were the literal and symbolic personifications of this complex unity that in the end is a foreshadowing of death.[18] Whereas in sacramental thinking the finite, material world and divinity are closely linked and presuppose each other, this other, contradictory, movement has underlined the distinctions and pointed out the gap between the natural and the supernatural. This eventuated in an ecclesiastical, cultural and theological dominance of fear and loathing of body and nature (and of sexuality, women, and death), and – since Medieval scholastic theology – in the gradual diminishing of general sacramentality in favour of a strong judicial-theological theory and praxis of the sacraments.

It seems to me that in the Christian history of sacramentality (and the same applies to the sacraments) we can find some similarity with the Christian history of the body. And the same holds true for the developments in contemporary appreciation of this history. About 25 years ago it was not uncommon among theologians to hold Christianity entirely responsible for an inherently negative view on the body because this view was based on a rigorous dualism. This conviction was demonstrated by persuasive quotations from Paul, Tertullian, Augustine or Aquinas. However critical these voices, underneath these accusations one could mostly find the opinion that these powerful dualism were a distortion of a more "original" Christianity that was often thought to be "less Hellenistic".

Since then, more specialised research on body, gender and Christianity has appeared.[19] These studies shed light on a far more complex Christian history of the body, on account of which it became clear that it is impossible to speak of a general body-hostility in Christianity. All this does not mean that we can speak of an uncomplicated, clear and univocal, positive Christian view of the body, but at least we have gained a better insight in the tradition's more positive affirmations of the body and all of creation. As there are no universal meanings of the body, there is a growing insight that there is no "Christian history of the body" either. This has induced a greater openness and sensibility for the undercurrents and side-lines of the tradition. It remains an important and indispensible task to continue to investigate the Christian history of the body, especially, in view of the impact that the teaching of the Churches has had on the daily lives of many people.

Although many theologians, myself included, do not accept the hypothesis of an – only to be discovered – "original" Christianity, we consider the acknowledgement of the polyphonic, ambiguous, contextual, and divergent ways in which Christians and Christian reflection have dealt with the body and the fact that humans are embodied persons, as an important sign of the relevance as well as the everlasting complexity of this subject. In the last few years the systematic reflection on the sacraments has shown a similar shift: from an either apologetic or extreme critical position, restricted to inner dogmatic-liturgical theorising on the sacraments, we gradually find more concern for the historicity of the sacraments, and also for renewed reflection on sacramentality in a broader sense, and, as a consequence of this shift in interest, we see more questions on the meaning of the sacraments for our time. It has been generally accepted that the far more symbolic and polyvalent interpretation of sacramentality and sacraments in the early church became more and more instrumental in the course of time,[20] without, as has only recently been discovered and valued, completely losing its symbolic, ambiguous dimensions. Currently we notice not only a retrieval of the marginalised, far less dualistic interpretations of the body in history, but also a retrieval of the less instrumental and more symbolic, metaphoric meaning of sacramentality.[21] I detect an inherent connection between those developments, a connection that relates bodiliness and sacramentality. I shall return to this below.

Sacramentality, Vulnerability and Finitude

All this renewed attention does not make sacramentality itself less ambiguous. It is true that nature and body are good, but only "in principle". It does not mean that reality always is a manifestation of the sacred. Ordinarily everyday experiences confirm this insight. Nature can be beautiful, peaceful, and experienced as overwhelming, transcending or sacred; but also and at the same time it can be destructive, violent and fearful. The ambiguity with respect to the body, concerns, for the same reasons, the whole of creation. In embracing sacramentality, Susan Ross therefore rightly warns against an uncritical glorification of creation, body and cosmos. However, the same warning applies, as she continues, to a reaction to the body, nature and cosmos in which fear and hatred are dominant. Both positions deny the given fundamental ambiguity.[22]

Theologians seem to run a risk in displaying sacramental enthusiasm, especially those who re-value the sacramental principle in their work. To counter an overly optimistic view on sacramentality, Sallie McFague introduced the notion of "negative sacramentalism". It is her way of being critical of the sacramental principle and of reflecting on the ways it is affected by sin. Out of the same suspicion, David Tracy argues that sacramentality needs to be balanced by proclamation. Paul Tillich was lead to seek this balance in opposing the "Protestant" dialectical principle to the "Catholic" sacramental principle.[23] I would suggest that this "sacramental suspicion or reservation" is haunted by the same dualism it seeks to overcome or by the historical effects of an uncritical or merely aesthetic sacramentality.

McFague illustrates the concept of sacramentalism in respect to human and non-human bodies, "not as an expressions of divinity, but as signs of human sin and destruction". Negative sacramentalism is the expression she uses for the negation and the oppression of the "vulnerabile and the needy [who] cry out for compassion and care".[24] She refers here primarily to the misuse of "other" bodies for "our" own good, which I interpret as the misuse of women's bodies, poor bodies, bodies of colour, homosexual bodies and all other kinds of bodies, including the non-human bodies of nature. In short, bodies in different gradations, deviating from the white, male and heterosexual body. These bodies, according to McFague, "appear to us not primarily as expressions of divine loveliness but as evidence of human neglect and oppression". They refer to "our refusal to acknowledge these bodies as valuable in and for themselves and to God".[25]

It is at this point that I want to clarify my own assumption. Without denying the political importance of her point, this plea to acknowledge the value of the vulnerable and finite body should not, in my opinion, be reserved only for the vulnerability of the oppressed or misused bodies. The oppressed and misused are always the "others", who "we" neglect or oppress. The privileging of the "oppressed" bodies, the suffering, wounded bodies whose characteristics are not only their suffering and vulnerability, but also that their suffering is caused by others, runs the risk of forgetting the vulnerability, the suffering and finitude of all bodies. To stress the value of the vulnerable, outcast bodies seems to take for granted the non-outcast, non-victimised but nevertheless suffering or broken bodies the value of which in and for themselves and for God is often also problematic and pressing.[26] I believe it to be very important, socially, politically, as well as theologically, first and foremost, to recognise and to emphasise the value as well as the vulnerability and finiteness of all bodies, regardless of the actual state of a body or the cause of that state.

McFague's negative sacramentalism seems to imply that the recognition of the sacramentality of the body also means that "positive" sacramentality would go beyond the vulnerability and finitude of bodies. To point out the sacramental presence of the Divine does not eliminate, as McFague seems to suggest, human (nor non-human) vulnerability or finitude, just as it does not eliminate human sinfulness, injustice or power, as she also seems to fear. As far as this fundamental aspect is concerned, I believe that negative sacramentalism is an improper concept because it diminishes the critical power of the necessary revaluation of sacramentality, notably in its material, bodily dimensions. The same applies to a completion of sacramentality with a "prophetic" or Protestant principle, if this completion aims at naming and criticising suffering, decay or death. Sacramentality, as I understand it, does not imply abolition of, nor is it a protection against suffering, decay or anything else that is a consequence of embodied, material existence. For that reason I would reject McFague's notion of negative sacramentalism, although I agree with her that sacramentality should not lead to an overly optimistic view on human behaviour. It is perfectly clear that the plea for a renewed sense of sacramentality, a sense of presence, does not release theologians from the responsibility to name and charge injustice and sin. But, as I want to emphasise, these are not mutually exclusive actions. The interpretation of sacramentality as presented here, implies a strong ethical involvement.

The inherent tension (ambiguity) in the concept of sacramentality is disregarded and overruled when sacramentality is put in contrast, even a productive contrast, with other notions, such as negative sacramentalism, or a prophetic or Protestant principle. The complex way in which McFague and others are dealing with their own positive valuation of sacramentality not only demonstrates that their renewed affirmation of the sacramentality of the body (and the whole of creation) is ambiguous. It also shows that they do not recognise their own ambiguity as well, let alone recognise the ambiguity of sacramentality itself.

In my view, the implied ambiguity of sacramentality is closely connected with our common understanding of the relation between materiality and the sacred, between the ever-changing, fragmented, fluid, finite bodies and the (unconsious?) pressumed unchangeable, whole, infinite divine. To put it differently, our understanding of sacramentality is linked with the traditional view of the relation between immanence and transcendence. In my opinions ultimately this relation is still thought of as a hierarchy. Emphasising immanence is seen as a counterweight to transcendence, without discrediting or diminishing transcendance itself.

Ambiguity and Everyday Life: Sacramentality as Embodied Knowledge

There are three different but strongly related aspects that associate bodiliness and sacramentality: The first regards the fundamental material and sensory character of sacramentality. Sacramentality is (inherently) material by definition and therefore implies – at least in principle – a sacramentality of the body. However, as a consequence of its material basis it shares the temporal and finite character of the whole material world.

But that is not all. The experience of transcendence, of divine presence, is caused by a sight, a smell, a shiver, a touch, a sound, an event. It is a bodily, sensory experience. Moreover, it is an experience that is not everlasting but finite. It is a momentary intensifying of reality by transcendence of that same reality: to see the same reality but in a new light.

> To see a World in a Grain of Sand
> And a Heaven in a Wild Flower
> Hold Infinity in the palm of your hand
> and Eternity in an hour.[27]

Like most sensory perceptions, these kinds of experiences are often overwhelming and for the most part uncontrollable. Hence, sacramentality is embodied knowledge. It seems to me that this element of correspondence between bodiliness and sacramentality is still present or preserved in the sacramental praxis of the Catholic and the Orthodox Churches.

The second aspect of bodiliness and sacramentality is concerned with the aforementioned similarity between the ambiguity in experiences of the body and the sacred. Not every smell, touch, sound or shiver is a manifestation of the divine. One moment a smell or touch can be sacramental, the next horrible. Therefore, insight into the embodied character of sacramental knowledge implies the acknowledgement that our experiences as well as our reflections on sacramentality and bodiliness are determined by the situated character of embodied knowledge. Situated by time and place, that is: by gender, class, and race, and culture. This insight should, among others, be a warning against speaking in too general or abstract terms about sacramentality, the body or sexuality.

The last element I want to highlight is the everyday character of both sacramentality and bodiliness. With regard to sacramentality, this element gradually got lost in the long historical process in which the church, emphasising the distinctive features of sacramentality in general, distinguished the seven sacraments. The same applies to the theological reflection on the sacraments, where the sensibility that firmly based sacramentality in everyday experiences, got lost as well. The often brilliant speculative systems seem to have no relation to the sacramental events being described, namely the sensory perception of the complex material world in which an event suddenly comes to light as a manifestation of divine presence. In theological (and other scientific) reflection, everyday life seems to be more and more excluded, as some feminists would say, from the patriarchal ordering of the universe. It is generally considered to be the place of women, children and the elderly. Consequently, theoretical reflection itself becomes a substitute for communication about the experience of the divine.[28]

As said earlier, a parallel can be found in contemporary reflection on the body. According to the Mud Flower Collective this has to do with the failure to recognise one's own life as a theological praxis.[29] Until recently, women were socialised to seek and to find God in everyday life and to identify their life primarily with their body. It is no coincidence that women start their reflection with their everyday life, with the highly complicated ways of dealing with their bodies and their God. It seems to me that this confrontation with and the reflection on day-to-day experiences also brings forth the insight into what has been the central perspective of this paper, namely the fundamental ambiguity and ambivalence of sacramentality and bodiliness. Everyday life is concrete, familiar, conventional and coincidental; it is ruled by routine and by improvisation at the same time, because no system or rule can foresee everything that might happen in a lifetime and because everyday life is an intersection of the diverse atmospheres that determine people's lives: family, work, nature, world, home town . In this sense, everyday life is messy, it is a kind of "orderly chaos". In short, everyday life is ambivalent and ambiguous.

A Broader Perspective on Ambiguity

Although I did not start from a philosophical but from a practical, everyday life point of view, I am inspired by Ruth Page's proposal to use ambiguity to indicate the whole metaphysical view; as an umbrella term for change, diversity and polyvalence and for the conditions which they create.[30] In Page's view, ambiguity is a component structure of reality: "Expressed in the starkest terms, any human attempt at order is a locally agreed cluster of values and interpretations involving a temporary simplification of complexity and the transient arrest of some aspects of change."[31] Yet, if indeed the world is ambiguous and neither simply lapsed from one original divine order, nor solely to be known from a scientific order, no expression, even of religious commitment and value, can escape the effects of that condition. However, as Page assures us, although ambiguity may be "the uncanny", it is not chaos, it is not the end of order but a change in order. The acceptance of that change "demands of humanity something like a Gestalt switch in metaphysical perception".

There seems to lie truth in this; that is, when speaking from a western point of view. I am convinced that "order", be it scientific, ecclesiastical or whatever, is not only imperative for interpreting the world and lending it a certain stability and coherence, but "order" can also be – in fact often is – a false security, a way of avoiding vulnerability, change, polyvalence and diversity. One of the most effective ways of gaining such a deceptive security is to make everybody and everything that differs from the dominant perspective an "outsider" or the "other". As Page asserts, ambiguity should not be feared or evaded. It is a challenge and, according to Mieke Bal, a certain amount of "messiness" has epistemological advantages. It avoids a priori categories and the biases in its wake.[32] However, if indeed ambiguity is an inevitable aspect of life, than it could be a justifiable thesis to state that in our Western, post-modern society, one can evade this ambiguity everywhere but in everyday life. It is, after all, the realm where constructions, conventions and order are being broken all the time.

If it is also true that at this moment in history women are more experienced in living the complexity of everyday life with its temporary and tempered, negotiated, messiness and order, Mieke Bal's statement that women may be better skilled to exploit or less fearful to handle ambiguity, makes sense. Whatever the veracity of the statement, it seems to me that being able to live in the messiness of everyday life makes visible the capacity to accept the limits of being human.[33] However, I would like to make clear, that this capacity does not mean, nor imply, resignation, apathy, or submission, but implies living your life, well aware of its vulnerable, finite, transient, and ambiguous character. Looking at the lives and biographies of so-called "ordinary people", or reading the works of Womanist and non-Western liberation theologians, gives me a better understanding of what I called earlier: the dangerous power of embodied sacramentality.

The experience of "Presence", in whatever form or event, under whatever condition, by whatever name it is called, originates in people's resilience, hope, resistance, durability and also such joys as the affirmation of life in the joyful eating, drinking, laughing and loving of everyday life. With regard to this, Elsa Tames speaks of a "proposal from the quotidian", an attitude she recognises in Qohelet and which she believes to be the greatest defiance to those who deny others a full and dignified life.[34]

When I searched for biblical support for the approach I presented here, I found that the Wisdom literature, a tradition that has long been neglected in Western Christianity, might be a good place to start. Although this is not the time and the place to elaborate the relevance of this ancient tradition, I would like to mention a few important and recently discovered and valued aspects of the Wisdom tradition. One of its most striking characteristics is that it arose from reflection on the patterns of everyday human experience and out of the trust that God is revealed therein. Directly related to this element appears to be the interesting fact that in the Wisdom tradition the immanence and the presence of God are emphasised. Traces of the old sacramental tradition, in all its material, sensory, sensual and embodied expressions can thus be found in the Wisdom literature. Without wanting to sound polemic, one can look at Wisdom literature as a kind of "natural theology".[35] The Wisdom tradition offers neither unequivocal interpretations of nor simple solutions for painful or complex, existential questions. On the contrary, according to Lefebure, Job and Qohelet suggest that the sages were able to live with conflicting, or as I would say ambiguous, views of God as well of human life. Furthermore, Wisdom literature displays an awareness of the limits of human understanding and openness to the surrounding culture. Today, one can also find more and more reflection on Sophia, the personification of Wisdom, and on the relation between the Wisdom tradition, Sophia and Jesus. Some scholars regard Jesus, like Sophia/Lady Wisdom, as the Wisdom of God.[36] Others speak of Jesus as Sophia's prophet.[37] In my view these developments offer challenging opportunities for rethinking fundamental Christian notions.

Sacramentality and Sexuality: A Shift in Focus?

I would like to conclude my contribution with a few brief remarks on sexuality and the Catholic tradition. It seems to me we ought to be careful in "embracing sexuality" without any further specification. Just as the body and sacramentality, sexuality is a far too ambiguous and problematic concept as well as praxis to embrace unconditionally. I understand and support the historical necessity to criticise the ways the Churches developed their teaching on sexuality and the biased theological, anthropological assumptions that underlie that teaching, as well as the highly negative effects it has had on the lives of many women and men. Nevertheless, I agree with Lisa Cahill when she states that it is important to hold a perspective in which sexuality is accorded the respect it deserves, without, as she adds, disproportionate emphasis. In emphasising sexuality, be it in the context of (a good) marriage or, in a liberal context, in any other monogamous one-to-one sexual relation often called "friendship", as one of the central human expressions for understanding the nature of the love of God, it seems to me we repeat and therefore reinforce – although in a more friendly way – the Roman Catholic fixation on sexuality. Also, speaking of one-to-one relations in their sexual dimensions hardly makes it possible to discuss either sexuality or relation without the "burden" of procreation or the (male) heterosexual perspective. There are more and more diverse ways in which people manifest love, care, emotion, even lust, than by means of an exclusively genital expression.

However, there are other arguments for a different perspective. One of the objections womanist theologian Delores Williams once made against white feminism was its focus on the male-female relation as the only and exclusive important form of relationship. She refers to the love, care and support system that is central to Black communities as a much broader model than the marriage-model. I wonder if she would feel the same about the western lesbian and gay movements in their struggle for equal rights, not with regard to sexuality but in their focus on the "equal to marriage" model, and therefore emphasising a specific and exclusive form of relationship as the most important.[38] Williams would probably also point at the highly complex and problematic situation of black women in regard to sexuality.

In recent feminist, womanist and mujerist theology we see a plea for the family as a central category, even as the fundamental category in sacramental theology as an alternative for the marriage or the nuptial model.[39] Fully aware of the limits and the dangers of the concept of family, Susan Ross is convinced, as is Lisa Cahill, that "family", as "a context for embodiment, has the potential to discover new riches in embodied human life".[40] Family, then, is not solely equated with marriage. Ross understands family as an institution that involves and affects all persons, even single people. She mentions several advantages of placing sacramentality and embodiment in a familial context.

First, the family is both grounded in history and biology. "While families have no fixed structure (that is, families can be biological, adoptive, multigenerational, extended) there is a cross-cultural and historical stability to the family that is grounded in human sexuality. (…) Human beings are linked both biologically and socially to parents, siblings, other relatives; they are also affiliated with others."[41] Embodiment, sexuality, affective relations, needs for physical and psychic nurturing, are experienced in a cultural context in which embodiment is not limited to sexuality but includes it, in gendered and relational form.

Family, according to Ross, is dynamic and not based on the interpretation of one exclusive sexual act that offers little or no room for flexibility of roles. It is multidimensional and includes all kinds of complex human interrelationship in contrast to the nuptial model that is dyadic by definition. The family-model opens up the fundamental inequality that is supported by the nuptial symbolism and is especially one-sided with regard to the roles of women in emphasising "receptivity". Consequently, Ross proposes an understanding of relationality as responsibility. Finally, the family, notably the family that goes beyond the biological family, can claim scriptural roots.

One of the great advantages of this model, as I see it, is that it firmly roots embodiment as well as sacramentality in a real, historical, social and cultural context that includes not only gender, but also race and class. It opens up the possibility to deconstruct a "natural", often false and unjust family-model, and to show the potential sacramentality of all biological and social relationships, without ignoring the complexities and ambiguity of embodiment and sacramentality. Although I have some reservations about this family-concept, I recognise and recommend its potential and its challenges.[42]

Notes

1 Carolyn Bynum, "Why all the Fuss about the Body? A Medievalist Perspective", *Critical Inquiry* 22 (1995) 1-33.

2 Paula M. Cooey, *Religious Imagination and the Body. A Feminist Analysis* (New York/Oxford: Oxford University Press, 1994).

3 See, among others, the influential work in this field by Mary Douglas, *Natural Symbols. Explorations in Cosmology* (3rd ed.; London: Routledge, 1996).

4 Thomas Luckmann, *The Invisible Religion: The Problem of Religion in Modern Society* (New York: Macmillan, 1967).

5 Linda Sexson, *Ordinarily Sacred* (Charlottesville: University of Virginia Press, 1992); Maaike de Haardt, *"Kom eet mijn brood..." Exemplarische verkenningen naar het goddelijke in het alledaagse* (Nijmegen/Tilburg: K.U. Nijmegen, 1999).

6 Heinz Streib, "Alltagsreligion oder: Wie religiös ist der Alltag? Zur lebensweltlichen Verorterung von Religion in praktisch-theologischem Interesse", *International Journal of Practical Theology* 2 (1998) 23-51.

7 Clifford Geertz, *Local Knowledge. Further Essays in Interpretative Anthropology* (New York: Basic Books, 1983) p. 16. I refer, among others, to the work of Ronald Grimes, Catharine Bell, Susan Starr Sered, and Paul Post, all of whom are working from either a ritual or more broad anthropological starting point.

8 Ada María Isasi-Diaz, *En la Lucha. In the Struggle: Elaborating a Mujerista Theology* (Minneapolis: Fortress, 1993); Delores S. Williams, *Sisters in the Wilderness: The Challenge of Womanist God-talk* (Maryknoll, NY: Orbis, 1993); Mary McClintock Fulkerson, *Changing the Subject: Women's Discourses and Feminist Theology* (Minneapolis: Fortress, 1994).

9 This is a fundamental insight in feminist and other liberationalist theologies, one that seems to be gaining ground in wider theological circles. See, Robert J. Schreitner, "Nieuwe contouren van geloven. Verkenningen van de stand van zaken in de huidige cultuur", *Tijdschrift voor Theologie* 39 (1999) 34-47. For a more elaborated reflection on this subject, see my text, *"Kom eet mijn brood..."*.

10 Regis A. Duffy, "Sacraments in General", in Francis Schüssler Fiorenza, John P. Calvin (eds.), *Systematic Theology. Roman Catholic Perspectives*, vol. II (Minneapolis: Fortress Press, 1991) 181-210, p. 181.

11 "Sacramentalia" are all kinds of blessings: persons, events, objects. They are an expression of the consecratio mundi and applied in very different situations and accommodated to different places and spaces. See, *Lexikon für Theologie und Kirche, Das Zweite Vaticanische Konzill*,

vol. I (Freiburg: Herder, 1993) p.72, "Anmerkung bei artikel 79 Sacrosanctum Concilium".
12 Richard P. McBien, *Catholicism*, quoted by Susan A. Ross, *Extravagant Affections. A Feminist Sacramental Theology* (New York: Continuum, 1998) p. 34.
13 However, although not every theologian refers at this point to "sacramentality" as a leading concept, the basic principles in (which) some theological alternatives (are described) can nevertheless be interpreted as "sacramental". See, for instance, Chung Hyung Kyung's description of an Asian feminist spirituality and theology in *The Struggle to be the Sun Again* (Maryknoll, N.Y.: Orbis, 1990).
14 Susan Ross, *Extravagant Affections*, p. 35.
15 *Ibid.*, p. 23.
16 Frans Maas, "Verkenning voor een hedendaagse sacramentele vroomheid", in W. Derkse, P.A.van Gennio and S. Waanders (eds.), *Ontmoetingen van geloof en wereld. Perspectieven op katholieke levensbeschouwing* (Best: Damon, 1999) 113-132.
17 Frans Maas, *Schoonheid vraagt om goed gezelschap. Katholieke cultuur tussen esthetiek en ethiek* (Vught: Radboudstichting, 1997).
18 See my, *Dichter bij de dood. Feministisch-theologische aanzetten tot een theologie van de dood* (Zoetermeer: Boekencentrum, 1993).
19 See, for instance, the works of Peter Brown, Margaret Miles and Carolyn Walker Bynum.
20 Regis A. Duffy, "Sacraments in General", p. 191.
21 This rediscovery of the symbolic meaning of the sacraments, mostly interpreted as their sign-character or representational image of the mystery of God (respectively Christ), can also be used as a plea for preservation of the status quo.
22 Susan Ross, *Extravagant Affections*, p. 37.
23 *Ibid.*, p. 35, note 39.
24 Sallie McFague, *The Body of God. An Ecological Theology* (London: SCM Press, 1993) pp. 185-186.
25 *Ibid.*, p. 186.
26 See my, *Dichter bij de dood*; also: "Transcendence, Finitude and Identity: Reflecting the Body Dying", in Jonneke Bekkenkamp and Maaike de Haardt (eds.), *Begin with the Body. Corporeality, Religion and Gender* (Leuven: Peeters, 1997) pp. 12-29.
27 From William Blake, "Auguries of Innocence", in John Hayward (ed.), *The Penguin Book of English Verse* (Harmondsworth: Penguin, 1968).
28 Ulrich Hemel. "Differenzierung und Transformation. Phänemenologische und structuranalytische Anmerkungen zum thema 'Alltagserfahrung und Transzendenz", in B. Caspar and W. Sparn (ed.), *Alltag und Transcendenz. Studien zur religiösen Erfahrunge in der gegenwärtigen Gesellschaft* (Freiburg/München, Alber Kreiburg, 1992).
29 Mud Flower Collective, *God's Fierce Whimsey. Christian Feminism and Theological Education* (Maryknoll, NY: Crossroad, 1985) pp. 64-65.
30 Ruth Page, *Ambiguity and the Presence of God* (London: SCM, 1985) p. 13.
31 *Ibid.*, p. 23.
32 Mieke Bal, "Methaphors He Lives By", *Semeia* 61 (1993) 185-207, p. 204.
33 *Ibid.*
34 Elsa Tamez, "When Horizons Close Upon Themselves". in D. Batstone et al (eds.), *Liberation Theologies,Postmodernity and the Americas* (New York: Routledge, 1977) 53-68, p. 64.
35 Leo D. Lefebure, "The Wisdom of God: Dialogue and Natural Theology", *Christian Century* 111 (1994) 994-999. There are many recent publications on Wisdom literature and, not coincidentally, quite a lot from a feminist perspective. Related to the growing interest in Wisdom literature in general there also is an emerging interest, stimulated by feminists, in Sophia, Lady Wisdom, the personification of God. For an overview of recent literature on this subject see my "*Kom, eet mijn brood*".
36 The work of Elizabeth A. Johnson is an example of this position, *She Who Is. The Mystery of God in Feminist Theological Discourse* (New York: Crossroad, 1995).
37 Elizabeth Schüssler-Fiorenza, *Jesus. Mirjam's Child and Sophia's Prophet. Critical Issues*

in Feminist Christology (New York: Continuum, 1995).

38 Delores S. Williams, "Women's Oppression and Life-Line Politics", *Journal of Feminist Studies in Religion* 1 (1985) 59-71; *Sisters in the Wilderness – The Challenge of Womanist God-Talk* (Maryknoll, NY: Orbis, 1993).

39 Susan Ross, *Extravagant Affections*, part 2.

40 *Ibid.*

41 *Ibid.*, p. 130.

42 I would like to thank Magda Misset-van der Weg for her help with this manuscript.

PART II

EXPERIENCING SEXUALITY

Chapter Four

The Female Experience of Sexuality

Mary Grey

How does one begin to confront the silence as regards the Christian/Catholic tradition on female sexuality? For it cannot be denied that prescriptive understandings of this have been developed and enforced by a male, celibate, clerical élite, within a patriarchal tradition and largely for motives of social control of women and children. As Judith Plaskow wrote in connection with the urgent task for Judaism:

> The need for a feminist Judaism begins with hearing silence. It begins with hearing the absences of women's history as shaping forces within the Jewish tradition.... Women have lived Jewish history and carried its burdens, but women's perceptions and questions have not given form to Scripture, shaped the direction of Jewish law, or found expression in liturgy.[1]

Is it not the same for Christianity? But if there was just silence to contend with, the task might be simpler. Unfortunately, when one combs the tradition for some clues, the negative thinking on female sexuality in Patristic thought as representing the shameful part of human nature that has formed the backdrop to official teaching – even if the line now is not explicitly misogynist – is an enormous stumbling block. As the novelist's imagination makes the mediaeval Héloise cry to Abelard (and their lives were surely victims to warped thinking on sexuality!):

> Do you think that I have not read what the Fathers have said about women since the beginning of the world? Do you think that it is easy for a woman to read that she is man's perdition?[2]

Thus the task of *hearing the silence into speech*[3] is complex, involving the way cultural constructions of gender identities – both masculine and feminine – serve the interests of the powerful; the internalisation by both women and men of the dominant understandings of sexual meaning; the distrust of bodily pleasure within the Christian tradition; the way thinking on sexuality has been used to justify the exclusion of women from ordained ministry; and the fact that the act of re-thinking is itself influenced by contemporary cultural factors both negative and positive. A salient factor in this case is the way feminist thinking – even moderate Christian feminist thinking – is encountering suspicion, mistrust and backlash from official authorities. It is accused of being anti-men, anti-marriage and family, and anti-Pope, pursuing a self-centred goal of fulfilment at all costs, even at the cost of a trail of abandoned children.

Mindful of all the many pitfalls, this paper attempts to sketch a way forward for understanding female sexuality specifically in its *conjugal* expression. I do not for a minute underestimate the importance of the lesbian discourse.[4] But there has been a tendency in recent feminist thought – as part of the ongoing struggle against hetero*sexism* – to focus all new thinking on sexuality around lesbianism, so that there is very little left that is inspirational about marriage itself. As Carter Heyward put it, "In feminism the lesbian word is made flesh"[5] – which leaves the question as to whether it can be made flesh at all within the married relationship.

"If I was you, I wouldn't start from here"

Postmodernism teaches that *there is no safe space outside our socialisation into patriarchally-constructed notions of sexuality and marriage,* within which to float free of all prejudices and presuppositions. Yet Christian feminist discourse, at the very least, offers points of critique from which to ask fresh questions. Whereas these are offered from "women's experience" there is no claim for any assumed universality. The discourse of the women's movement has increasingly made space for diversity, trying hard to make amends for the early days when a Euro-American analysis assumed a false superior position. Context makes all the difference as to whether economic, social-cultural, racial, traditional and religious factors offer genuine opportunities for heterosexual relationships to be experienced as loving, just, egalitarian partnerships. My list is far from exhaustive.

Egalitarian Re-thinking

The context of this re-thinking is a culture characterised by individualistic narcissism, stress on self-fulfilment, and a cult of pleasure, where sexual pleasure is frequently conceived of as immediate self-gratification, not necessarily within committed relationships. Immediately this has to be qualified as being a Euro-American feature, one not characteristic of many other parts of the world. (In this context the Vatican reaction of stressing sex exclusively within life-long monogamous marriage is intelligible.) That is the negative side. The positive side is that goals of fulfilment and freedom for all human beings are seen as achievable in and through the sexual relationship. Put in the context of a Christian sexual ethic, as Lisa Cahill rightly states:

> For Christian sexual ethics to have more than a future as more than a sectarian relic it must ground sexual freedom and fulfilment in some account of human goods at stake in sex and in the relationships built upon it.[6]

Contemporary stress on egalitarian partnership, on the hope of an integrated human life within marriage must be the hopeful beginning of what is at stake – but only a beginning.

Romance

The romantic myth in which marriage is frequently packaged – in novel, TV, film and advertising – still maintains its grip. See the continuing popularity of stories such as *Gone with the Wind*. Marie Fortune describes it thus:

> Rhett Butler and Scarlett O'Hara are arguing: he tries to kiss her; she resists; he picks her up and carries her up the grand staircase. The film cuts to Scarlett waking up alone in bed the next morning; smiling, radiant and happy; although the movie was produced before sexual scenes were explicit, the dramatic implication is clear: Butler took O'Hara to her bed despite her resistance and forced her to have sexual intercourse. The next morning she is delighted by the whole affair. This is the picture now repeated over and over; only now in films the sex scene is explicit and usually more violent.[7]

But does this mean that there is no place for romance within a renewed sexual ethic? Clearly not in this form, but there are other possibilities within a Christian framework which deserve attention.

"Happy-ever-after…?"

Following this, it is a sad fact that classical literary imagination stops short when the hero captures the heroine and the stage is set for "happy-ever-after". The hunt is over; existence freezes with the "capture". But partnership is not the same thing as a single event.

Not only is it almost impossible to find examples of married holiness in Christian tradition, but, more specifically, to find couples whose path to holiness was nurtured specifically through sexual intimacy. (I am convinced that this has frequently happened, but it has not been held up to us as a path to follow.) Nor do mothers with small children fare any better, although there is sentimental idealisation of the young mother who has just produced the son and heir. Tolstoy's epilogue to *War and Peace* describes his heroine Natasha, a few years after marriage in a most unflattering way.[8]

Reproductionism

One of the sexual goals of marital intercourse within patriarchal constructions is undoubtedly ensuring the continuation of the line, thus achieving a particular form of immortality – although this also can lead to more discrimination against girls.[9] Maternal deaths in childbirth have been so much part and parcel of Christian marriage tradition that they have often simply been assumed to be part of "women's lot". Nor was this confined to poor women: a recent biography of Jane Austen – a clergyman's daughter – casually mentions that her three sisters-in-law died in childbirth. One had been married at 18, produced a child a year until she died with the birth of the last one at the age of 26 years.[10]

Surrender and Obedience

An important problem area for feminist discourse is that the principal model of heterosexual love inherent in patriarchy is that of penetrative genital intercourse, the expression of domination and submission, presumed to be the height of sexual pleasure. This is subsumed under the rhetoric of marital bliss. In Christian tradition, it is confused with notions of women having to perform the "marital debt" (not to render the debt was material for Confession). Marriage was seen as the surrendering of a woman's will to that of her husband, although procreation was always presumed to function as the justification for the sexual act in the first place. In many instances, this has resulted in the instrumental use of women, with callous disregard to female inability or disinclination to respond sexually. Sexual excitement in terms of the hunt/capture/surrender is not only the motif of the bodice-ripper romances, but has been and is the tragic reality of married life for many women the world over. Unquestioning obedience to the will of a husband, servicing his sexual need whatever the drudgery of a woman's life, even enduring abuse and violence, is far from a reality of the past. Carol Adams writes:

> According to the US Bureau of Justice National Crime Survey, in the US a woman is beaten in her home every 15 seconds. Testimony before the Senate Judiciary Committee indicates that as many as 4 million women are affected each year by woman-battering (US Congress, Senate 1990). In the US, a woman is more likely to be assaulted, injured, raped, or killed by her male partner than by any other assailant.[11]

Against this background it is no wonder that this understanding of the meaning of sexual intercourse is questioned by feminist thought. It has even to be asked whether the new, contemporary personalist meanings of sexual expression such as mutuality, sex as healing and sustaining, can really work if the dominant model is still in place and if the underlying misogyny is not addressed. For example, much of the Church rhetoric in encouraging women to understand their role as home makers, providing a nurturing ambience to the man as breadwinner, who is stressed-out from the strains of the "real world", has been geared towards preserving the man from temptation to extra-marital infidelity. Little attention was given to what women need in terms of nurture. But again, the double standard regarding marital fidelity has been a constant feature. The fact that, for Augustine, masculine sexuality needed control ignored the fact that for women, uncontrollability of sexual desire is seldom a problem. The assumption has continued to be that compulsory maternity is a woman's destiny. Thus, sexual expression, seen as separate "acts", was necessarily linked with procreation as a manner of controlling masculine sexuality, but it simultaneously functioned as an excuse for constant availability to serve male sexual needs.

Biological Model

Against this background it has to be asked if the suffering of many women within marriage – unquestionably linked with economic factors of poverty, unemployment, housing, lack of education and social desperation – is not exacerbated by the restriction of sexual expression to this biologically-based penetration model of intercourse, one which in these circumstances could be conducive to male aggression, or at least to male assertion of power over women.

All these factors can be developed cross-culturally. For black American women the picture is complicated by racism and colonialism: it was particularly their sexuality that was victimised by the white slave trader. It is the marriage traditions that make the lives of many Indian women a torment. Bride-burnings are on the increase – as is infanticide of the female girl-child. The position of widows in many cultures is a desperate one; their right to a human existence is diminished at the death of their husbands.[12] Although it has to be said that all these factors coalesce in expressing an underlying misogyny (experienced by women in numerous ways), the marriage relationship can be a site of intersection where, owing to the weight of tradition and the inflexible nature of authority, many women experience themselves as totally trapped.[13]

Signposts for a Way Forward

Of the many currents in contemporary feminist thought, in the context of attempting a dialogue with Roman Catholic teaching on the marriage relationship, certain choices are necessary. There are at least three radical currents to be mentioned but not developed in this paper. First, Judith Butler's project is the deconstruction of the binary oppositions of maleness and femaleness – which she sees as only intelligible within compulsory heterosexuality:

> This socially constructed system links and regulates sex, gender, and desire in stipulated constellations of "male" and "female", "masculine" and "feminine" for purposes of reproduction. Butler is interested not only in "achieving the denaturalisation of gender as such", but even in confounding the very binarism of sex, and exposing its fundamental unnaturalness.[14]

To suggest such a radical agenda in the current attempts at dialogue with the Roman Catholic authorities, sadly, might eliminate common ground.

Secondly, the project of the Italian philosopher Luce Irigaray also attempts to disrupt the binary system by trying to develop a specific female imaginary, a new symbolic system which advocates,

> a multi-faceted strategy of eliciting of women's voices, listening for the silences, the lacunae, the sounds from the margins, listening not just to fathers and sons but to mothers and daughters, even as the question of women subjects is thereby destabilised.[15]

This project, potentially the most exciting around at the moment, takes as starting point the realities of the female body, asking what is female bodily pleasure and how women becoming subjects outside the "economy of the same", if they refuse to fit into the traditional male discourse:

> So for woman it is not a matter of installing herself within this lack, this negative, even by denouncing it, nor of reversing the economy of sameness by turning the feminine into the *standard* for sexual difference; it is rather a matter for trying to practice that difference.[16]

The wide-reaching parameters of the discussion of sexual difference lie beyond the aims of our particular task. What is important is the stress on a symbol system arising out of women's experience based on birth-giving. Birth-giving – *natalité* – is meant in a wider sense than simply physically giving birth. It stands as the core of a symbol system inspiring creativity, life, care for all living beings, replacing patriarchal images focused on warfare, power-as-dominance and violence.[17]

Thirdly, arising from French feminism, in particular from the work of Julia Kristeva arises a discourse of female *jouissance*, sexual pleasure, which, it is claimed, can be detected in the gaps and fissures of patriarchal discourse. *And Sarah laughed* (at the announcement of the conception of Isaac), is sometimes thought to be an example of this. How is this *jouissance* to be detected?

> But listening, by recognising the unspoken within all discourse, however revolutionary, by emphasising at each point whatever remains unsatisfied, expressed, new eccentric, incomprehensible,

that which disturbs the mutual understanding of the established powers.[18]

A Christian Feminist Perspective

A specifically Christian sexual ethic springing from feminist, liberationist thinking and congruent with much contemporary thought, is grounded first in the New Testament vision of the Reign, or Kingdom, of God. Significantly, the *mujerista* theologian Ada Maria Isasi Diaz prefers to speak of the "*kin-dom*" of God, because "we are all brothers and sisters in the new creation".[19] Within Jesus' vision and proclamation of the Reign of God all relationships are placed within a framework of justice, peace and the reconciliation of all creation. How we relate is not only a matter of personal happiness but of significance for the "upbuilding of the Body" as a whole.

It is interesting that Jesus never speaks about orgasmic fulfilment, but does preach *love* as the ethic of the Kingdom. Nor is love an abstract, spiritualised concept. For a spiritual healer, Jesus is extraordinarily interested in *bodies,* particularly when they are sick, despised, outcasts and with no legal rights. He wants bodies to be fed and to be healed: his eating practices are one of the key characteristics of Kingdom ethics. Specifically as regards women, it is remarkable that they are valorised specifically not as procreative vessels of patriarchy, but as hearers and doers of the word: "Yea rather, blessed are they who hear the word of God and keep it!" (Lk 11:28) Women are also valued as co-workers in the spreading of the Good News – another indication that, however one's sexuality is lived-out, the priority is that it is subsumed into the ethics of the Kingdom.

So, marriage is for the Kingdom – a special (but not exclusive) embodied, incarnational way of living out of just relationships. Rather than beginning with Genesis – Fall, and subsequently blaming of Eve – a trajectory beloved by the Fathers – a Christian feminist ethic begins with Resurrection: if all creation is invited to participate in new creation, the Risen Life of Christ, this applies also to human sexuality. Women and men can embody a diversity of transformed relationships, playing an integral part in transforming society. It cannot be too strongly emphasised: patriarchy is *disordered relationship* spawning diseased patterns of *both* maleness *and* femaleness. Re-conceiving these patterns enables both women and men to balance tensions between pleasure and responsibility, between interpersonal fulfilment and commitment to community.

Building on this, one of the insights of feminist thinking is the intrinsic connection between love and justice. (This is an integral to liberation theology, essentially grounded in *praxis*.) Mindful of the multiple, global contexts in which sexuality is lived out, it is impossible to define sexual meaning and purpose without reference to economic, social and environmental context. A simple example would be the enforced sterilisation programme put in place by the Indian government. Forcing family planning onto poor rural communities, whose primary concern is the survival of enough children into adulthood to ensure the survival of the family, was a venture doomed from the start. As Carter Heyward put it:

> We must begin to see that love is justice. Love does not come first, justice later. Love is not a "feeling" that precedes right relation among the persons in a family or the people of the world. We do not feel our way into doing what is just. We act our way into feeling.... Sexuality is the undercurrent of the love that flows as justice in close friendship; in the victory salutation of a Sandinista rebel in Nicaragua.... when there is no justice – between two people or among thousands – there is no love.[20]

Hence any discourse of interpersonal sexual pleasure can never be isolated from the backdrop of global justice.

A second current running through feminist thinking is that of the centrality of *embodiment*.[21] This is congruent with the New Testament focus on the healing of bodies (never separated from the healing of soul/spirit). Feminist pastoral theologians and ministers often focus on the healing of the violated bodily integrity of women. But within the Pauline understanding of the Body of Christ, this must be a concern of the whole Church. As Sally McFague has put it: if the world can be seen as the Body of God, the shape of the body is *Christic*.[22] The focus of the Christic body today, as in the ministry of Jesus, must be on the well-being and flourishing of the body (in the most integrated meaning of body, personally and communally): redeemed from the androcentric, patriarchal constructions, there is much within the Catholic/Christian tradition to support this widened notion of flourishing. But one cannot side-step the need for transforming the way official teaching on sexuality refuses to listen to a specific female experience, ignoring the continuing violation of women's bodies, even if violence and discrimination are now officially condemned, and interpersonal meaning now extolled.

Feminist understandings of embodiment show that female sexuality is more diffuse, not so mono-focused on genitality as is often presumed. The affective dimension of sexuality, as tenderness and intimacy is expressed in a plurality of ways. Women, often stereotyped as less intelligent, are no less prone to loving *mindfully*. The idea of loving with body and intelligence is an ideal of feminist theorists, theologians and poets, such as Adrienne Rich.[23]

Childbirth and breast-feeding can be experienced as a source of sexual pleasure – but many women are hesitant to admit this, feeling somehow guilty, as it seems far from the dominant understanding of sexuality (usually dismissed as purely hormonal!), and not directly linked with their partner's pleasure. The female clitoris is also a site of great sexual pleasure – which makes the practice of female genital mutilation practised in some Muslim countries, and now, increasingly, in Britain, such a brutally cruel and unjustifiable practice.

Embodiment and Eros

Linked with this is the way eros is understood. The late Audre Lorde is usually credited with expressing this in an inspirational way as "the creating, enlarging and sustaining of relationships", the "assertion of the life-force of women, of that creative energy empowered". It is the power which at its deepest roots understands joy and refuses injustice,

> because the deepest celebration is the union with others, and the clearest protest against oppression comes not from an abstract commitment to principles, but from the experience of suffering caused by oppression.[24]

Others link eros with the creative energy pulsating through the whole of creation. Carter Heyward names erotic power as sacred, finding its home ultimately in God:

> As we come to experience the erotic as sacred, we begin to know ourselves as holy and to imagine ourselves sharing in the creation of one another and of our common well-being. As we recognise the faces of the Holy in the faces of our lovers and friends, as well as in our own, we begin to feel as ease in our body-selves – sensual, connected and empowered. We become resources with one another of a wisdom and a pleasure in which heretofore we have not dared believe. We begin to realise that God moves among us, transcending our particularities.[25]

It is common today to challenge the sharp distinction in Christian tradition between eros and agape, especially given the classical expression by Anders Nygren.[26] Augustine's sense of being drawn towards God by the desire of God is one way of enlarging understanding of erotic desire as focused on pure self-satisfaction. *Agape* – traditionally seen as "disinterested love" is often understood less as totally other-centred than as including an element of pleasure within the process of service of others. Thus Sally Purvis has written of motherhood as model of agapic love in the sense of a mother's joy and well-being (yes, suffering and sorrow too), being bound up with her child: her self-giving, pleasure and pain, focused on the child, are yet integrally bound up with her very life-purpose.[27]

Whereas it is helpful to Christian thinking to challenge the sharp boundaries between self-seeking and other-centred love, and to widen the eros discourse to include creative energies, this needs careful attention. In the first place, it is a discourse of the First rather than Third World. Third World women suffer so much from degraded and pornographic forms of eros – for example in the trafficking of women – that such language is out of place. Secondly, in placing eros in a rather idealised context of "relational power", in a rather free-floating manner, the specifics of married sexuality are not addressed. A Jewish tradition suggests a helpful context: at the Passover Haggadah, two texts are read: the Exodus story and the Song of Songs: a suggestion that liberation and committed sexual love can be combined as a community ideal.

An area not to be neglected – alluded to but not yet addressed specifically – is how feminist theological thought on sexuality copes with the tradition's essentialist interpretation of a woman's vocation as that of motherhood. As is well-known *Mulieris Dignitatem* understood motherhood to be lived out either biologically or spiritually (with a special dignity being attributed to consecrated virginity). In each case, the accent is on the mother's body as oriented to "total self-giving".[28] Acknowledging the progress made in this document in outlining women's role in the New Testament and in condemning discrimination, Feminist theology still rejects its blatant essentialism and attempts to move beyond the way motherhood has been used as a means for the of social control of women's lives (motherhood has even been thrust upon us as means of salvation – 1 Tim 2:15).[29]

There are many ways of being a woman – as there are of being man – and the challenge to live responsibly eludes no one. But Feminist theology insists that if women are fully human subjects, then self-determination in areas of sexuality must be encouraged and promoted. Of course within a Christian, relational ethic, this takes place in the context of responsibility to community and gospel. One of the strengths of Christian tradition is to take responsibility for the way marriages and family life can flourish according to Gospel values. Undoubtedly, motherhood has brought many women lives of unremitting drudgery, poverty, and early death. But – misogyny apart – this is often because society in general devalues caring roles – such as nursing and social work. The recently-developed ethics of care and responsibility[30] (and the years of ensuing discussion) has demonstrated the gender division in the area of care.

Jean Baker Miller pointed out the socialisation of women to empathy and relational sensitivity.[31] Carol Gilligan, in her later work, described the development of two types of self, a self developing through autonomy and independence, and a self developing through intimacy and connection. The nature/nurture divisions here are blurred.[32] But, as Miller asserts, if it is true that women have been socialised to be more relational and empathic, this is a torch carried in the name of all humanity. If women have lived out marital love as caring – for husband, children, home – the challenge is for this ethic of responsibility to be shared by both partners and by the Christic body as a whole.

But it is also a call for an ethics of care to be linked with ethics of justice and to be part and parcel of becoming responsible sexual beings. Care as rooted in the dynamic energies of growth and sustenance of all living things. I think this is what has given many women strength to sustain hope while enduring lives of drudgery. The ethics of care stretch far beyond an act-centred approach to sexuality.[33] The act of conceiving a child may not have been pleasurable for a woman; the act of giving birth may have been pain-filled. But frequently the joy is in the day-to-day sustaining of life – viewed in an inter-generational way. Women derive pleasure in handing on cultural traditions, in the knowledge that they are handing on life's energies.[34] Hence their role in story-telling, in keeping the feast, in taking trouble to cook for special occasions – food which will disappear in minutes. I recall my grandmother, a First World War widow, who had to bring up eight children in poverty, whose joy became caring for myself and siblings and the pleasure that life was continuing.

But what of interpersonal joy, heterosexual desire and conjugal sexual pleasure? I am aware that these have become somewhat lost in the focus on problematic areas and gender roles. Here I would like to return to the romantic relationship, which I had viewed negatively within a patriarchal construction. If we – the Christian-Catholic community – now operate within an ethics of care, and responsibility, new possibilities emerge, which, I believe, also give sexual pleasure a more scriptural grounding (rather than simply being a concession to uncontrollable desire).

Conclusion: Imagination and Conjugal Love

Earlier, I lamented the lack of imagination in literature in regard to marital love. It seemed that we could get our imaginations aroused by courtship, but any "happy-ever-after" shrouded lives of daily boredom, only worthy of mention on the occurrence of extra-marital affairs or divorce. Rosemary Haughton offers another possibility for romantic love. Using as source the Arthurian poems of Charles Williams, and the inspiration of Dante and Beatrice, she uses romantic love as paradigm of love-as-exchange, "the loveliness of every day exchange".[35] Romantic love is a symbol of the exchange of life between all spheres of existence. Romantic love pinpoints this exchange because love is concentrated at one point where it is ennobled to break though all the defence mechanisms and barriers which human beings erect to block mutuality with each other. Theologically, we are brought back to the energies of Resurrection, because the flesh-taking of Jesus was the breakthrough of divine love into human existence.

Jesus' passionate love opened up the way of exchange for all who believe in him and reached a culminating point in his death and Resurrection:

> The cry of Jesus was the cry of awareness that all indeed was accomplished, brought to consummation. He knew that he could, at last, give back to the One he loved, the unshackled fullness of love, and in so doing, carry with him on the surge of that passion the love which is the essential being of all creation.[36]

Romantic love – freed from cheap commercialism – offers the promise, innocence, freshness, idealism and calling to love with the passion embodied by Christ in the proclamation of the Kingdom. Not as a quickly-forgotten springtime, absorbed into the trivialities of living, but as a challenge to experience all of these as the very matter of sacramentality.[37] In the context of moving deeper into cherishing each other, the romantic moment can be experienced with astonishing diversity as the flow of exchanged love, widening its capacity, yet always grounded in the realities of bodily sharing. Hence I think there is a language of marital desire yet to be discovered. Not merely the classical, male-centred expression:

> But then there came another hunger
> Very deep and ravening;
> The very body's crying out
> with a hunger more frightening, more profound.
> The hunger for a woman.[38]

Nor even the desire embedded within an fertility context: as Eliot put it:

> – see their dancing around the bonfire
> The association of man and woman
> In daunsinge, signifying matrimonie
> a dignified and commodious sacrament.[39]

Nor even the obligatory invocation of Trinitarian relationality, to symbolise the trio of man, woman, child. The language of eros of the Flemish mystic, Hadewych, captures the sensuality of hungering for God; a hungering put in the context of human passionate love in a contemporary prayer:

> And there were no words
> and there was no terror only stillness
> and I was wanting nothing and
> it was fullness and it was like aching for God.[40]

Such a language would be fully personal, gendered yet expressive of mutuality, imaginative in exploring love's possibility for just relation. And at the same time would be fully consistent with the spirit of the Church's moral teaching: incarnational, sacramental, incorporated in a theology of sexuality widened and developed to honour the bodies of both sexes, promoting accountability and self-determination of both, in the context not only of responsible generativity and care for the future of community, but in the full materiality of responsible caring for the flourishing of all forms of shared common life.

Notes

1 Judith Plaskow, *Standing again at Sinai: Judaism from a Feminist Perspective* (New York: Harper and Row, 1990) p. 1.
2 Helen Waddell, *Peter Abelard* (London: Constable 1933) p. 103.
3 The phrase, "hearing the silence into speech", is crucial for feminist theology and derives from the late Nelle Morton, *The Journey is Home* (Boston: Beacon 1986).
4 See the chapter by Elizabeth Stuart, below. There are a range of issues around this, as well as areas such as pre-marital sex, single parent families, and so forth.
5 See Carter Heyward, "Heterosexist Theology: Being Above it All", *Journal of Feminist Studies in Religion* 3 (1987) 29-38.
6 Lisa Cahill, *Sex, Gender and Christian Ethics* (Cambridge: Cambridge Univ. Pr., 1996) p. 11.
7 Marie Fortune, *Love does no Harm: Sexual Ethics for the Rest of Us* (New York: Continuum, 1998) p. 56.
8 Leo Tolstoy, *War and Peace* (Harmondsworth: Penguin, 1997) pp. 1272-1275.
9 In rural Rajasthan (Northwest India) the killing of the girl child is on the increase and there is a growing disparity between the male and female population.
10 Claire Tomalin, *Jane Austen: A Life* (Harmondsworth: Penguin, 1997).
11 Carol J. Adams, *Woman-Battering* (Minneapolis: Fortress, 1994) p. 12. The literature is prolific. See, for example, Marie Fortune, *Is Nothing Sacred? When Sex Invades the Pastoral Relationship* (New York: Harper and Row, 1989); Aruna Gnanadason, *No Longer a Secret: The Church and Violence against Women* (Geneva: WCC, 1993). The latter includes a particularly useful list of resources for Christian Churches on a global basis.
12 In India, for example, even though the practice of sati is outlawed, it still occurs. More widespread, however, is the discrimination of widows after the death of their husbands, their bracelets – symbols of their marriage – are stripped from their arms. They must spend 12 days in the dark as an initiation to their new status. Poor food is given them and they are sometimes confined to the house, ostracised from family events.
13 In many parts of the world divorce is not an option. Women rarely enjoy any economic independence.
14 Lisa Cahill, *Sex, Gender and Christian Ethics*, p. 4.
15 Luce Irigaray, as cited in Grace Jantzen, *Becoming Divine: Towards a Feminist Philosophy of Religion* (Manchester: Manchester Univ. Press) p. 11.
16 Luce Irigaray. *This Sex Which is Not One* (trans. Catherine Porter, Ithaca, NY: Cornell Univ. Pr., 1977; 2nd. ed; 1985) p. 159.
17 This discussion is creatively developed by Grace Jantzen, *Becoming Divine*. The contention is that the theological interpretations of fall/guilt/sin/atonement belong in a constellation which has been interpreted and lived out within patriarchy with disastrous results.
18 Julia Kristeva, "About Chinese Women", in Toril Moi (ed.), *The Kristeva Reader* (Oxford: Blackwell, 1986) 138-159, quotation 156, translated by Sean Hand.
19 Ada Maria Isasi-Diaz, En La Lucha, *In the Struggle: Elaborating a Mujerista Theology* (Minneapolis: Fortress, 1993) p. ix: "the word kin-dom makes it clear that when the fullness of God becomes a day-to-day reality in the world at large, we will all be sisters and brothers – kin to each other."
20 Carter Heyward, "Sexuality, Love and Justice", in Judith Plaskow and Carol Christ (eds.), *Weaving New Visions* (New York: Harper and Row, 1989) p. 295.

21 See, for example, Lisa Isherwood and Elizabeth Stuart, *Body Theology* (Sheffield: Sheffield Academic Press, 1998); Elisabeth Moltmann Wendel, *I Am My Body* (trans. John Bowden; London: SCM, 1994)); Melanie May, *A Body Knows* (New York: Continuum 1995); Jonneke Bekkenkmp and Maaike de Haardt (eds.), *Begin with the Body: Corporeality Religion and Gender* (Leuven: Peeters, 1998).
22 Sally McFague, *The Body of God: An Ecological Theology* (London: SCM 1993).
23 Adrienne Rich, "Splittings", in *The Dream of a Common Language* (New York: Norton, 1978) p.11.
24 Audre Lorde, *Use of the Erotic: the Erotic as Power* (Brooklyn: Out and Out Books, 1978), as cited by Rita Nakashima Brock, "The Feminist Redemption of Christ", in *idem.* (ed.), *Visions of Christian Feminism* (San Francisco: Harper and Row, 1984) p. 64.
25 Carter Heyward, *The Erotic as Power and Love of God* (San Francisco: Harper and Row, 1984) p. 102.
26 Anders Nygren, *Eros and Agape* (London: SPCK, 1953).
27 Sally Purvis, "Mothers, Neighbors and Strangers", *Journal of Feminist Studies of Religion*, 7 (1991) 19-34. The author is well aware of a lurking essentialism here and does not claim for a moment that all mothers actually behave like this!
28 John Paul II, *Mulieris Dignitaetem* (London: CTS, 1988).
29 A history of the exegesis of this text shows that its contextual meaning was the defence of procreation against gnosticism. However, that it was subsequently used as a means of social control. See Mary Grey, "Yet women will be saved through bearing children" (1 Tim 2:16): "Motherhood and the Possibility of a Contemporary Discourse for Women", *Bijdragen* 52 (1991) 58-69. [Ed. note: the cited text is actually 1 Tim 2:15.]
30 See Carol Gilligan, *In a Different Voice: Psychological Theory and Women's Development* (Cambridge, MA: Harvard Univ. Pr., 1982).
31 Jean Baker Miller, *Toward a New Psychology of Women* (Boston: Beacon, 1978).
32 Clearly in a fast-changing society, where in many countries women take a large share in professional roles and are entering many new spheres, men are also freely assuming caring roles.
33 See the chapter by Joseph Selling, below.
34 Yet the concern for handing on cultural traditions may involve women in the very cruel practices from which they themselves have suffered; for example, genital mutilation.
35 Rosemary Haughton, *The Passionate God* (London: Darton, Longman and Todd, 1981) p. 318.
36 *Ibid.*, p. 153.
37 See the chapter by Maaike de Haardt, above.
38 Cited by Rosemary Haughton, *The Knife Edge of Experience* (London: Darton, Longman and Todd, 1972) p. 127.
39 T.S. Eliot, "East Coker", in *Collected Poems 1909-1962* (London: Faber and Faber, 1974) p. 197.
40 Janet Morley, "And you held me", in *All Desires Known* (London: WIT, 1988) p. 56.

Chapter Five

A Young Person's Perspective on Authority and Sexuality

Anna Roper

Understanding a Cappuccino Culture: Authority and Challenge

In the cult American TV show, *Ally McBeal* is a successful young lawyer, an intelligent, witty young woman who is attractive, skinny and suffering from the neurosis of modern youth. She believes in justice, love and freedom, and in a strange sense of destiny in her personal relationships. Her legal and personal philosophy is at once "issue" based and deeply person-centred. She embodies the belief that no authority is beyond challenge. One of the unusual hallmarks of this slightly wacky comedy is the portrayal of a woman with a vivid and imaginative inner life. This quirky internal world of conflicting fears, desires and fantasies plays a central role in this drama-comedy. She certainly seems to believe in a spiritual life, but rejects much of what might be considered "Tradition". In court and in her other relationships she establishes authority through a combination of personal relationship, emotional manipulation, flirtation and reasoned argument. Sex plays a central role. Much of the visual text is an exploration of the experiences of sexuality and the attempt to find a permanent soul mate with whom to share intimacy and in particular someone who will affirm and balance her inner world. Like the equally popular *Friends* it draws a considerable youth audience, especially women. Both represent the cappuccino culture of instant and continuous leisure. Both represent a neatly seamed world of Western, middle class values. Both speak to the confusion, neurosis and fragmentation of consensus in Anglo-American society, both portray something of the range of values from which young people pick their own philosophy of life. Both shows drip feed their values through the powerful medium of light entertainment and humour.

There is a temptation to make this discussion of young people in the context of the Church and its teaching on sexuality a somewhat complicated and negative affair. There are many negative things said about young people in the context of the Church, and so I shall begin with some of the "positives". Firstly, for many young people the Church remains an important source of authority. For many it provides leadership, guidance, teaching and support. Secondly, many young people listen with interest to much of what the Church has to say on moral and social issues. Many feel that the Church takes a clear stance on important moral issues, and sets itself apart from the apathy and relativism of much secular thought. Thirdly, a good number of young people are daily employed in furthering the mission and teaching of the Church through their friendships, their example, and also through more institutionally focused involvement in teaching, chaplaincy, pastoral care and missionary work, to mention a few of a growing number of areas of involvement in the life of the Church. Young people are actively involved in disseminating and passing on this faith to others. In our parishes young people are involved in catechesis, special Eucharistic ministering, prayer and faith sharing. Finally of particular note, some are involved in supporting their peers as they navigate the complexities of modern relationships. The growth of peer support ministry is in my opinion, significant.

Where is the focus in the debate on young people and sexuality? Perhaps it is most correctly on the points of contrast and contradiction, that for each young person who remains in touch with the Church many more have passed out of reach, for each that is interested in the moral and social teaching many more have ruled it irrelevant and lacking in authority, that for each young person that continues to give time and attention so many more have stopped listening. Perhaps most sadly, for each young person who feels supported by the Church and its teaching many more feel hurt, patronised, unsupported or damaged by their experience of the Church in the area of sexuality.[1]

When one asks what is considered authoritative in the lives of the majority of young people, it would seem that the Church comes far down the list, and for many young people it simply does not figure in their thinking or the practical daily exercise of their lives. Ally McBeal is a symbol of an age that has a very great preoccupation with self-representation, true across the gender divide. Ally, like the culture that she represents, seems to focus almost exclusively on what is named "experience" as its main teacher and guide, thus experience largely forms the conscience. The self-preoccupation of youth has much to do with the insecurity that most suffer, exacerbated by the fragmentation and disintegration of values and resulting in a lack of moral consensus, which is so much a part of our contemporary society. In this context experience is treated as a straightforward and universal category and is used frequently without any attempt to discern its structures, its history or its potential.

Experience: A Tale of Two Worlds

In reality "experience" for young Catholics can be a deeply divided and confusing affair. There is, in my experience, often a dualistic mind set that is present in many young people, socially and spiritually as Roman Catholics in our society. Young people live in a world that demands conformity and from which it is difficult to stand alone or as part of a minority group. Young people feel at once at home in a world of opportunity for knowledge, leisure, travel and achievement and many accept the values that accompany this package. However, they also experience the Church and its call to be different. This call to be different requires that they stand out amongst their peers by attending Mass, by informing their faith, by receiving the Sacraments and by accepting a different way of practising loving relationships. Many feel torn between what they feel are conflicting values, and in this context they do not perceive the Church as offering a positive ethic for the living of modern relationships. One student in conversation said: "I think about the things I'm taught and what the priest says at Mass; but when I go out, to a club or a pub it's a different world and I'm a different person."

Many young people find themselves dipping into the Christian tradition and jumping out of it when the water becomes too deep and troublesome. Many times I have listened to my students explain how they become a different person when they go to Church, how they prepare themselves for the experience mentally, for the appearance of conformity and required piety. This is not an unusual story. However, I would suggest that there is a real danger inherent in the socialisation of young people in the methods of splitting experience and spirituality, the creating and splitting of the public and private self. To illustrate my point I'd like to make reference to a case study from a book about the challenges facing Catholic education.[2]

The passage is about a young girl of university age who presents herself for counselling. In conversation she claims that she is the perfect product of a Catholic education and upbringing. Her father and mother are high profile within the Catholic community and in fact contribute to the Marriage Encounter programme. Her father donates money to the Catholic University he attended, and he is also on the parish council. Lisa herself attends a Catholic University, studies some theology, and is involved in many student organisations. She is also the elected representative of her halls. Surely a success story?

As she explains to James Day, she is a model Catholic because she embodies the extremes of division that can be present and yet hidden and secret within our community. Lisa argues that our faith gives us the authority to maintain personal divisions that promote the appearance of virtue as opposed to its actual practice. It is a mode of practice she suggests is present from top to bottom in our structures. She argues that it stems from having espoused one thing and done another, to having talked rather than listened and to having focused upon standards rather than truth.

Her unheard story was that her father had abused her from 11-18. She had begged him to stop but he had refused. Her mother had refused to believe her, insisting that she was lying. She had told a priest at school and then at university, both had told her to pray and forgive her father's mistakes. One had said: "focus on yourself ... what is it in your own sinfulness that draws your father to you and which makes him do these things?"[3] The same priest later, on retreat, tried to kiss her, touch her breasts and suggested that they have sex. This is her testimony as introduced by James M. Day:

> I have learned to have a life that is perfectly split, on the one hand made for the public view and for the appearance of virtue and being sociable, on the other hand angry, frightened and horribly alone. I have learned along the way that reason and faith are good, that feelings don't count and that the latter are a danger to the first. When I've tried to think about what to do, what I should do, I've only heard this chatter of voices, confused, detached from myself and my feelings, because I don't have a real voice of my own, no-one who's me I can turn to in trying to figure out what should come next. It's weird, you'd think that natural, to have a way to talk to yourself, but I've just learned not to be a person, in the sense of this, you know what I mean? I mean, when I've needed, needed someone in myself to turn to, I've had no way, I mean no words, no real possibility of finding that. Maybe that's really what I'm here for, to find a self who can help me morally. (She continued...) I'm the good girl, the one whom my teachers and parents have always been proud. But this is only because they know neither me, nor themselves, nor the truth about how we relate to one another. As far as I'm concerned, the whole Catholic world is a conspiracy of silence, punctuated by occasional bouts of warmth that don't really go anywhere.[4]

Lisa's case is at least an exaggeration of the norm, in its detail it is not the norm. However we fail if we do not recognise the trend. No one wanted to listen and to engage with her or her context. She claims that it is the systematics of her case and not the particulars that are most significant. How many young people, struggling with ambiguous experiences of sexuality would echo the words of Lisa: "I kept looking within the Church for someone who would listen instead of tell, who would care instead of instruct, who would let me say my own story."[5]

One of my own students asked me some weeks ago, why he was taught so often that his body was a negative thing, something to be wary of and to fear? He asked me why his faith had not taught him to celebrate what he had been given.

He often comes to see me and discusses feelings that he feels have no place in any Catholic morality that he has come across, the feelings of desire to be known and to know, the odd realisation of one's own embodiment and of how his sexuality relates to his identity, both as a young man and as a Catholic. This leads me to reflect on Grace Jantzen's assertion that bodilness generally has been seen as opposed to life in the Spirit in much traditional Christian thought.[6] Kenneth Leech describes this as a "Gnostic contempt for the flesh".[7] Sadly in many cases this has led many to reject the paradigm and seek to move on. Another male student seeing things more simply commented "it's been so influential, I mean being brought up in this country in the Church, it's all around you, it's there as nurture, but we reject it now, it's not relevant for us, it's not the way we see things". A female student who had come for advice and help, a theology student, explained the friction at home caused by her need to be away from the Church to find her own voice and to work out something of her identity as an embodied individual. "My mum doesn't understand that the things that are important to me are not there. Other things are important. I know the priest, he's lovely, he's a friend, I can talk to him, but it doesn't make any difference. I'm bored, so much of it seems wrong and it's not relevant, I feel that I need to move away to find space to breath and to learn to be myself."

Secular Fragmentation: Deep Uncertainty, Rapid Change

Authority is a contentious term for most young people, irrespective of their context. It connotes the idea of limitation and containment of freedom. It suggests an established structure and way of being, the existence of a challenging and powerful force. In the search for idealistic independence and a bright new future, authority doesn't really figure. Authority is the old order. The questioning and critique of authority is a key part of the process of becoming a moral individual capable of exercising moral choice. It is also part of the process of finding one's own identity or "voice". However, this process has been complicated by the turbulence within institutions that symbolise this authority. This has occurred quite separately from the rebellion of youth. As young people seek to explore their relationship with these structures of authority and engage with tradition, they are finding that their experience of life brings both the teaching of the Church and the structures that mediate this truth into question. An experience of deep and unresolved contradiction confuses and alienates many who wish to maintain their relationship with the Church.

The fragmentation of values at political and ecclesial levels has added to the pressures of living in a pluralist society. This fragmentation has occurred at local, national and international level, and this has been mirrored politically by the gradual erosion of many of the institutional features of our traditional community life. Many young people would argue that the movement of people and the resulting exchange of ideas and cultural values have come to define our epoch. Beyond this, the undermining of traditional truths and the ossification of many of the traditional structures, if authority and governance, especially in the Church, is commented on and discussed. The Church is often perceived as an institution more interested in political self-preservation than the humble search for the authentic Christian life. Few would see the Church entering into the implication of Christ's Incarnation and responding to this by a true commitment to the ongoing transformation of this world and a witness to the promise of life in the next world.

What is certain is that young people have been born into an era of deep uncertainty and rapid change. A feature or consequence of this has been the decline in active membership of the Christian churches; the laity has left the pews in their droves. And where they remain, many practice behaviour that contradicts official teaching. Our present generation of young people are more likely to practice sex before marriage, use contraception, have many more children outside marriage, and are more likely than any recent generation to separate and re-partner. Serial monogamy is the likely pattern of their intimate relationships. They are more likely to be openly homosexual and to expect these patterns of relationship to be recognised socially, legally and spiritually. In terms of the breakdown of previous patterns of social life one would not hesitate in naming a crisis of relationships and of structures of authority. The Church can be painted in this scene as one of a number of ancient and crumbling institutions alongside Marxism and particular forms of patriarchy, shadowing against a skyline revealing the chaotic scaffolding of an emerging post-modern age. In a pluralist age, many see the Church as sidelined, isolated and marginalised and consider their message to be socially and culturally outdated. The provider of the "God of gaps"[8] has now become largely obsolete. The language of universal ideas, such as "redemption", "truth" and "transformation", has itself been so undermined by post-modern critique as to be rendered useless for many. The values of the Church can, at very best, be seen as values alongside other values.

A Crisis within the Church: Faith and Institution

Fragmentation is not simply the lot of the secular world. I followed with interest the dialogue between two senior Cardinals, following an address to the Sorbonne in Paris.[9] Both Cardinals named a crisis of faith and of institution in the Roman Catholic Church at present. However, the matter for disagreement was the order and causation of these crises. I would disagree with Cardinal Ratzinger when he argues that the crisis of faith precedes the institutional crisis. I would argue with Cardinal Eyt that the institutional crisis has fed the crisis of faith and that the institutional crisis remains a causal factor in the crisis of authority. Certainly both need to be addressed with urgency if we are to reach the present generation of young people. In particular it is very difficult for the Anglo-American Church whose practices and teaching on relationships seem to ring so hollow. To speak and inspire, with authority, of the relevance of Catholic social teaching is one thing. To address the actuality of modern relationships and to encourage young people to see and realise the potential inherent in their relationships is quite another. "The Western Christian Tradition has been hard on passion and pleasure, strong on control and abstinence. Sexuality has been seen largely in terms of its problems, not its potential. Yet love-making and justice making are closely connected."[10] The daunting task of approaching the reality of relationships and looking to their potential socially and spiritually faces the whole body of the faithful. The Church must ask itself a series of questions. What part of the Church's teaching is being rejected by young people and why? How has the Church become detached from the lives and experiences of young people? Why is the Church no longer seen as an inspiring source of authority in the area of sexuality and in particular in the area of intimate personal relationships?

As a starting point in this debate, it must be recognised that there is no single "young persons" experience of the Church and of its teaching. Context matters. I must stress that it is the contextualised stories of young people that the Church needs to listen to. It is an understanding of the fabric of the lives of those who are facing the challenges of growing up into a twenty first century world that the Church must actively seek.

We live in a culture that has seen unprecedented social and scientific changes over the last fifty years. These changes have affected not only the material conditions of our lives but also the attitudes and values that we accept as normative. New horizons and possibilities have exploded and confused our mindset, and presented significant challenges to the truths that we have accepted as fundamental. We have greater opportunity for travel and cultural exchange, for annihilation and mass destruction, for cure of disease, for control of the reproduction of life, for the involvement of women in secular structures of authority and governance, to highlight but a few of many paradigmatic shifts.

Changes in the fabric of our social and familial lives have also been significant. Serial monogamy is on the increase; unmarried co-habitation, divorce, single parenthood and the greying of the wedding couple have also been noticeable social trends. Our lives as individuals in this social context have continued to change apace. Johnson, et al, note in their 1994 UK study of sexual lifestyles that the median age for sexual intercourse amongst the age group 16-24, born between 1966 and 1975 was 17 for both males and females. The median age for first sexual experience was 14 for females and 13 for males. The authors note that this suggests that first sexual intercourse is happening "some four years earlier than for those born four decades previously". In addition "the interval between first experience and first intercourse seems to be diminishing over time, more markedly for women than men". The median time for the 16-24 age group in 1994 was two years for women and three for men. It is also worthy of note that an increasingly sizeable minority of young people are experiencing sexual intercourse before the age of sixteen. "Of women aged 16-19, 18.7% had experienced sexual intercourse before the age of sixteen compared with fewer than 1% of those aged over 55-59, for men the equivalent proportions are higher." In case there is any doubt over the relevance of such a general survey of UK attitudes to the Roman Catholic population, there is also a breakdown of the statistics in term of religious affiliation. The authors state: "More surprisingly perhaps, given the position of the Roman Catholic Church on sexual behaviour, those reporting Roman Catholic affiliation are no less likely than those reporting other affiliations to report intercourse before the age of 16, and if anything slightly more so."[11] The Church has been slow and often seemed unwilling to respond or engage with these changes. It has seemed particularly unable to sift the beneficial aspects of these cultural advances and to speak out against its truly abusive aspects. This has been particularly noticeable in the case of sexuality.

Society accepts and even promotes a culture where the control of fertility and sexual experiences before and outside marriage are seen as legitimate, where homosexuality is increasingly seen as a relationship amongst relationships. This is a deeply pervasive culture. Many young people find themselves drawn into this culture and find it deeply attractive. There are, of course, many who are also deeply hurt by their experience of our culture and its contradictions and paradoxes. Above all, many experience a deep ambiguity at the heart of the modern and religious understanding of sexuality. The increasing gap between puberty and the establishment of permanent relationships and the conflicting norms that govern sexual behaviour and the establishment of sexual identity during this time contribute greatly to this ambiguity.

The Church, in contrast to these trends, champions the values of fidelity, sexual dignity and the need to practise periods of celibacy and abstinence. It highlights the danger to the individual's integrity and dignity involved in the exploitation of the gift of sexuality. The Church privileges the institution of life long, monogamous marriage and the place of fruitful sexual union in this context. Sex is for procreation and the expression of love in that order, sex is understood in terms of its functions. In broad terms most young people would welcome the valuing of integrity and dignity in the context of sexuality and most would see the value of permanent stability and loyalty.

The Johnson, et al, study noted earlier reports that first sexual intercourse happens within the context of an established relationship, however, only 6.1%

of men and 15.9% of women were married to their first sexual partner. This reduces to less than 1% for men and women in the 16-24-age bracket in 1994.

A Widening Gap

There is clearly a widening gap between the received teaching of the Church and the pastoral experience of this teaching in the lives of young people. The conduct of adults who embody the contradictions between Church teaching and the behaviour patterns of the laity more generally (in a Western European and certainly in an Anglo-American context), fundamentally undermines the credibility and thus authority of the Church's attempt to regulate sexuality. As young people begin to form meaningful relationships and to explore their sexuality, many feel that the paradigm the Church offers does not allow them to freely interpret and explore the gift of sexuality. Many feel that sexuality is viewed as an abstraction rather than a contextual experience. It seems to allow for neither the ambiguity of sexual exploitation nor the joys of deep human encounter possible. In response, many simply reject the whole paradigm offered by the Church. However, there is a significant number of young people who seek to remain broadly within the paradigm offered by the Church, and who embody a sense of critical loyalty to the Church's teaching on sexuality. In between these positions, many feel alienated and confused by the gap between pastoral practice and teaching. For many it is an issue of great pain and hurt when they feel unable, in all conscience, to remain loyal to the teaching of the Church. In this context many seem to suffer from low spiritual self-esteem. Teaching is rarely as easily dismissed as many think.

The Church must actively engage with this reality and it must seek to nourish and support those who feel these contradictions acutely. An active engagement with the world is a prerequisite to its transformation. This engagement in the case of sexuality, must be twofold. First, it must involve a clear and audible rejection of the abuse of sexuality that so damages and scars our communities, both religious and secular. This will necessitate the Church examining its own role in the abuse of sexuality and the offering of healing and comfort to those within the Church who carry a sense of failure, hurt and brokenness as a result. The Church must then raise its voice and speak out against the production and use of alienating and pornographic images, the use of sex as a panacea, the trade in sex and especially prostitution. Perhaps one of the Church's most difficult tasks (especially in the light of its own complicity) is to speak about and condemn all forms of sexual prejudice and oppression, most notably the structures of patriarchy and paedophilia.

The issues outlined above have been well discussed in the press in recent times and are perhaps considered obvious needs. However, there is a deeper ambiguity that the Church must seek to enter into if it is to speak to the heart of the experience of brokenness and sexuality in contemporary society. Sex has come to occupy a central role in public life, cultural life, the media and the Church. Sex has variously been over-glamorised, trivialised, objectified, distorted and viewed as panacea. Both Church and society can be accused of promoting a narrow understanding of sex. Society can be considered guilty of focusing on the physicality of sex, of promoting an event-based attitude to sex, of stripping sexuality down to its physical power dynamics. Sex has become the ultimate "must have" consumer commodity and its image and style are heavily prescribed and readily and frequently explored and described. This does much to damage the experience of sexuality mediated to young people. In particular it promotes the view that sexuality boils down to sexual intercourse, heterosexual or homosexual, and that this in turn boils down to physical pleasure and orgasm. In contrast one can argue with the philosopher Gillian Rose,

> Love making is never simply pleasure. Sex manuals or feminist tracts which imply the infinite plasticity of position and pleasure, which counsel assertiveness, whether in bed or out, are dangerously destructive of imagination, of erotic and spiritual ingenuity. The sexual exchange will be as complicated as the relationship in general – even more so.[12]

It can also be argued that at times the Church has promoted as narrow an understanding of sexuality as society, albeit on different terms. The narrow focus of the Church upon the procreative function of sex at the expense of other "functions" and experiences adds to the ambiguity of the moral message received by young people. This narrow focus reinforces much of the physicality and concern not with what bodies and embodiment are about but rather a concern with what bodies do. The focus of what has been called an "act centred morality" can be argued to represent another negative face of an obsession with the physicality of sex. A sexual morality that fails to recognise the importance of context in meaningful human experience echoes with little authority for many. I would argue that both Church and society offer little for young people to aspire to in terms of their personal relationships. In order to confront this reality, the hierarchy of the Church needs to enter into the actuality of the lives of the laity. The potential richness of personal relationships needs to be set as an aspiration for all Christian people, and the experience of sexuality is part of this. Gillian Rose argues that,

> Kiss, caress and penetration are the relation of the relation, body and soul in touch, two times two adds up: three times three is the equation. The three I harbour within me – body, soul and paraclete – press against the same triplicity in you.[13]

Teaching on sexuality must be grounded in values and not upon acts or functions, and not predicated exclusively upon particular patterns and structures of kinship. If the Church chose to be an agent of dialogue between the world, its people and their perfection, if the Church chose to sit firmly at the meeting place between the potentiality and actuality of the world, acting as an agent of dialogue, it could do much to empower and encourage young people to strive for the Christian life.

The Woman at the Well: A Scriptural Paradigm

To return briefly to the experience of Lisa, the American student, she mentions the account of the woman at the well (Jn 4:1-43). The meeting between Jesus and the Samaritan woman represents for me many of the things that the Church should be in its encounter with young people, in its approach to authority and sexuality in this context. The story of so many young people tells us that this kind of rich encounter is sadly too rare. There are many points of reflection that the passage has to offer us. Jesus is present as the woman arrives, waiting, he engages with her despite the fact that she is morally marginal. The quality of this engagement is made obvious when we see that the encounter is based upon a dialogue between a man and a woman, Jesus listens as well as talks and he is not concerned with her degree of public or private virtue in itself, but rather her openness to recognising the quenching water he has to offer, to his message of salvation. Jesus was waiting for the woman at a meeting place, a point of connection, and he uses the everyday, the ordinary reality of her life to engage with her in her own context. He transgresses his own cultural boundaries to make the connection possible. He does not try to remove her from her own context. He offers her a new vision of what had previous to that moment been ordinary: the water is now seen as a life force capable of transforming and sustaining towards eternal life.

I think the water could also be a good metaphor for our relationships. In a dynamic encounter between the Church and its youth (of all ages), we could together be agents in each other's transformation in terms of looking for the potential of our sexuality as individuals and in relationships. How does the woman respond? Jesus has drawn near to her and in turn she draws near to him. She leaves her jar and returns to tell her community what she has discovered about herself, her own voice returned in that of Jesus' words to her, and so she brings her people to him. Her conversion comes in part from the engagement that both Jesus and the woman make with her story.

Encounters on this model with young people could begin to move us toward the healing of the rift between the public and private self, towards reaching out to those who have rejected the contradictions of our community. It is the integrity of this surprising encounter that we must value and seek to make real in our relationship with young people. In my experience, I have found that to reengage with young people it is necessary to work one to one and in small groups, working both in their daily contexts and encouraging time away from their contexts. Retreats and pilgrimages offer a great chance to engage personally with faith journeys and to gain a positive sense of universal Church. Creating a space away from the demands of everyday living for rest and for the rebuilding and re-imagining of relationships can be greatly helpful. For those in schools and colleges some excellent provision is already available through good RE departments, chaplaincies, parish links and counselling services. However, once young people enter the workplace there is little outreach by the Church and little chance locally for young adult faith formation and Church based pastoral care. Relationships with key individuals, usually by luck and links with good parishes are able to offer nourishment and support to some, but not to all. The Church is perhaps at its weakest when seeking to offer sustenance for the day to day lives of the young.

Beyond some of the positive moves that are already afoot in the church to minister to youth, there is a need to begin a genuine and open dialogue, not simply a one-sided restatement of current thinking on controversial issues such as contraception, homosexual relationships, women's role and sexual experiences outside marriage. This dialogue must take into account the contradictions between Church teaching, the lived experience of the laity and the demands of modern culture. In addition it must go far beyond these and seek to enter into the heart of the confusion of what one philosopher has aptly titled the "broken middle"[14] of modernity. This will speak to young people of the values that lie behind the use and abuse of sexuality not simply the abstracted functions of sexual union. A relationship of mutual trust will not be easy to establish with many young people. Many have learned quickly not to attempt to dialogue and to look elsewhere for support in exploring the meanings of their sexual identities. However, building on the excellent good practice of schools, colleges and parishes would be a significant starting point.

It is my opinion that any such dialogue might lead to discussion of an understanding of sexuality that privileges love, mutuality, respect, dignity and sacrifice and might consider promoting an understanding of sex within this context as joyful, mysterious, healing, comforting, loving and as such fruitful in manifold ways. The procreative gift would sit beautifully within this context. The Church would perhaps be encouraged to restate the need to privilege truth as more than a value amongst values. It may be encouraged to understand sexuality as part of its focus upon justice, peace and the integrity of creation. Young people would encourage the Church to enter into the complex relationship between the actuality of the world and its potentiality and be present at its heart, offering a teaching of true transformation through Christ. The Church would be exhorted to proclaim its message simply, clearly and joyfully and with a clear conscience. Such an idealised dialogue might present the possibility that together, as agents in each other's perfection, the Church and its people could thus move forwards in faith to a reconfiguration of the living out of sexuality in our communities. And perhaps in turn this might evangelise the Church to move toward making real a sense of dynamic, collaborative and conciliar authority, to replace structures of restricted clerical hierarchy.

Re-establishing Broken Ties

Finally, a few practical reflections on engaging with this kind of model. This model would be about partnership, in the sense of focusing our teaching on the challenges of journeying together. It is notable that the Association of Catholic Chaplains in Education uses the Road to Emmaus story to express something of this. We must seek an active presence in the lives of young people, we must go into their environments and we must speak in a language of mutuality and personal growth that they will respect and for which many will have been seeking. We must spend time listening and learning as well as teaching and guiding. This way we will begin to re-establish ties that have been broken. In the famous children's book *The Little Prince*,[15] the Prince and the fox have to learn to establish ties, to relate to each other. The Prince tells the fox that he is looking for friends and the fox replies that he cannot play with him, as he has not yet been tamed. "What does that mean – tame?" Well "it is an act too often neglected", said the fox, "It means to establish ties", "To establish ties?" "Just that" said the fox. "To me you are still nothing more than a little boy who is just like a hundred thousand other little boys. And I have no need of you. And you, on your part have no need of me. But if you tame me, then we shall need each other. To me you will be unique in all the world. To you, I shall be unique in all the world…"

Practically speaking, the Church must be an active community, one that opens itself to the participation of youth in all areas of its life. It would do well to harness the concern with justice that many young people have. This needs to be done through parishes, schools, pastoral centres and chaplaincies. "Reach out" needs to be the enterprise of all within our communities and not just paid or voluntary workers, although they provide an excellent support function that is fragile and must also be nourished and valued. It is through an active, positive, non-judgmental dialogue, that has its roots in valuing and listening, that we may begin to enable our community to reach an understanding of its contradictions, and through scripture, prayer and the guidance of the Holy Spirit we may walk forwards to resolving some of these contradictions. Beyond this, there is the hope that through honest search and a genuine effort we may reach out towards the transformative potential that exists within any area of our humanity and surely especially within a justly lived and experienced sexuality.

Notes

1 William Rademacher discusses this paradox between renewal activity in the Church and decline; see his *Lay Ministry* (New York: Crossroad 1992).
2 Terence McLaughlin, Joseph O'Keefe and Bernadette O'Keefe (eds.), *The Contemporary Catholic School: Context, Identity and Diversity* (London: Falmer, 1996).
3 James M. Day, "Recognition and Responsivity: Unlearning the Pedagogy of Estrangement for a Catholic Moral Education", in Terence H. McLaughlin, et al. (eds.), *The Contemporary Catholic School*, 162-173, p. 167.
4 *Ibid.*
5 *Ibid.*, p. 168.
6 Grace Jantzen, *Power, Gender and Christian Mysticism* (Cambridge: Univ. Pr., 1995).
7 Kenneth Leech, *The Sky is Red: Discerning the Signs of the Times* (London: Darton, Longman & Todd, 1998).
8 For a discussion of the crowding out of a false "God of gaps", see Richard Holloway, *Dancing on the Edge: Faith in a Post Christian Age* (London: Fount, 1997).
9 Reported in *The Tablet* (29 January 2000) p. 125.
10 Kenneth Leech, *The Sky is Red*, p. 31.
11 Anne Johnson, *Sexual Attitudes and Lifestyles* (Oxford: Blackwell, 1994).
12 Gillian Rose, *Love's Work* (London: Vintage, 1997) p. 63.
13 *Ibid.*, pp. 63-64.
14 Gillian Rose, *The Broken Middle* (Oxford: Blackwell, 1992).
15 Antoine de Saint-Exupery, *The Little Prince* (London: Mammoth, 1991).

Chapter Six

Authority, Sexuality and Friendship

Elizabeth Stuart

In Martin Scorsese's interpretation of Kazantzakis' *The Last Temptation of Christ*, the dying Christ experiences his last temptation in the form of a hallucination in which he takes Mary Magdalene as his wife, enjoys sexual intercourse with her and together they procreate. In his dying moments, Jesus is enticed to become just the sort of man the Pope, the Archbishop of Canterbury and most of the modern Church would regard as a good Christian disciple. The film, by summoning up the temptation and drawing attention to the necessity of its rejection, exposes and questions modern Christianity's easy identification of domesticity, marriage, the family and discipleship. In what follows I want to press the question further by suggesting that the crisis over ecclesial authority and sexuality (particularly homosexuality with which I shall be mainly concerned) is largely due to an inadequate handling of what is authoritative in the Church, namely its scripture and tradition, the thick richness of which has been diluted to a thin soup incapable of nourishing anyone.

The Nature of Authority

In his study on the nature and practice of authority in the Roman Catholic Church, David J. Stagaman makes a number of key points which are essential to bear in mind in any discussion of authority and sexuality.[1]

- Authority is not an attribute of a person[2] or an object but a binding practice in a particular community. It is that which gives a community an identity.
- Authority is always grounded in the authoritative, i.e. the foundational beliefs and values of a particular community.
- Authority is transparent in that the promotion of a particular mode of being or action has to be explained and justified.
- There have been certain paradigm shifts in the understanding and exercising of authority in the Roman Catholic Church in the twentieth century. These shifts include the understanding of official offices in terms of charism rather than status and their holders as servants rather than legates, the exercise of authority in terms of persuasion rather than obligation, dialogue rather than

hierarchy. In short there has been a shift in understanding authority as fixed in essence and exercised juridically, to an understanding of it as fluid, relational and sacramental in character.

- Authority is not a threat to freedom because, contrary to the modern myth, freedom is not identifiable with independence but with community in which an individual is able to flourish as a relational human being.
- Authority is owned by a whole community and exercised in its name:

> when an authoritative communication imposes an obligation on someone, it does so in such a way that the mutuality of the interaction is preserved as well as the agency of the person who assumes the obligation. To attribute obligation is to attribute agency. Neither coercion nor manipulation are consonant with the practice of authority in normal circumstances ... Authentic authority enhances individual freedom. In fact, a general principle for evaluating authoritative acts involving mature and decent actors, is that authority and voluntary assent mutually enrich one another.[3]

- Authentic, thoughtful dissent is essential to the proper exercise of authority; without it "a community soon faces a Hobson's choice between tyranny and anarchy".[4] Dissent is an attempt to restore authenticity to authority because I can only be obedient to that with which I believe to be true.[5]
- Christian authority is authentically Christian if it is exercised under and within the mysterious character of God and is eschatological in character, attempting to concretise the hope of the people of God whilst realising that it will never be entirely successful and sacramental in its power.
- Baptism is the foundation stone of the Church's sacramental life and authority. All those who are baptised are given the authority to participate in the Eucharist and proclaim the word of God, to authorise the exercise of authority by pastors and to give a sense of the faithful.
- In order to do this the baptised draw upon what is authoritative to the Christian community, its tradition which "bears the past into the present, but also critically assesses that heritage in light of the demands that the future makes on the community".[6] Tradition is the matrix of the community, providing it with its grammar. Tradition is simultaneously past, present and future, and we are both formed by it and responsible for its formation. It and it alone provides us with the tools for revolution against part of itself. As Stagaman notes, it is as essential as the air that we breathe but like that air it is polluted and constantly in need of purification.
- Finally, in answer to the question, "why do we need authority?" Stagaman provides two answers. First, authority unites a community in common action, saving it from the paralysis of pluralism. Second, authority exists for the purpose of friendship,

> in a sense familiar to the way in which Aristotle saw friendship as the goal of his fellow Greeks living together in the *polis* … Freedom aims not at isolation, but at union. This union is achieved when people come into mutual understanding and actualisation in the process of communicating with and revealing themselves to one another.[7]

Authority exists to create the kind of community in which people can relate to one another as friends.

Several books could be written on the failure of the Christian Churches in general and the Roman Catholic Church in particular to exercise such an authority with any competence over issues of sexuality in the latter half of the twentieth century. This refers to the whole baptised community, not only those who exercise episcopal or papal authority on their behalf. I wish to focus on the failure of authority to engage sufficiently with the richness of the authoritative tradition of the Church in its reflection upon same-sex relationships. And I include my own work in this indictment. Since the Congregation of the Doctrine of the Faith has reminded us that it is the "duty" of the theologian "to make known to the magisterial authorities the problems raised by the teaching in itself, in the arguments proposed to justify it or even in the manner in which it is presented"[8] in order that the magisterium will be better able to represent Church teaching, my approach should not be regarded as hostile to the magisterium but rather as a loving attempt to help it exercise its authority more competently, whilst of course acknowledging that I may be wrong.

Swings and Roundabouts: The Vatican and the Redemption of Sexual Desire

One of the most extraordinary turns in the Roman Catholic Church in the twentieth century has been that towards modern understandings of sexuality and sexual identity. Even whilst claiming not to,[9] the Vatican in general and Pope John Paul II in particular have absorbed almost uncritically and sanctified the modern discourses of sexuality. Although often hailed by liberals as a positive advance, in that it included at least a partial embrace of a personalist understanding of married love and an acceptance of the homosexual as a "person" with a distinct identity, the consequences have not been entirely constructive. The Pope's construction of the nuptial meaning of the body[10] privileges heterosexual desire and reflects the thoroughly modern belief that all desire has its origin and *telos* in male/female relationships (rather than in the pre-modern belief that desire had its origin and *telos* in God) so that even the religious life seems to have been relegated to a lesser vocation (this is strenuously denied but if you are going to use nuptial imagery of the body then the obvious impression is that marriage is the ideal to which all Christians are called).[11]

Homosexual persons, even whilst they are acknowledged to exist at least in some parts of the 1986 "Letter to Bishops" and therefore must share in some sense in the personhood of God and the dignity that comes in bearing God's image, are effectively denied moral agency by being judged incapable, by virtue of their sexual orientation, of being able to manifest the nuptial meaning of their bodies in sexual relationships and therefore given only one real option – celibacy. This idealisation/idolisation of heterosexual desire makes it extremely difficult for the Church to deal publicly and effectively with abuse within heterosexual relationships or manifestations of homophobia.[12] It also defeats its own purposes by idealising marriage even at the expense of the religious life. The appeal of the religious life or even simply a celibate life becomes even harder to comprehend.

The Silencing of Tradition

What is particularly striking about the 1986 Letter is the (lack of) appeal to what is authoritative, the scripture and tradition, which for a community which lives off and in the presence of its past, is thin and narrow. The theory of complementarity, based upon Genesis 1-3, developed in this letter has no grounding whatsoever in the Church's tradition and owes more to Jung than to Yahweh.[13] The other passages from scripture focused upon are those which condemn same-sex relations within a context of clearly defined and fixed gender roles – man as one who penetrates and women as one who is penetrated[14] – which is an understandable choice considering the fact that the magisterium has built is own theology of sexuality upon similar if not exactly parallel constructions of gender. But what are silenced in this reading of the tradition are other, more prevalent dimensions of the tradition which call into question both ancient and modern constructions of gender, desire and sexuality. If these were taken seriously, they would enable the Church to assume a proactive rather than reactive position in the inevitable reconfigurations of gender and sexuality in the twenty-first century. Because it would constitute an authentic appeal to what is authoritative, it might go some way to restoring the Church's authority on these issues.

It is perfectly legitimate to argue that at the heart of the Christian tradition in the person of Jesus Christ we are presented with a figure who both enters into gender and then radically subverts it. If we reverse the standard liberal approach of attempting to measure Christ against our current categories of the human, and instead measure our understandings of what it is to be human against the revelation of true, redeemed humanity in the person of Jesus, we will find ourselves dealing with unstable and multi-variant notions of gender that render the current ecclesial discourse on sexuality largely meaningless. As Graham Ward has noted, the body of Jesus is from the moment of its incarnation present, in the sense that it is gendered and performs its gender within the social context of its time and place. It is also backward-looking to a pre-fallen corporeality and eschatological in that it looks forward to the resurrection.[15] Jesus is born male but from purely female matter, he emerges from the womb in a complex web of symbolic relationships with his virgin mother.

> The baby boy is husband and bridegroom, spouse and prefigured lover of the mother who gives him birth, whose own body swells to contain the future Church. The bridal chamber is the womb which the bridegroom will impregnate with his seed while also being the womb from which he emerges. The material orders are inseparable from the solid and transcendent orders, the orders of mystery. The material orders are caught up and become significant only within the analogical orders. And so here Jesus' body is brought within a complex network of sexualised symbolic relations that confound incest and the sacred.[16]

The instability of the body is further played out in the displacements of the transfiguration, the Eucharist, the resurrection and finally the ascension. In the transfiguration, the body of Christ becomes transparent to divinity – our attraction to this figure is taken through the male gendered Jew towards God in whom desire is finally satisfied. In the Eucharist, Jesus' body is transposed, extended into the gender neutral form of bread and, as Ward notes, bodies are revealed as things not only transfigurable but also transposable and "in being transposable, while always being singular and specific, the body of Christ can cross boundaries, gender boundaries for example. Jesus' body as bread is no longer Christ as simply and biologically male".[17] In the crucifixion and death, Jesus' body becomes liminal and soaked in iconicity, it becomes a floating signifier which the medieval Church could represent as a maternal body, the side wound representing a womb from which the Church springs, and nourishing breast.

The resurrection recapitulates and plays out all previous displacements, revealing the body as essentially mysterious, beyond grasp because the body is finally transposed into the Church at the ascension. Jesus becomes the multi-gendered body of the Church. As the revealer of true humanity, Jesus reveals this because all bodies are situated within and given significance within his body they too are "permeable, transcorporeal and transpositional".[18] Or, as Richard Rambuss has put it, because Christ's body is both human and the body of God, it is always situated at the limits of cultural boundaries, "Christ's body, in other words, is one that by its very nature keeps exceeding, keeps transcending the bounds of the licit..."[19] Christian living then becomes a participation in this "permeable, transcorporeal and transpositional" body in an individual and corporate arena. A consistent strategy among some Christians has been the parodying (and therefore subversion) of gender codes in each age and in each cultural context in order to constantly realign the telos of desire. We see that suggested in Galatians 3:28, and played out in Ephesians 5, where the male Christ has a female body. The Church and men within that body are then gendered female, even as women who are part of it represent a male Christ to the world. This is more subtly, but no less radically, performed in Paul's representation of Jesus the perfect female (because perfectly submissive) whilst also the perfect male (because he displays perfect self-mastery).[20]

Christianity and Gender

This view of the body often brings the practice of Christian living within the realm of transgressing the established gender codes and therefore in open defiance of some readings of the tradition itself. As Bataille has noted, "the underlying affinity between sanctity and transgression has never ceased to be felt. Even in the eyes of believers, the libertine is nearer to the saint than the man without desire".[21] This is evident in a long tradition of what one might call "gender bending" in the Christian devotional and mystical traditions in which women become male and men become female, particularly maternal.[22] In my childhood this became evident in the women who were presented to me with male names such as Sister Bernard Joseph and in the celibate men whom I had to address as "Father", who performed the maternal roles of bringing to (new) birth and regular feeding.

But it is also evident in the vast and consistent homoerotic tradition of devotion in the Christian tradition. As Richard Rambuss has noted, Catholicism, by centralising within its devotional matrix the semi-naked male body of Christ, has induced homoerotic desire in a manner for which it now refuses to take responsibility. As the central character in Antonia Bird's 1995 film, *Priest*, confesses concerning his struggle with his homosexuality, "I sit in my room sweating. I turn to him for help. I see a naked man, utterly desirable. I turn to him for help, and he just makes it worse." This utterly desirable Christ is the object of homoerotic devotion in art and literature across the Christian centuries. Rambuss focuses on the manifestation is this devotion in the metaphysical poets, some of whose work lurks at the back of my copy of the *Divine Office*, including Donne's *Holy Sonnets* which pleads for the "three personed God" to "batter my heart" and "ravish me".[23] It is, however, traceable throughout Christian history.

Although overwhelmingly male, there are also elements of a female homoerotic devotional tradition. Crawshaw could represent Teresa as receiving erotic "darts" not merely from Christ but also from the Virgin. Catherine of Siena urged her sisters to put on the nuptial garment of Jesus whose body is represented as female and maternal.[24] This "gender bending" and homoerotic tradition, which is part of what is authoritative for the Christian community, must be allowed to impact upon contemporary Christian reflection upon issues of sexuality.

Queering Theology

Within the lesbian and gay communities the horrors of the AIDS pandemic revealed the hopeless inadequacy of the modern discourse of sexual identity and led to the birth of what is known as Queer Theory. Queer theory is chiefly associated with Michel Foucault and the development of his ideas by Judith Butler.[25] Foucault questioned the two central notions upon which post-Enlightenment theory and theology of sexuality have been based. The first is the notion of a fixed, essential identity, sexual or otherwise. Foucault argued for the social construction of sexual identity through discourse and constant redefinition. The second is the idea that power is something held by dominant groups and used against others who had less power, for instance, women, gay people, the poor, and so forth. Foucault argued that power was fluid and present in all parts of society and could be deployed by any group. Where power was exercised, there was always resistance to it, which itself was a kind of power. These ideas are developed by Judith Butler. She argues that feminism has made a fundamental error in continuing to assume that there is an identity of "woman"somehow bound up with the female body which is stable enough to formulate some, though perhaps not many, generalisations. This is a paradoxical position for most feminists to take, considering their antipathy to the "biology is destiny" approach to gender.

Butler seeks to question the "natural" connection between sex, gender and desire, arguing that gender and desire are unstable. Indeed, she famously asserts that gender is not expressive of some inner nature but performative. We learn to become a woman or a man by following the gender scripts that our culture hands out to us, and each performance re-inscribes that gender upon our bodies. It is only when some people throw away the scripts or perform them badly or subversively that the non-natural nature of gender is revealed. Butler argued that the parodic performance of gender by drag queens or butch and femme lesbians most clearly demonstrated and disrupted the connection between sex, gender and performance. She called for a resistance to the gender scripts and a proliferation of subversive performances of gender. She simultaneously noted the difficulty of resisting such scripts because no one stands completely outside of them. This is the "essence" of queer theory, that there is no essential sexuality or gender.

"Queer" then is not actually another identity alongside lesbian and gay (although it is sometimes rather confusingly used to convey a radical coalition of lesbian, gay, bisexual and transgendered persons)[26] but a radical destabilising of identities and resistance to the naturalising of any identity. Queer theory mirrors and recalls to us the Christian tradition in which through baptism we are taken up into the life of Christ and his body, the Church, in which all culturally given identities are radically destabilised and open to redemption through parodic performance. But whereas queer theory threatens to dissolve the self into postmodern nihilism, the Christian tradition offers a *telos* for destabilised desire, and that is God. Traditionally, the celibate stands as the most potent reminder of this Christian truth, which is why the crisis in religious vocations in the West is evidence of a crisis in Catholic sexual theology, but it is also a vocation to which all Christians are called in their performance of marriage, family, singleness and homosexuality.

Lesbian and Gay Relationships

Eugene Rogers, Jr., operating from within what we might call the queer tradition of the Church, offers what I consider to be the most convincing theological argument ever articulated for lesbian and gay marriage. He argues that the central symbol of the Christian tradition is God's marriage with humanity in Jesus Christ, and therefore marriage is the state of every one of those who becomes part of Christ's body through baptism.[27] It is manifest in two forms of existence in the Christian community, in covenanted sexual relationships and in monasticism. Both are a form of asceticism and both are a form of each other: monasticism a marriage to God and marriage a form of self-denial and a place of sanctification in which God takes our worst and most wayward desires and begins our redemption just there.

Following a number of contemporary theologians in locating the procreative principle within the overarching virtue of hospitality, Rogers argues that there is no theological reason to deprive lesbian and gay people of access to the sacrament of marriage and every reason not to do so, particularly as the married relationship mirrors and participates in the homo-social relationship between God and Christ.

> The "family resemblance" by which same-sex unions deserve to be called marriages is not primarily their resemblance to opposite-sex unions ... The family resemblance by which same-sex unions deserve to be called marriages is the same resemblance by which Christians justify calling opposite-sex unions marriages: their resemblance to the marriage of Christ and the Church ... The problem is not that gay and lesbian couples are denied satisfaction,

> although that is bad enough. The problem is that they are denied true asceticism.[28]

If we want to follow the Holy Father in stating that our bodies have nuptial meaning, then that meaning is grounded not in the complementarity of the sexes, because baptism destabilises gender, rendering complementarity as a concept extremely problematic, but in the relationship between God and Christ.

Rogers's use of the nuptial imagery is ingenious and extremely challenging but in seeking for an overarching Christian symbolic with which to make sense of sexuality he has excluded an alternative discourse which has also been all but silenced in modern Catholicism but which dominated pre-modern Christian thought – the discourse of friendship. Since Stagaman argues that it is one of the purposes of authority to create the kind of society in which friendships are possible, one simply cannot ignore the pre-modern tradition's valorisation of same-sex friendship. This privileging of friendship to the extent that both Augustine and Aquinas could talk of marriage as a form of friendship,[29] is largely constructed in same-sex terms and frequently elides into the passionate and amorous, from the passionate friendship between David and Jonathan through the tradition of Christ's relationship with the Beloved Disciple, and onwards. Friendship is frequently constructed as an ecstatic ascent to God, the site of the development of *theoria* (contemplation of goodness, truth and beauty) and a relationship of mutuality (often conceived as mutual and reciprocal consciousness) in which friends bear each other's image.[30] It is easy to understand why contemporary lesbian and gay theologians, myself included, have argued for a locating of same-sex relationships within this tradition of friendship.[31] If Augustine and Aquinas could understand the married relationship as a type of friendship, comparable to the monastic form of friendship which was of necessity homo-social, then in a tradition which destabilises and de-naturalises gender the Church appears to have no authority to deny to same-sex relationships the respect and theological support it has given to friendship for centuries.

But … Theology and Metaphor

An objection could be levelled at my argument in that I have failed to appreciate the metaphorical nature of both the homoerotic tradition of devotion and the construction of Jesus' body. If I am guilty of that charge then so are all those theologians, including the present pope, who fail to appreciate the metaphorical nature of the nuptial tradition. Along with Sallie McFague and others, I want to emphasise the metaphorical nature of theological language which "always contains the whisper, 'it is and it is not' like this".[32] It is the latter part of that whisper that is so often inaudible or only heard around certain metaphors. So I would want to resist a heterosexist reading of the tradition that emphasises the metaphorical nature of the homoerotic material but not the heterosexual nuptial. As McFague points out, “thinking metaphorically means spotting a thread of similarity between two dissimilar objects, events, or whatever”.[33] The fact that within the Christian tradition some have seen a thread of similarity between homoerotic desire and the desire of the soul for God suggests a valorisation of homoerotic desire which has been erased from the body of Christ’s consciousness and which it might be helpful to recall in our attempts to wrestle with difficult issues surrounding sexuality. I would also want to resist the gulf that modernity opened up between heaven and earth, the literal and the metaphorical, the mysterious and the historical, the physical and the spiritual, at a time when contemporary western culture is rejecting such dualism in favour of a much more mysterious, stranger and “thicker” understanding of reality that enables the mysteries at the heart of the Christian, Christological tradition to be heard once again and applied to issues that our culture wrestles with but cannot grasp, such as the nature of the body and sexuality.

Conclusion

It has been my intention to suggest that, following Stagaman’s taxonomy of authority, the proper exercise of ecclesial authority in relation to issues of sexuality involves a communal attention to the thick nature of the Church’s authoritative tradition relating to the radical destabilising of gender (and indeed all identity) that takes place in the baptised. This attention will lead back to the valorisation of friendship as the moral matrix within which to evaluate sexual and indeed all other relationships. Authority must recognise that “the authoritative” demands the same rejection of the idealisation of heterosexual domesticity that tempted Scorsese’s Christ.

Notes

1 David J. Stagaman SJ., *Authority in the Church* (Collegeville: The Liturgical Press, 1999).
2 The single exception to this is the person of Christ from whom all authority in the Church flows and to whom the Church is responsible for the exercise of its authority.
3 Stagaman, *Authority in the Church*, p. 46.
4 *Ibid.*, p. 63.
5 *Ibid.*
6 *Ibid.*, p. xv.
7 *Ibid.*, p. 36.
8 Congregation for the Doctrine of Faith, *Instruction on the Ecclesial Vocation of the Theologian* (London: Catholic Truth Society, 1990) para. 32.

9 "Today, the Church provides a badly needed context for the care of the human person when she refuses to consider the person as a 'heterosexual' or a 'homosexual' and insists that every person has a fundamental identity: the creature of God, and by grace, his child and heir to eternal life." Congregation for the Doctrine of Faith, *Letter to the Bishops of the Catholic Church on the Pastoral Care of Homosexual Persons* (London: Catholic Truth Society, 1986) para. 16.
10 John Paul II, *Original Unity of Man and Woman: Catechises on the Book of Genesis* (Boston: Daughters of St Paul, 1981).
11 *Ibid.* A similar impression is given in the House of Bishops of the General Synod of the Church of England, *Issues in Human Sexuality* (London: Church House Publishing, 1991).
12 This matter is further complicated by the fact that the Church's moral and pastoral tradition, which demands a more nuanced, specific and compassionate approach to these issues, is rendered invisible in recent Vatican pronouncements and therefore relegated to private discourse to which some people for a variety of reasons never have access.
13 For a thorough critique of the concept of complementarity, see, Gareth Moore, *The Body in Context: Sex and Catholicism* (London: SCM Press, 1992) p. 118.
14 For a full discussion of this construction of sexuality see Martti Nissinen, *Homoeroticism in the Biblical World: A Historical Perspective* (Minneapolis: Fortress Press, 1998).
15 Graham Ward, "Bodies: The Displaced Body of Jesus Christ", in John Milbank, Catherine Pickstock and Graham Ward (eds.), *Radical Orthodoxy: A New Theology* (London and New York: Routledge, 1999) 163-181.
16 *Ibid.*, pp. 164-165.
17 *Ibid.*, p. 168.
18 *Ibid.*, p. 176.
19 Richard Rambuss, *Closet Devotions* (Durham and London: Duke University Press, 1998) p.19.
20 So argues Stephen Moore in a paper given to Society of Biblical Literature Annual Meeting 1999, "Que(e)rying Romans, or How Paul's Jesus is a Woman Forever in The Process of Becoming a Man".
21 Georges Bataille, *Eroticism: Death and Sensuality* (trans. Mary Dalwood; San Francisco: City Lights, 1986) pp. 21-22.
22 Gillian Cloke, *This Female Man of God: Women and Spiritual Power in the Patristic Age, AD 250-450* (London and New York: Routledge, 1995); and Caroline Walker Bynum, *Fragmentation and Redemption: Essays on Gender and the Human Body in Medieval Religion* (New York: Zone Books, 1992).
23 See also, Pat Pinsent, "'My Joy, My Love, My Heart': Sexuality and the Poems of George Herbert", in Michael A. Hayes, Wendy Porter and David Tombs (eds.), *Religion and Sexuality* (Sheffield: Sheffield Academic Press, 1998) 135-144.
24 Richard Rambuss, *Closet Devotions*, pp. 41, 47-48.
25 Michel Foucault, *The History of Sexuality, Volume 1: An Introduction* (New York: Random House, 1978); Judith Butler, *Gender Trouble: Feminism and the Subversion of Identity* (London and New York: Routledge, 1990).
26 This is certainly how Goss uses it in his work and how it is used in Elizabeth Stuart with Andy Braunston, Malcolm Edwards, John McMahon, and Tim Morrison, *Religion is a Queer Thing: A Guide to the Christian Faith for Lesbian, Gay, Bisexual and Transgendered People* (London and Herndon: Cassell, 1997).
27 Eugene F. Rogers, Jr, *Sexuality and the Christian Body: Their Way into the Triune God* (Oxford and Malden: Blackwell, 1999).
28 *Ibid.*, pp. 210-211, 232.
29 Adrian Thatcher, *Marriage After Modernity: Christian Marriage in Postmodern Times* (Sheffield: Sheffield Academic Press, 1999) pp. 138 and 219.

30 David Moss, "Friendship: St Anselm, *Theoria* and the Convolution of Sense", in John Milbank, Catherine Pickstock and Graham Ward, *Radical Orthodoxy: A New Theology* (London and New York: Routledge, 1999) 127-142.
31 See my *Just Good Friends: Towards a Lesbian and Gay Theology of Relationships* (London: Mowbray, 1995).
32 Sallie McFague, *Metaphorical Theology: Models of God in Religious Language* (London: SCM, 1982) p. 13.
33 *Ibid.*, p.15.

PART III

EVALUATING SEXUALITY

Chapter Seven

The Catholic Church and Sexuality: The Tensions of Love, Freedom and Law

James O'Connell

Theology and History

This essay is principally concerned with the issue of the authority of the Church in the area of sexual morality. In principle, however, the same conclusions apply to other moral areas. I will begin with a discussion of the scriptural roots of morality, and then introduce an historical view of the evolution of moral thinking in the Western Church and examine the claims of authority over morals that popes and others have made. After a short philosophical reflection,[1] I will describe what I believe to be the role of the Church in relation to morality. Finally, I suggest that we will not reach a new understanding of the Church and sexuality unless the Church manages to come to new understandings of its mission. It might well be remarked at the outset that there seems to me no other sphere in life where ecclesiastical rulers have been so tempted to maintain order at the expense of love, to look to past models when circumstances have changed, and to insist on rules and ritual as a condition of salvation.

In effect, this essay argues three contentions, though not in consecutive order. First, the Church does best to limit itself to principles and practices that are linked to a basic law of love. Within this approach its fundamental moral function is to bear witness to Christ in fostering love for the individual and in building community. For that reason also, it may on occasion rebuke or exclude those who harm an individual or who violate community. Inversely, except in exceptional circumstances the Church does best to stay away from seeking to specify or control the detail of morality.

Second, for historical reasons – and in this connection the leaders of the Church belong to the same tradition as did the leaders of the Synagogue – churchmen play a role not only as leaders of a religious community but as notables/elders of society. Simultaneously, there is constant danger that office-holders in the Church may confuse – or at least not disentangle – their roles as clerics (ecclesiastical administrators) from those of notables/elders (persons wielding political and/or social influence in secular society). Consequently, church administrators or officials do well to remain aware of the need always to distinguish, and sometimes to separate, roles.

Third, since it takes time for people to come to grips with changes brought about in human living and thinking by science and technology, elders or notables of societies, especially religious elders and notables, have a tendency to hold on to earlier moral opinions from periods when behaviour appeared more stable and less complex and authority surer and less questioned. Built into the conservatism of elders is a temptation to uphold historically inherited organisational structures and forms of decision-making that face revision as technological and modernising changes take place in societies.[2]

The Foundations of Christian Community and Judgement

Christ: Example, Orientation and Attitude

In relating to his Father and his contemporaries Jesus provided a religious example from his person and life. He taught by conveying attitudes and giving advice, sketching principles and illustrating them. His basic rule and summary of Jewish morality was:

> "You shall love the Lord your God with all your heart, and with all your soul, and with all your mind". This is the greatest and first commandment. And a second is like it, "You shall love your neighbour as yourself." On these two commandments depend all the law and the prophets. (Mt 22:37-40)

He suggested a crucial relativising of law: "The Sabbath [law] was made for humankind, not humankind for the Sabbath" (Mk 2:27). He went generously beyond accepted sentiments: "I say to you, Love your enemies and pray for those who persecute you, so that you may be children of your Father in heaven" (Mt 5:44-45).

Beyond emphasising love and putting law in its place, Jesus turned a face of compassion toward human frailty. One commentator[3] observes that he does not seem to have gone around condemning people for their minor lapses and that he worked not among the powerful but among the lowly; and he did not want to be a censorious judge who would only add to their burdens:

> Come to me, all you that are weary and are carrying heavy burdens, and I will give you rest. Take my yoke upon you, and learn from me; for I am gentle and humble in heart, and you will find rest for your souls. For my yoke is easy, and my burden is light. (Mt 11:28-30)

Jesus left Baptism as the ritual entry to his community and gave the Eucharist as the central commemoration of himself and his sacrificial work. Broadly speaking, he proposed values but did not lay down rules, just as he did not set up a bureaucratic organisation. He did establish through his disciples a Church or community that had a minimal organisation, that proved it could evolve structurally as new historical circumstances required, and that established a powerful tradition of worship, reflection and integrity. Yet it is right to say that the Church that Christ set up is mission before it is administration; it is preaching and witness more than prescription; and it is service rather than domination.

If with time the Church has grown into a great and world-wide society that embraces many and diverse communities and cultures, it needs organisation to mobilise energies and talents; and it needs rules to avoid disputes and conflicts. In principle, however, the Church is a society of conscience rather than law.[4] It depends on those who freely follow Christ (discipleship): "Follow me" (Mk 1:17); who are willing to bear witness in truth, worship and integrity (prophecy): "The commandments are summed up in this word, 'Love your neighbour as yourself'...love is the fulfilling of the law" (Rom 13:9-10); and who form a distinctive community (body of Christ): "I am the vine, you are the branches" (Jn 15:5). Yet, while this scriptural essence of the Church has belonged to the Church all through history, one cannot pretend that the historical church has, or indeed could have, entirely coincided with its dynamic and joyful, if austere, essence. For that reason the "Church as such is always in need of radical conversion to the Gospel".[5]

Hence, although organisation that operates through rules is necessary to religion, nothing is more inadequate. Example, orientations and attitudes, if they are properly human and loyal to Christ, can endure. But organisation and rules in the Church which at any historical period are lived in a creative tension with freedom tend to grow obsolete. In practice, we have in every generation to win back the freedom of the gospel from the encroachments of organisational demands and the rigidities of law.

Paul: Freedom and Law

Paul's teaching on freedom and law was crucial for offering a theological foundation for Christian community and behaviour.[6] In preaching against the Judaisers, Paul argued that the gospel drew on the power of Christ and brought freedom from law. In that way he taught that Christians were entitled to set aside the Jewish rituals and rules of his time. Initially with the Galatians Paul took a stand against the Law being imposed on Christians. The Galatians, who were newly converted, had apparently turned for guidance in their situation to Jewish Christians who were following the Law. In consequence, they began to follow not only the moral laws of the Jewish scriptures but also the ritual prescriptions of the Law. Their Judaising mentors thought that the Mosaic Law was given by God and should go on being observed. Paul understood that Christians who drew on the strength of Christ did not need the crutches of the works of the Law. His language to the Galatians in favour of freedom is the strongest in any of his letters. Paul realised that Judaising behaviour would take away the freedom that Christ had brought and would land the new converts in a quagmire of prescriptions and prohibitions. He also realised that Gentiles generally, and the Greeks in particular, were not easily going to accept circumcision.

Later, in writing to the Romans, he would at much greater theological length explain and justify the stand that he was taking. He wanted to end once and for all any view that did not accept that salvation was through Christ alone. Essentially, he was arguing that Christians had to take responsibility for themselves and could not hide behind the futile certainties of regulations. "The essential difference [between Christians and Jews] lies in the source of moral knowledge. For the Jew it was derived from the Law, but for the Christian it is derived from love."[7] Christians had a commandment to love; they had to work out the responsibilities of that commandment; and they were assured of the strength of the freedom that Christ had won for them. For that reason the work of salvation did not depend on observing the Mosaic Law.

Murphy-O'Connor sums up Paul's general stand on law:

> There is one obvious way of ensuring that the practice of the members reflects the unity of the Body to which they belong, namely, tight regulation of their acts by means of binding legislation. The solution was unacceptable to Paul.... for Christians to give full obedience to a new law would place them in the position of the Jews whose exaggerated respect for the Mosaic Law condemned them to inauthenticity. All that legislation can achieve is uniformity of action. It is incapable of bringing about the gift of self which is the very essence of unity.[8]

Paul never speaks of obedience to a specific law or precept. In his epistles obedience is always a synonym for faith (Rom 6:16; 10:17; 15:18; 16:26; 2 Cor 10:5; 2 Thess 1:8), i.e., acceptance of the mode of existence demonstrated by Christ (Rom 5:19; Phil 2:8). He states his own preferred approach to authority: "...though I am bold enough in Christ to command you to do your duty, yet I would rather appeal to you on the basis of love" (Phlm 8-9). Paul's directives are essentially educative. His approach has little in common with the Judaisers who arrived with the 613 precepts of the Law.[9] For that reason he prays: "And this is my prayer, that your love may overflow more and more in knowledge and full insight, to help you to determine what is best..." (Phil 1:9-10).

Obviously, Paul saw that one of the biggest problems that his Christians faced was that they had to live in a society that did not provide congenial conditions for living in love, and that indeed very often contained structures highly hostile to such living. Paul seems to have conceived of sin as a massive disorientation of society or, more specifically, as the corroding pollution of a corrupt environment. In consequence, Christians had to be detached from the grip of a society that almost despite themselves moulded them to its own image. "Do not be conformed to this world but be transformed by the renewing of your minds, that you may discern what is the will of God – what is good and acceptable and perfect" (Rom 12:2).

Paul saw however that protection could be provided only by the setting up of an alternative environment in which we would be subject to inspiration supportive of our quest for authenticity. This environment is nothing other than the local Christian community, which is not only the embodiment of freedom and salvation but is also the critical instrument for change in the world. But this interdependent and supportive environment is created by the freedom and responsibility of love and not by the imposition of laws.[10]

When we look at early Christian practice in sexual ethics, we find that Christians accepted existing structures and practices while introducing their own nuances, building on a radical equality of men and women, and seeing all life in the light of the coming of the kingdom. Countryman writes:

> The New Testament writers did not try to construct a new sexual ethic from the ground up. They took over the existing cultural patterns and refocused them, pushing some elements from the centre to the periphery, altering the balance of powers allotted to various members of society, and, most important, relativising the familiar life of this world by subordinating it to the reign of God. The result was that Christians could, in many ways, continue to conform to familiar cultural mores while, at the same time, understanding these familiar institutions in ways which undermined their absolute claims.[11]

Sturzo sums up the basis of Christian morality:

> Christianity in the sociological field brings about an inversion and reordering of values... sociality is a projection of the individual. Every social foundation is laid by the individual. The superimposing of the social form on the individual, as in the pre-Christian societies, was a deviation and in many cases a perversion; the return of the individual as the basis of every social value is a conversion and restoration.[12]

The Primacy of Orientation over Regulation

From the sections above that deal with Christ's approach and Paul's teaching I want to draw the conclusion that the ethic proclaimed in the gospel and the epistles is "directive" or "orienting" rather than "regulative" – though Paul might at times not appear to be entirely consistent in his views or behaviour.[13] What is clear is that the main Christian ethical directive is to love God and our neighbour. These two commandments not only contain the whole Law in Christ's opinion but once he had given them exemplary content through his own life and teachings, not least in the sermon on the mount and the discourse after the last supper, they go far beyond anything laid down in the Law. The double commandment to love is the touchstone by which all other commands are to be judged.

The Paths of Christian History: The Changing Clerks and the Death of God

In pre-scientific epochs, God's power was invoked for much that would later be explained through science. He – and he was very much a he – was a God in a rural mould. He was for long the God of nature, even in the new Western cities which were time and again beset by plagues and diseases, wars, internecine strife, and the vicissitudes of commerce. Under such conditions he was too often the God of the gaps. He supplemented human powers, and when science and technology expanded human powers, the powers of God shrank. When Nietzsche declared the death of God, it was the death of that God that he proclaimed.[14] In declaring the death of God, Nietzsche also implicitly recognised the concomitant shrinking of the authority of that God's church. The Church's authority has diminished for various reasons: there has been a decline in faith because the Church has coped badly with the advent of science as well as with the new urban developments of the 19th century; the balance of secular education has shifted from clerics to lay people; and the contemporary state has mostly taken over the functions of social welfare, health and education that had been pioneered and organised by clerics and religious.[15] Yet on the positive side belief has been purged of much sociological and historical clutter.

Claim to Moral Judgement

Do these changes bring with them a revision of the Church's long sustained authority over morality? Historically, in legitimising its moral judgements and interventions the Church has tended to claim an authority that belonged to its divine founder as well as to follow the example of his great apostles such as Paul. Yet if we examine scripture and history carefully, the authority claimed by the Church in moral issues can be seen to have been formulated historically in good part from a conflation of the roles of cleric and elder/notable. In other words, for a long time in the West (and the same is in large measure true of the making of the Muslim world) clerics were the main literate groups in society (our word "clerk" comes from this capacity and function) and exercised accordingly a great power of moral reflection and judgement. Generally, clerics could influence political authority but not exercise it directly – except where they were political leaders in their own right rather than church persons (popes and prince bishops wielded straightforward political authority for a long time; and churchmen, including abbots, exercised judicial functions over many kinds of local crime). In a more internal forum, however, clerics were accepted as authorities on individual morality, especially once the practice of private confession had become widespread.

Such clerical judgements on morality have come from three sources. The first source was the watchfulness that office-holders of the community of Christ exercised over ways of life meant to embody love which was the defining code of the Church and which was linked with the way in which Christians would recognise one another. This watchfulness was however strongly conditioned by a selective adoption of moral codes from the Jewish scriptures which were prescriptive with a detail that was entirely missing from, and indeed alien to, the Christian scriptures. The second source was the authority that came from being joined with temporal power, whether linked with political rulers or linked with local notables/elders within traditional communities. This second source was heavily conditioned by the long, influential and respectable sojourn of the Church in Western, Central and Eastern Europe. The third source of morality was the ethnic and purity customs of Western peoples.[16]

That Christian moral thinking and Church practice drew heavily on these three sources seems to me to explain why – in spite of significant continuity – there is a great historical and theological distance between the Church as founded by Jesus and taught and organised by Paul, and the ecclesiastical claims of jurisdiction over morality today. In our time the Code of Canon Law (which is cited and amplified by the *Catechism of the Catholic Church*[17] makes a careful, if extensive, claim:

> To the Church belongs the right always and everywhere to announce moral principles, including those pertaining to the social order, and to make judgements on any human affairs to the extent that they are required by the fundamental rights of the human person or the salvation of souls.

There is less difficulty in this statement with the enunciation of "moral principles", which can in any case be relatively banal, than with the elucidation of "judgements on any human affairs". The statement also seems to assume that "the fundamental rights of the human person" possess an easily acknowledged content and are not greatly influenced by social and cultural factors. But alongside these insistences runs another set of claims that bristle historically and theologically with even greater difficulties. According to the *Catechism*:

> ...from generation to generation, under the aegis and vigilance of the pastors, the "deposit" of Christian moral teaching has been handed on, a deposit composed of a characteristic body of rules, commandments and virtues proceeding from faith in Christ and animated by charity. Alongside the Creed and the *Our Father*, the basis for this catechesis has traditionally been the Decalogue which sets out the principles of moral life valid for all men... (2033). The authority of the magisterium extends also to the specific precepts of the natural law, because their observance, demanded by the Creator, is necessary for salvation.(2036)[18]

These are vast claims. No wonder John Mahoney[19] refers with some astonishment to "the Church's claim to competence over the whole field of morality". Such claims blissfully ignore, among other things, doubtful or wrong-headed judgements such as the strictures of Boniface VIII on secular rulers, the sanctioned use of torture by ecclesiastical judges, the intolerance meted out to heretics and Jews, and the opposition of Pius IX to democracy. Popes and theologians have as well been obliged to revise opinions on interest-taking; they have come to regret the unjust burdens laid on the consciences of Italian citizens within the new Italian state; and they remember with some embarrassment their slowness in the early stages of the industrial revolution when other thinkers and activists had moved much sooner to challenge the institution of slavery or to condemn working conditions. Also, the last sentence in the passage cited that links salvation to observing specific precepts of the natural law is hardly consonant with Paul's strictures on law – or for that matter with Aquinas' views on conscience. If instead of speaking of "authority" the Catechism had referred to "witness",[20] it might have been on surer and less contestable ground.

To understand the background to the claims in the Code and the *Catechism*, however, we have to look at Western medieval history, where ecclesiastical attitudes took on much of their present shape. These claims are, in turn, linked to a philosophical theory of natural law that derives from the ancient and medieval worlds and that cannot readily be taken for granted as consonant with the Christian scriptures or modern insights into behaviour.

The Role of History

The early Church communities were small, marginal groups that were preoccupied with their own organisation and morals. They often passed judgement on the pagan societies around them but they mostly avoided giving offence. This situation changed as Christianity spread, especially after

Constantine, and by the Carolingian period the Church already formed part of the moral and organisational fabric of society in Western and parts of Central Europe. One distinguished historian writes about the kind of bishop who emerged in the wake of the Carolingian order

> ...he was a man endlessly exercised in the care of temporal and spiritual things, a chief agent in the royal government of the kingdom. In many ways the practice and theory of the ninth century stamped a character on the episcopate in the West which it has never lost ... rulers who had difficulty in securing loyalty and obedience from others needed the support of their bishops. At the same time the great spiritual and temporal resources of the episcopate, their clear aims and well-defined laws, gave them a growing sense of their corporate power.[21]

Once the small ecclesial communities of the first centuries that had overseen the behaviour of their own members expanded immensely, and society and Church had seemed in the concept of Christendom to become coterminous, the social roles and authority of Church leaders changed and enlarged. The upper clergy formed part of the ruling nobility and influenced policies in kingdoms and fiefdoms. Mundy writes somewhat elliptically: "From the days of the Gregorians until the turmoil of the fourteenth and fifteenth centuries, what led Europe was an inadvertent, rarely conscious, but very real alliance between Europe's aristocracies and the see of Peter."[22] In their new roles as organisers of society, bishops and abbots exercised secular authority. They and the superiors of religious orders distributed considerable patronage through the political and social power that they held. Moreover, though medieval secular rulers lost with time the aura of sacredness, Church rulers at every level retained it.[23] Hence, popes and bishops, when they intervened with moral judgements and sanctions, tended to claim sacred as well as moral authority. "The ideal church of the twelfth and thirteenth centuries was a society of disciplined and organised clergy directing the thoughts and activities of an obedient and receptive laity – kings, magnates, and peasants alike."[24]

The lower secular clergy, even during the Middle Ages but especially after the Tridentine reforms, were mostly a relatively educated group that formed part of decision-making structures in town and countryside. Also, alongside the secular clergy, down to the reformation period (and beyond in some countries) monks were not only spiritual witnesses but great landowners who exercised powers of life and death over tenants and workers; and they were agricultural innovators who contributed crucially to feeding the expanding population of Europe. This situation was buttressed by the skills of the new orders and congregations that came in with the Counter Reformation and that provided many, if not most, of the social welfare and educational facilities in Catholic and other countries. Well into the nineteenth century and beyond, clerics, including religious brothers and sisters, were not only sacred but they were secularly powerful and educated.

In such historical contexts the influence of the Church overflowed into many spheres of social and personal living. Clerics and theologians meditated on and preached the scriptures and maintained worship. In that way, they worked spiritually to enrich and redeem lives that were often hard and short. In the making of Europe, bishops and priests, monks and friars assisted small town and peasant communities to look beyond the harshness of their daily lives, bore witness in their service to disinterested generosity, provided far more support for women's status and rights than they are often given credit for, and offered a way up for many who came from the lower strata of society. They also preserved a universalism that linked isolated communities with one another and kept them open to the influences of high culture, whether functional, as in the agricultural methods, or aesthetic, as in the beauty of ritual and the building of great cathedrals and abbey churches, as well as those gorgeous small town and village churches that stretch right across Europe.

In short, from the 6th to the 12th centuries the Church was constantly being called upon to deal with conflicts of laws and customs and sheer disorder among small and scattered communities. It alone had a sense of universal law that reached out beyond the feudal, ethnic and other groups. "Most would agree", writes a recent historian of Europe, Norman Davies, "...that the unifying feature of the medieval world is to be found in organised Christianity".[25] Churchmen mediated between the surging Germanic tribes and Gallo-Roman society. They ran local courts which gave reasonable justice. They assisted monarchs and others acting on their own account to establish a blend of Roman and customary law to resolve conflicts through established courts rather than by the arbitrary use of power or trials by ordeal. They promoted the peace of God in turbulent feudal societies. They linked communities through clerical organisation, the acceptance of law, and the gradual growth of a wider sense of humanity within Christendom; and they sponsored the universities and the development of intellectual life.

At the centre of such development was a growth in papal power and law. An able papal historian writes:

> Rome had originally been conceived [in the West] as the court of final appeal: in the course of the twelfth century it took on the role of a court of first instance. The pope became the "universal ordinary", exercising direct jurisdiction in every corner of Christendom, dispensing judgements which were built into the precedent books and became the basis of law.... It was the work of the medieval papacy to transform this religious perception into legal reality. Canon law became one of the principal fields of intellectual effort and advance in the Middle Ages, and the

> codification of law put the papacy at the heart of the Church, as the monarch and his courts lay at the heart of secular legal systems.[26]

Overall it would be a mistake not to appreciate the highly positive, if largely nobility-linked, role of churchmen as elders during the long years of the making of Europe and beyond. The trouble, however, was that clerics did not always keep their religious role distinct from their role as elders; and they grew accustomed to, and comfortable with, wielding secular authority. Also, in the traditional societies where ecclesiastical attitudes were formed; skills were not highly differentiated, roles were much fewer than in our modern situations and usually maintained for life. For such reasons it was easy to confuse certain broad forms of conduct that were crucial to gospel witness with moral norms based on concepts of social order. Administrators and thinkers did not keep historical customs and theological and philosophical analysis distinct from one another. In other words, Church judgements on morality tended to come from a mixture of reflections on biblical texts, traditionally received values and clerical vested interests as well as from the interests of the ruling groups to which the clergy were linked.[27] Witness to the purest values hobbled along on occasion side by side with a crass lust for power or encrusted ethnic customs. Moreover, a traditional conservatism in morality was deepened by the older than average age of Church leaders and their celibacy.

A sketch of Western history suggests how profoundly conditioned moral judgements were by the social context of each period, how much clerical judgements were influenced by caste interests as well as by the corporate interests of the Church as an organisation, and how conflated were the roles of cleric and notable/elder. Long after the medieval period was over influences from this blending of the religious and the secular lingered on in many countries.

After Trent, a religiously revitalised papacy went on to accrue enormous power within the Church itself; it set up a rigorous seminary system for training clerics; and it created a new, highly regulated and bureaucratic religious society. In fact, a reformed Catholicism with a disciplined clergy managed to exercise a powerful influence on personal behaviour right across the Catholic regions of Europe – and in the Americas, Asia and Africa once migrations and the missionary movement took off in the wake of colonialism – that was Roman, centralising and highly and traditionally moral. The scholastic revival under Leo XIII and the impetus that he gave to concern with social conditions simultaneously appeared to offer a new intellectualism and a renewed relevance of Church teaching to the secular world.

The culmination of this movement came as the papacy gained general control over the appointment of bishops. The new power was formulated in the 1918 Code. To quote Duffy again:

> The overall effect of the code was a massive increase of centralisation. It owed more to the spirit of the Napoleonic Code than to scripture or patristic tradition (scripture is rarely quoted in it), and it canonised as permanent features of church life aspects of the papal office which were very recent developments. In particular, canon 329 declared that all bishops were to be nominated by the Roman pontiff, setting the seal of legal timelessness on a radical extension of papal responsibility which had taken place virtually in living memory.[28]

Concomitantly with the extension of papal authority over episcopal appointments came a deepened sense of pervasive control over the whole life of the Church and a great part of the lives of the faithful.

Codifying the Claim to Moral Judgement

It is against such historical background that one must situate the controlling authority over morality claimed for the magisterium. That claim is flanked in the same *Catechism* context by the following assertion: "The Magisterium of the Pastors of the Church in moral matters is ordinarily exercised in catechesis and preaching, with the help of the works of theologians and spiritual authors." If it has been so exercised, it has been exercised very much in the context of, and with the consent of, the elders of society; and it is marked at least as much by the moral views of these elders, of which the clergy form part, as by the values of the gospels.

What the preceding paragraphs argue is that three crucial factors greatly influenced the judgement of clerics on social and individual morality. First, they often behaved as social elders when they believed they were acting as Christian guides. Second, they esteemed the worth of conserving Church organisation because the Church was the vehicle of salvation. Third, in pre-Freudian eras less overtly concerned with personal sexuality than our times, they remained in greater or lesser degree insensitive to the influence of professional celibacy and the part it played in the pressures, tensions and defences of the judgements of clerics in sexual matters. One result was that sexual morality tended to be given a disproportionate place in moral teaching and preaching; and a theology of the confessional that had gained ground over other loci of moral thought deepened the emphasis on individual sexual thoughts and actions.

What has been written about the principal architect of the law of marriage, Pietro Gasparri (1852-1934), in the 1917 Code of Canon Law might well be used to describe generations of Church rulers and jurists:

> He inherited the qualities of the classical Roman lawyers; his legal works are marked with clarity, conciseness and balance. His theological horizon, however, was rather narrow. His main concern

> was to uphold and to protect the institution of marriage. Hence, the Code drafted under his direction paid little attention to the legitimate desires and needs of individual persons. It stressed throughout the propagation of children as the primary end of the institution; it made the acts apt for the generation of the offspring the principal object of the contract. As long as this institutional end could be achieved, it made virtually no concession to personal dispositions and mistakes, not even when they were induced by wilful deception. In mixed marriages the conscience of the non-Catholic could not be taken into account. This attitude extended into the field of judicial procedures: individual persons often had to wait for years before ecclesiastical courts were ready to pronounce a judgment.[29]

When the Church claims to invigilate and to describe and in measure to designate the natural law (not least, through the work of officials such as Gasparri), she does so in good part in relation to sexuality, much more so, for example, than in the case of social justice. There have been three broad consequences of the Church's claims and emphases. First, sexuality has tended to be dealt with juridically rather than psychologically or sociologically – or for that matter scripturally.[30] Second, a concentration on the narrowly teleological dimensions of sexuality – or if you wish, on the physiology of sexual intercourse – has both diminished the human side of sexual relations and reduced much moral judgement to a biological basis. Third, in attempting to dictate morals, especially in the area of birth control and demography, in what appears as an outmoded fashion the Church has in the contemporary intellectual world created disarray among some of her own best moral theologians, cowed bishops into a tacit and gloomy acceptance of Roman directives, issued confused messages on the meaning of the ordinary magisterium and simply stayed apart from some of the most crucial discussions that are taking place on the future of biological and genetic research and its implications. In the process, the Church has been unable to come to terms with or to reflect sensibly on the technological and genetic advances that have been taking place within medical and other sciences.

Analysing the Roots of Morality

To complement the previous historical section it is useful to take a brief philosophical look at the human roots of morality and to examine critically moral norms drawn too readily from natural law theories. It has to be remembered that the roles of pontiffs, bishops and clerics that were forged during the Middle Ages were flanked from the 13th century on by concepts of natural law that have come close to dogma in the contemporary Roman Church.[31]

Society and Order: Function, Solidarity and Aesthetics

There are some salient features of society/living together that we all want to control or to organise or to have organised in such fashion that they are or become acceptable to, or tolerable for, us. First, we want society to function so as to fulfil our basic needs, not least those of security, welfare, and freedom. Second, we want it to form a social whole within whose boundaries we can expect social support from others, interact benignly with others, and identify with them. Third, we want social living and habits to be aesthetic or congenial to our tastes.

In other words, I am contending that the content of morality is usually conditioned by three central behavioural dimensions: function, solidarity[32] and aesthetics. I am also contending that these three dimensions – together or singly – provide eminently useful guidelines for ethical behaviour. Equally, I want to say that they do not constitute morality. I accept that they also in some measure overlap with one another.

Each one of the three dimensions that I have just mentioned – the sources of practical morality, if I may so call them – is related to order. The first dimension (function) is related to the order of achievement which involves the relationship between the use of means and the securing of a given or proposed end. The second (conformity or convention) is the recognition of shared and established relations between persons and between groups: it is related to the sense of wholeness and solidarity of a society. The third dimension (aesthetic) is taste or style: it is the manner with which situations and issues are dealt with. The last dimension may be more subjective, that is, it may depend more on personal and social taste than the first two dimensions, but it comes constantly into play not only as familiar conduct is carried on or dealt with but as changing situations elicit reactive or exploratory behaviour and as new relations between persons, actions and things are discerned or proposed.

Taking these features of society as the context within which moral reasoning and behaviour take place, let us come back to them in a way that is closer to moral reflection. The first feature of practical morality is functional. Deep within moral attitudes there is support for the purposeful working of society and the relations of its members to one another – functioning in the broadest sense of co-operating for security, maintaining law and order, and working for interests that include economic efficiency and growth; and functioning also in the sense of individuals respecting their own psychological and biological make-up. The Western classical and medieval understanding of nature, essences and natural tendencies draws on this criterion. It is a criterion that is made use of, for example, to underpin human needs of survival and procreation and to examine the use of human biology in achieving such ends. But it also takes in the care of children by parents, and it is employed to require truthfulness in terms of the function of speech.

What is at the heart of the second criterion, the communal or conventional, is not simply conformity. The latter is secondary. What is fundamental is the concept of wholeness or community: the latter includes, positively, members with a sense of belonging to one another, offering one another support and accepting interdependence within the social whole. Negatively, it means avoiding actions that do not betray the community or involve severance from the other members. At the heart of this criterion lie the exigencies of order: patterned and agreed relations between persons and groups. By such criteria are judged, for example, on the one hand, citizenship and the right to vote and, on the other hand, the strangeness that makes some persons non-citizens, outsiders or (depending on the shape of the exclusion) pariahs. By such criteria, in fact, persons are identified as belonging but others are not only set apart from the grid or structures of society but are put outside the group itself, at least in a moral sense, even if such persons physically or territorially or legally remain part of the group.

The third dimension of morality, the aesthetic, is often dressed up as pure morality. Such aesthetic judgement is closely related to the previous dimension and is heavily based on and interlaced with what in social affairs persons are accustomed to - though aesthetic judgement from time to time moves beyond accepted taste and adds something to the latter. However, too often once persons encounter culture or behaviour to which they are not accustomed and which they dislike, they react with attitudes that range from unease and distaste to straightforward moral condemnation and rejection. In referring to this aesthetic criterion I am not talking about what is thought beautiful – though that is not excluded – but am rather referring to styles of being and doing that are much wider than beauty and relate to what is thought fitting for individuals and society. Much of the traditional sumptuary legislation in medieval European society came from a sense of what was fitting, as has legislation on clothing and nudity in modern times. To take a light but interesting example: there have been until very recently few new forms of dancing introduced into Western culture that have not met with some moral rejection. The waltz, for example, which now looks so staid and old-fashioned, was the first European dance in which partners held one another closely, and it endured decades and more of theological and moral opprobrium. In short, the aesthetic dimension is closely linked to function and conformity but it does take on a life of its own. In the case of homosexuality, for example, my impression is that though arguments are used from function and solidarity, it is aesthetic revulsion (the charge of obscenity) which now dominantly endures and which may prove a more formidable source of opposition to tolerance than objections based on non-functionality in terms of procreation (perversion) and non-conformity to majority behaviour (deviancy).

The Patterns of Moral Behaviour

What these three criteria or dimensions do when they are used together is to suggest patterns of social and individual interrelationship. They serve to create or maintain a basic social order. They issue in the observance of those behavioural codes that are needed for predictability in the actions of members of a society as well as for their experience and confidence in adapting to change. They also establish patterns that obviate the necessity for each generation to think out issues afresh; and so they reduce reliance on the obvious frailty of newly formed opinion, not least moral opinion. Out of such criteria come, on the one hand, a will to protect life, to promote social intercourse and assistance, and to respect the sensitivities of strong and weak alike, and, on the other hand, a willingness to drive on the agreed side of the road, to pay politically levied taxes, and to accept the results of elections in democratic societies.

But if the criteria outlined in the previous paragraph are crucial to guiding the detail of individual and social morality, underlying them and giving them moral meaning is a reverence for the whole of creation/existence and for each of its parts, not least its human participants. Without such mutual respect among humans the logic of human living – doing to others what we would have them do to us – loses consistency, and, in consequence, rationality.[33]

To use somewhat different language: I am saying that the three criteria that provide a guide/content for individual and social behaviour take on moral meaning when they are animated by a judgement which involves a respect both for the individuality, and for the inter-dependence, of everything that exists. Only through such logic can humans not only co-exist with one another but co-exist participatively.

Principles of Orientation and Practice for the Church

In an attempt to synthesise, let me put forward, first, some *principles of orientation* that suggest applied approaches which support the faith and role of the Church in relation to sexuality and marriage. Second, let me propose by way of *principles of practice* statements on law and ideals.

With regard to principles of orientation, the love and respect inherent in good interpersonal relations provide the foundations of morality, including sexual morality. While useful guidelines exist in the shape of functionality, social integration and aesthetic taste, these must be tested against the foundations of human and Christian morality: respect for persons and love of neighbours. In light of this, laws in the Church have always to be judged by how much they foster love for individuals and serve to build Christian community. In other words, every law has itself to undergo the test of love. Laws are not to be multiplied without necessity; and they have to be changed/modernised as technology, society and economy change, that is, as people and their relations change.

Principles of Practice

1. A pastoral function of the universal Church and local churches is to provide support for teaching and training in sexual deportment or to assist those, including parents and others, who provide formation. It needs to help those entering marriage and those who are in marriage. In this connection, the Church has an obligation to use its influence and resources to influence laws and benefits that support marriages and benefit children. At the same time, however, I believe that it is now time for the Church to cease its undue preoccupation with sexual morality and treat sexual morality as part of the general morality of interpersonal relations.

2. Marriage lies at the heart of sexual morality. Some marriages may however decay or may have been unsound from the outset. For such reasons local communities may need to devise guidelines for their circumstances and work with individual persons and/or couples to see how such guidelines apply in particular cases of marital breakdown. Christ set an ideal of indissoluble marriage. But from the time of the apostle Paul, Christian communities have accepted that marriages may be dissolved.

3. The witness of the clergy and the blessing of marriage in Church are highly desirable without being necessary.[34] The Church should foster such witness without imposing sanctions on those who consider it unnecessary. The Church needs also to come to terms with a phased giving of consent in marriage, especially in those African cultures, for example, where the Roman concept of an instantly contracted union runs counter to traditional custom, or in Western countries where young couples have refused to distinguish sharply between loving cohabitation and formal marriage.

4. Same-sex partners need to be given support. The Church has to set aside its public opposition in certain countries to more liberal laws for homosexuals. In such legal changes there is no degeneracy but only the recognition of the role of changing behaviour and new aesthetic tastes in society.[35]

5. It does not belong to the domain or powers of the Church to impose through law a secular concern for social order or the values of ruling groups on sexuality and marriage. In the event the Church should consider reducing its marriage legislation to a minimum of rules that are meant to serve the unity of the community and the support of families.

In suggesting broad principles of orientation and practice, let me add that the Church is faced with a perennial task that must of its nature always remain full of tension. On the one hand, the Church must seek to understand the values, hopes and tasks of our contemporaries and must speak to them in their language. It has also to learn from its contemporaries if it is to speak to them. In this sense, the Church is all things to all people (1 Cor 9:20-23). On the other hand, the Church has to confront the too easily accepted wisdom of the day, challenge values that run counter to those of the Gospel and create communities within which the example of Christ can be followed and the hope of the resurrection shine through (Rom 12:1-3). In this sense, the Church has to uphold with determination and courage the ideals that Christ and the apostles bequeathed. But it has to hesitate before translating those ideals into laws without allowing that hesitation to harm the ideals.

In putting the case for reforms in understanding the authority of the Church and its exercise in sexual matters the resistance to change should not be underestimated. Historically the problem is that it has taken a long time for doctrinal development to take place in many moral issues – one has only to think about the relations between faith and politics, the economics of interest taking, the acceptability of slavery, and the role of women in Church and family. Living as we do in a time of rapid change, revised theological thinking has tended to threaten the security of many Western clerics who are already on the defensive against trends in the modern world that range from the higher criticism of the scriptures to advances in bio-genetics. Such new thinking exasperates Third World bishops who in struggling with practical difficulties see changes in the theology of sexual morality as one more problem foisted on them by the former colonial West. It disconcerts many concerned lay persons in every part of the world who have been unaware of changes in theological thinking and little informed about newer hermeneutical approaches that undermine the concept of scripture envisaged as a set of moral norms.

Yet if we argue for a reduction in the legal role of the Church in respect to sexual morality and marriage, then we can more easily return to the spiritual role of the Church in sexual and other forms of morality. The Church's crucial role in morality is that of prophetic witness: witness in teaching (including reflecting, preaching and persuading), witness in the nobility of practice, and witness in the facilitation of individual and community integrity as well as in organised support for human living, whether through community development, education or hospital services. Mahoney, in an eloquent passage writes about such witness and eschews mentioning the role of law:

> For here again, recent theological reflection on sacramental theology and on the nature of the Church has resulted in a fresh appreciation of the function of the Church within God's unitary enterprise of creation and redemption. It is to give witness in human society to that fellowship of individuals to which every man is called and to give evidence of the degree to which he is already

> enabled, by the Spirit of Christ, to live in communion with God and his fellow men. To live its witness is the prime task laid upon the Church. But to preach that witness, in words as well as example, is also its charge. It is to be both a symbol and an agent of human community.[36]

Such witness presupposes saintly discipleship and efficient social organisation within the Church, especially though not only among its organisational professionals, but also a continuing, pervasive, free and open reflection on moral matters.

A Movement toward Broader Reform: Where will Orientation and Practices Go?

I have throughout this essay avoided the question of the legitimacy of ecclesial authority. I have suggested where authority has performed useful functions, where it has in Christian terms failed, and where it might usefully bring in or accept changes. The legitimacy of authority depends on three factors: that the rightful people are ruling – in this case those who have inherited the powers of the apostles; that they are ruling rightly, that is, efficiently, justly and within their ecclesial powers; and that those ruled who form the community and who in the last resort share in the government of the community accept that those with the powers of governing are rightful rulers and are ruling rightly. In the case of a society of conscience, which is what the Church is, legitimacy is even more important than in a secular society which can have recourse to sanctions that touch on physical security, property and freedom. In a profound sense, the Church has to win the allegiance of people.

The need of the Church to rely on consciences is a great strength because conscience, especially if working within sensible structures, acts powerfully on behaviour. It looks, however, a weakness in the eyes of those who rely on organisation and rules to keep the community intact. The truth is that we are in a period where not only has conscience become more important through education and technological development but where mass communication quickly spreads ideas and values faster than ever before in history. What once might have remained elite views now quickly become generally accepted. If one wants evidence of the growth of conscience in contemporary political circumstances, one can find it clearly in the growth of single issue campaigning and the proliferation of environmental groups.

Against this background three changes in the practices of the faithful show how Christian conscience and practice are changing. First, by and large people no longer go to confession, and they settle their own consciences with God. Second, they no longer accept that going to Mass on a Sunday or a holiday of obligation is obligatory, and they attend as they think fit. Third, young people in many countries cohabit before marriage, and they do not accept that they are living in sin. Waving rules at such people will not work, telling them that they face eternal fire will only evoke amusement or derision, and arguing that a return to traditional practices is the best way of doing things will fall on deaf ears. We are dealing with changed people in a developing context and face new problems that call for new methods of approach.

Yet in drawing attention to conscience within the working of the Church, I am not seeking to devalue ecclesial institutions. Conscience itself works best within a Church whose structures reflect evangelical values, that are adapted to the technology of a period and that respond to free and faithful discussion. In other words, in a spiritual organisation it is crucial to rely on conscience, and yet to note the interplay of conscience and institutional structures. Spiritual reformers for that reason neglect at their peril the construction and operation of institutions. Mary Douglas in a secular context makes a crucial point on how decisions that affect the body corporate are made:

> For better or worse, individuals really do share their thoughts and they do to some extent harmonize their preferences, and they have no other way to make the big decisions except within the scope of the institutions they build.[37]

Finally, let me say that I do not believe that we will evolve an evangelical, traditional and relevant approach to sexual morality unless other aspects of the Church's life are put into better order or reformed.

Given the need to win allegiances in a society of conscience, that is to say, to create a blend of freedom, collaboration and obedience, what is likely to happen in the future to Church authority, whether in sexual morality or in anything else? There are several possibilities that are not mutually exclusive.[38]

First, in line with the ambitions of Pope John Paul II and his immediate collaborators we may have an ecclesial community that is highly centralised, that is clerically controlled at every level, and that accepts traditional sexual morality within a legal apparatus of control. In the context of the modern world, such a community would go on diminishing in numbers. It would live in some alienation from its own best theologians, it would mummify liturgically, and it would lose the collaboration if not the allegiance of many educated Catholics.

Second, we may have a church that is made up of a traditional grouping such as in the first possibility but whose traditional membership is flanked by those who stay within the same Church but choose its rules and values with some freedom, distancing themselves from more rigid attitudes, drawing on the example of Jesus, and stressing the more humane aspects of Church and tradition. With time, the more liberal group may find it harder to stay central to the life of the Church, may face some harassment from ecclesiastical authorities, and may decide to find a more personal and individual way forward. In other words, a large group that is profoundly upset by what appear to them to be unchristian and anachronistic viewpoints may gradually cease to contribute actively to the Church, leaving the latter profoundly weakened. Perhaps the biggest danger in this second scenario is less that some fine and sensitive individuals may leave – though this is a danger that should give authorities pause – but that clerical and educated ranks may split and that the general laity may become confused by bitter in-fighting among professionals and that the more theologically sophisticated lay activists will join them in what could come to a form of civil war.

Third, we may have a Church that in a much more plural approach to contemporary societies and cultures may gradually devise relevant liturgies for various groups and bring back into worship an awareness of the presence of God, a sharing in sacrificial offering, and a sense of small-scale and large-scale community. It may re-think its witness of integrity in relation to great social and personal issues, ranging from bio-genetics and birth control to international cooperation and social justice, that are pouring in on us. In the process, its leaders may speak in dialogue with its members, that is, to speak to them rather than claim to speak for them. The Church may well revise its organisational structures, not just the papal curia but the workings of the dioceses, the recruitment and formation of clerics, the diversifying of episcopal and priestly structures, and a deepened appreciation of the role of the laity.

We are, in practice, not going to get a Church that resists all change; and we are unlikely to get a Church that embodies all the reforms that are envisaged in a pluralist Church that welcomes continuing change. We may well get, for a time, a divided Church that is composed of traditionalists and modernisers. What one can say with some certainty is that the future of the Church depends on its faithfulness to its origins as well as on the mixture of tradition and modernity that we put together. In this connection, too, the life of the Church and human sexuality are distinct but not separate from one another.

Notes

1 A philosophical reflection is needed for several reasons. First, it sets a parameter for a theological approach because while faith and theology can offer historical and speculative insights to reason, they cannot contradict reason; and theology itself is essentially reason working analytically and historically on the data of scripture, tradition and the living life of the Church. Moreover, implicitly, if not explicitly, I want to suggest in this opening paragraph that the Church needs to be cautious in relying on theologies that use philosophical theories that are heavily marked by the intellectual climate of the ages in which they were elaborated. In the present context I believe that a reliance on natural law theory

which comes from the Greeks and the medievals and which assumes pre-Newtonian scientific conceptualisation is highly inadequate for understanding contemporary morality.

2 It is worth remembering that the contemporary concept of homosexual orientation, for example, is as alien to the scriptures as is the Copernican/Newtonian/Einsteinian universe, the system of venture capitalism or the science that is able to clone living beings. In short, once technology changes not only do new problems – and for that matter new solutions – arise but ways of thinking may need to be refined.

3 E.P. Sanders, *The Historical Figure of Jesus* (London: Penguin, 1993) pp. 202-203.

4 One may contrast the concept of a society of conscience with the comment of a modern analyst on a society of law.

> Recent analyses of the "corporate state" or bureaucratic-technological society have pointed out that the social world in which we live is highly legalistic; however, law serves no longer primarily as an instrument of justice and delimitation of power but as the value-free medium which permits the bureaucratic system to function smoothly and to maintain a high degree of institutional control. Laws are enacted primarily to satisfy the exigencies of administration rather than to protect the rights of individuals.

Peter G. Hodgson, *New Birth of Freedom: A Theology of Bondage and Liberation* (Philadelphia: Fortress, 1976) p. 190.

5 Richard P. McBrien, *Do We Need the Church?* (New York/London: Collins/Harper and Row, 1969) p. 147.

6 For interpreting Paul I have drawn heavily on two works of Jerome Murphy-O'Connor, *Paul: A Critical Life* (Oxford: Clarendon, 1996) and *Becoming Human Together: The Pastoral Anthropology of St. Paul* (Wilmington, Del.: Glazier, 1984).

7 Murphy-O'Connor, *Becoming Human Together*, p. 235.

8 *Ibid.*, pp. 213-214. Peter G. Hodgson, *New Birth of Freedom*, p. 190, extends this contention to law more generally:

> But it may be asked, is Paul's rejection of the law as binding on the believer as radical as this? Is not the "law" he rejects simply an external code, a list of thou shalts and thou shalt nots, in particular the code of Judaism? Whatever may seem to be implied in some of his practical teaching, I feel sure that in his "theory" of the Christian life Paul went much further than this. Although undoubtedly he is frequently referring to the Jewish law, one cannot deny the presence – often, if not always – of a more radical, more inclusive reference.... Law, as such, is no longer valid for the Christian.

9 Gasparri, for Benedict XV, produced 2,414 canons (not to mention sub-divisions). The legal collaborators of John Paul II have managed to reduce the previous total to 1,752. I cannot help thinking that the two codes confuse in some fundamental way prescribing for order, for morality and for salvation.

10 See Jerome Murphy-O'Connor, *Becoming Human Together*, p. 13. In a study of Paul's life and teaching the same historian and commentator writes, in *Paul: a Critical Life*, p. 214:

> Only when the pattern of...Pauline passages is perceived does it become clear just how radical Paul's antinomian stance was. He would not give obedience to any law, and he would not exact submission from his converts. He would indicate what he expected of them. He would attempt to persuade them to modify their behaviour.... For Paul there was only "the law of Christ" (Gal 6:2b; cf. 1 Cor 8:13).... Now God's will is embodied in the comportment of Christ, who both exemplifies the demand made on, and models the response of, humanity.... "Bear one another's burdens" (Gal 6:2a) – love is the sole binding imperative of the new law. It was the salient feature of Christ's humanity, and is the content of the one true precept which remains (Gal 5:14; Rom 13:8-10; 1 Cor 7:19), because it is of the very essence of Christian life (2 Thess 4:9; 1 Cor 13:2).

11 L. William Countryman, *Dirt, Greed and Sex: Sexual Ethics in the New Testament and their Implications for Today* (London: SCM, 1989) p. 239.

12 Luigi Sturzo, *Inner Laws of Society: A New Sociology* (New York: P.J. Kenedy & Sons, 1944) p. 85.

13 There is, for example, tension, and practical contradiction, between Paul's refusal to have women

placed over men and his assertion of the fundamental equality of the sexes.

14 Historically too many preachers had failed to come to terms with the God of the paradoxes who is everywhere and is nowhere; who does everything and does nothing; who hears our prayers and yet never intervenes; who achieves his will and still leaves us free.

15 In itself this process would however without a concomitant growth of unbelief have been less a secularisation than a declericalisation of society.

16 The history of the convoluted and inconsistent canonical decrees on the taboos/bars to marriage, for instance, that were based on consanguinity and affinity owed nothing to the New Testament but a great deal to Jewish, Roman and Germanic legal codes.

17 See, the *Catechism of the Catholic Church* (London: Chapman, 1994) 2030-2040. The quotations in the text come from these sections. For the weighty authority given to the *Catechism* by the Roman authorities one may consult the Apostolic Constitution, *Fidei Depositum*, by Pope John Paul II which serves as a foreword to the catechism, pp. 1-6.

18 I have remarked in passing above the limitations of the use of the term "deposit". I cannot help wondering also how 19th century ill-nourished and badly housed slum dwellers in Manchester and Birmingham observed "the specific precepts of the natural law" so as to work out their salvation.

19 John Mahoney, *The Making of Moral Theology: A Study of the Roman Catholic Tradition* (Oxford: Clarendon, 1987) p. 115.

20 I take 'witness' in the sense of reflecting on issues, debating them with others, and where need be acting on them with integrity.

21 Richard W. Southern, *Western Society and the Church in the Middle Ages* (London: Hodder and Stoughton, 1972) pp.175-176.

22 Cited in Robert Bartlett, *The Making of Europe: Conquest, Colonization and Cultural Change, 950-1350* (London: Penguin, 1993) p. 244.

23 Richard W. Southern, *Western Society and the Church*, p. xx, writes: "...the whole broad spectrum of society which he [the king] particularly represented – the laity – suffered a corresponding demotion. Henceforth it became increasingly natural to speak of the ecclesiastical hierarchy as 'the church'. Of course everyone knew that there was another, more ancient sense of the word which embraced the whole body of the faithful, but even when the word 'ecclesia' was used in this wide sense the role of the laity began to be seen as a very humble one."

24 Richard W. Southern, *Western Society and the Church*, pp. 38-39.

25 Norman Davies, *Europe: A History* (Oxford: Univ. Pr., 1996) p. 292.

26 Eamonn Duffy, "Papal Authority", *Priests and People* 11 (1997) 301-305, p. 302.

27 Clerical leaders often sought to protect the interests of their organisation by claiming sacred rights to curb or reject the powers of other organisations, not least the state, whether it was in England the rejection of the right of Henry II to try clerics in civil courts, the penalties inflicted on Church members in the Codex of 1918 who took bishops to court, or the organisational withholding of paedophile priests (without much regard to the rights of their victims) in the U.S., Canada, Ireland and elsewhere from the jurisdiction of civil law and punishment for their crimes.

28 Eamonn Duffy, "Papal Authority", p. 304.

29 Ladislas M. Orsy, *Marriage in Canon Law: Texts and Comments, Reflections and Questions* (Dublin: Dominican, 1988) p. 35.

30 I can only briefly refer to the harm done to church thinking on sexuality by the influence of St. Augustine who linked procreation to the concept of original sin; and who misunderstood the function of sexual pleasure and its fundamental goodness.

31 There is not enough space available here to go into the issue in full detail but those who wish may consult what I have written elsewhere: "The Sources of Morality: Function, Conformity and Aesthetics", *The Heythrop Journal* 34 (1993) 160-170.

32 Other terms may be used to describe the worth of social cohesion, including concepts of the common good, that are involved in this dimension of morality.

33 Kant's moral imperatives sum up the complexity of that kind of respect and offer slightly more detailed directives for human living.

34 Technically this is called "the form" of marriage.

35 A longer and fuller exposition of my views on homosexuality can be found in, "On Loving All Our Neighbours: Notes toward a Theology of Homosexuality", *The Month* 33 (2000) 95-97.
36 Mahoney, *The Making of Moral Theology*, p. 346.
37 Mary Douglas, *How Institutions Think* (London: Routledge and Kegan Paul, 1987) p. 128.
38 I have suggested elsewhere in a more developed way these various scenarios for the future of the Church, see, "The Future of the Church", *The Month* 31 (1998) 222-229 and 275-281.

Chapter Eight

Authority and Sexuality in the Protestant Tradition

Adrian Thatcher

The topic I have been asked to address is impossibly broad, so I have narrowed it in order to do five things. In the first section, some of the acrimonious sexuality debates in various Protestant churches during the last decade are described. Attention to these might show, empirically, how Protestantism handles, or rather fails to handle, questions about sexuality. Secondly, some tentative conclusions are drawn. In section three, appeals to the Bible as a source of authority are examined. Some remarks are made about the models of authority and tradition in the recent ARCIC document, *The Gift of Authority*[1] in the fourth section. Finally, it is suggested that the Catholic and Protestant traditions should address common problems afflicting both of them.

The Sexuality Debates

Many of the Protestant denominations in the USA, Britain and elsewhere, held acrimonious debates over sexuality issues in the late 80s and early 90s. Attention to these has the advantage of turning abstract questions about authority into empirical descriptions of bureaucratic manoeuvrings, shoddy tactics, political battles, and so on. If anything is to be learned about authority in Protestantism, it will be found in the way Protestants behave. I have selected three, from many possible case studies.

The Presbyterian Church, USA

In 1987, the General Assembly of this church appointed through its Moderator a special committee with a mandate to "review and update previous General Assembly studies of human sexuality" and to include "biblical-theological guidance in light of our Reformed tradition", and an "understanding of the variety of expressions of human sexuality".[2] Previous studies had barred "practising" lesbian and gay members of the church from being ordained. This was the issue that aroused most fears in this church. The committee took six months to set up because so many people wanted to be appointed to it and so many sub-groups sought representation.[3] The denomination was divided theologically from the beginning, and these divisions were certain to be reflected in the committee and its report.

As the committee undertook its research it concluded that previous reports had articulated only the views of its "greying" membership (average age 55) who were mainly opulent, white, middle class, and married. The committee was "stunned by the scope of sexual violence in America", and "surprised to realise the scope of the problem of clergy misconduct". They found great prejudice against AIDS sufferers and "a final thing which sobered us was the role of patriarchy in the shaping of American society". They held hearings in nearly every North American city to discuss, *inter-alia*, whether there was support for the ordination of lesbian and gay people with partners, and as their Chairperson noted, "We came to see that there are many myths and stereotypes which the heterosexual culture has about gays and lesbians, and we decided to name those myths".[4] This was just what the church did not want to hear.

The report, *Keeping Body and Soul Together*, was ready for the 1991 Assembly. Perhaps there has never been a more positive church sexuality report for advancing a self-critical understanding of the gender inequalities, patriarchal influences, sexual violence and attempts at social control which can be found in Christian thought and practice, together with a deeply Christian affirmation of people who have suffered from these malign influences or who are found beyond the customary parameters of approved sexual behaviour. But before it appeared, a minority resigned from the committee and produced their own report. There was thus also a rival report.[5] Before the report was debated there were many threats of resignation from individuals and threats of secession from churches, should the report be approved. There were acute differences in the Assembly and on the Committee about the problem of biblical interpretation. The Assembly attracted national media attention. The Assembly threw out both the majority and the minority reports, and the Moderator was required to send a pastoral letter to all congregations, saying (among other things): "We affirm the Scriptures to be the unique and authoritative word of God, superior to all other authorities.... We strongly affirm the sanctity of the marital covenant between one man and one woman to be a God-given relationship to be lived out in Christian fidelity.... [and] we continue to abide by the position of the General Assemblies of 1978 and 1979 regarding homosexuality."[6] This "position" barred from ordination all "practising" homosexuals.

A major reforming document was produced, but a moment for reform was lost, and the divisions which were present before the Assembly met were aggravated. The hopes of sexual minorities in and on the fringes of the church, for greater understanding and acceptance, were raised, and dashed. The 1993

General Assembly called for a further three-year study "of human sexuality as it applies to membership, ministry, and ordination".[7] The 1996 General Assembly sent a resolution to all the churches which, if passed, would be inserted into the denomination's *Book of Order*. It said,

> Those who are called to office in the church are to lead a life in obedience to Scripture and in conformity to the historic confessional standards of the church. Among these standards is the requirement to live either in fidelity within the covenant of marriage of a man and a woman, or chastity in singleness. Persons refusing to repent of any self-acknowledged practice which the confessions call sin shall not be ordained and/or installed as deacons, elders or ministers of the Word and Sacrament.[8]

The rationale for the resolution was the familiar distinction between orientation and practice.

> Through listening to the pain of its members, the church has learned to distinguish between homosexual orientation and practice. Homosexual orientation is not a sin; neither is it a barrier to ordination. However, the refusal to repent of any self-acknowledged practice that Scripture, interpreted through the confessions, calls sin, bars one from office.[9]

Evangelical Lutheran Church of America

In October 1993, the Evangelical Lutheran Church of America produced the "first draft" of a social statement, *The Church and Human Sexuality: A Lutheran Perspective*. A "Task Force on Human Sexuality" had been set up in 1989 and had spent four years of reflection and consultation in "what probably has been the most extensive, impassioned discussion of sexuality in the history of American Lutheranism".[10] The draft was distributed to the churches for study and comment with a deadline for responses. The Task Force intended to revise the document in response to the feedback that had been solicited, and then to send a second draft to the Board of the Division for Church in Society, and to the Church Council. It would then be considered at the 1995 Church-wide Assembly. This lengthy procedure had already been used for other issues in the church and was devised as a teaching and learning method which was genuinely consultative, democratic, inclusive and participatory.

The Task Force, conscious of the Reformation roots of the Lutheran Church, included a bold assertion of the right of that church to make doctrinal and moral changes: "The Gospel message of freedom allows us to change positions we have held in the past when such change enhances the ministry of the Word of God, as part of the ongoing reformation of the Church."[11] Masturbation was generally fine – "a means of self-pleasuring" which "is generally appropriate and healthy, unless it becomes compulsive or hinders development of life-fulfilling relationships".[12] I am told one mocking tabloid headline read "Masturbation? Lutherans don't give a toss". A realistic section on teenage sex warned against its harmfulness and encouraged the use of contraceptives where it was known to occur. There were sympathetic, but not approving, statements about living together before marriage and about sexually active single adults. The draft noted three responses to the divine command to love "neighbours" who are lesbian and gay. These were, "to love the sinner but to hate the sin": to show compassion and understanding "of the dilemma facing those who do not have the gift of celibacy", and "open affirmation of gay and lesbian persons and their mutually loving, just committed relationships of fidelity".[13] It was clear the report favoured the third approach.

The document caused an uproar in the Church. The Task Force Director, Karen Bloomquist, was sacked ("asked to step aside").[14] The Church Council disowned the document (it "underscored the fact that the draft is not official ELCA policy"). It commissioned a new consulting panel (packed with safe names chosen mainly by the Bishops' Conference) to produce a new "possible social statement" on human sexuality, "with the content to be in keeping with the ELCA's bland (*sic*) confessional foundations". The document, it was implied, was *not* "in keeping" with the preferred blandness. It stated that "trust in the current task force has been impaired".[15] It was reported that "more than 1,300 clergy and lay leaders endorsed a response statement that takes issue with the sexuality draft".[16] It is very interesting that *a majority of women clergy were in favour of the draft*. By April over 8,000 responses had been received.

> 15% of lay responses were positive while 64% were negative. Nearly 25% of clergy responses were positive and 42% were negative. More female clergy respondents (62%) than male clergy (22%) registered positive reactions. Negative clergy responses by gender were 44% male and 29% female.[17]

Within a year a second sexuality document appeared.[18] Whereas the tone of the first one was warm, compassionate and inclusive, the second one was dogmatic and icy.[19] Reading it is akin to the experience of opening the door of a freezer.

Karen Bloomquist wrote subsequently about her experience as Task Force Director. She thinks the controversy was prompted by a pervasive fear of sexuality.[20] "A conference of all-male church leaders can spend five days hearing and talking about sexuality issues, but without ever focussing on their own experience as sexual beings." She understands the conservative reaction to be fuelled by a loss of control over the church by a male hegemony. Heterosexism, she says, is an idolatry. "There is an urgent need for communities of faith to be safe places, havens from the continual wounding of judgment. We need to shift from equating the gospel with liberal tolerance/acceptance to a gospel-formed community of faith that is able honestly to face and grapple with ethical dilemmas as people actually face them in their lives as sexual beings."[21]

The Church of England

The third and last example of a church struggling with sexuality issues is the Church of England. We will look briefly at three documents before reflecting on all three case studies together. The 1978 Lambeth Conference of Bishops had called on all bishops of the Anglican Communion to undertake a "deep and dispassionate study of the question of homosexuality", and this call was reaffirmed a decade later.[22] The House of Bishops published *Issues in Human Sexuality* in 1991, as "partly a response to that call as well as being our reflection on the pastoral situation we face in our own Church and society".[23] Whatever authority bishops have in the Church of England, was invested in this document. Chapter 3 set out "The Christian Vision for Human Sexuality", but 2 of the 5 chapters were on homosexuality, and there is no doubt that the subject was the major preoccupation of the report. This preoccupation was hardly new. The General Synod had published *Homosexual Relationships in 1979*. A Working Party of the Church of England Board of Social Responsibility had produced a further report (the "Osborne Report") in 1989. The House of Bishops refused permission for its publication.

In 1991 the House of Bishops concluded:

> There should be an open and welcoming place in the Christian community both for those homophiles who follow the way of abstinence, giving themselves to friendship for many rather than to intimacy with one, and also for those who are conscientiously convinced that a faithful, sexually active relationship with one other person, aimed at helping both partners to grow in discipleship, is the way of life God wills for them.[24]

This is a considerable gain, years ahead of the Presbyterian asseveration that a homosexual act is a sin because it always has been. Living together is fine for lesbian and gay people, *as long as they are not ordained*:

> The Church exists also to live out in the world the truth it has been given about the nature of God's creation, the way of redemption through the Cross, and the ultimate hope of newness and fullness of life. We have judged that we ourselves and all clergy, as consecrated public and representative figures, entrusted with the message and means of grace, have a responsibility on behalf of the whole Body of Christ to show the primacy of this truth by striving to embody it in our own lives. But we also wish to stress the Church's care for and value of all her clergy alike, and that where

> the Church's teaching results for any ordained person in a burden grievous to be borne we, the bishops, as pastors to the pastors, will always be ready to share in any way we can in the bearing of that burden.

The bishops did *not* say that homosexual "acts" were sinful. They set out two principles and drew conclusions from them. The first principle is "that homophile orientation and its expression in sexual activity do not constitute a parallel and alternative form of human sexuality as complete within the terms of the created order as the heterosexual". The second is that "homosexual people are in every way as valuable to and as valued by God as heterosexual people".[25] Some "Christian homophiles" feel an obligation to a life of abstinence, while others "are conscientiously convinced that this way of abstinence is not the best for them, and that they have more hope of growing in love for God and neighbour with the help of a loving and faithful homophile partnership, in intention lifelong, where mutual self-giving includes the physical expression of their attachment". On grounds of *conscience* (i.e. of "homophiles", not bishops!) and

> while unable, therefore, to commend the way of life just described as in itself as faithful a reflection of God's purposes in creation as the heterophile, we do not reject those who sincerely believe it is God's call to them. We stand alongside them in the fellowship of the Church, all alike dependent upon the undeserved grace of God.[26]

This is an ingenious way of postponing trouble. Lesbian and gay couples are outside Christian moral norms, but on the grounds of their own convictions, they are to be affirmed and welcomed in the churches. A Church of Scotland report wryly observed this solution was "allowing a maximum of pastoral discretion while officially affirming traditional standards as the ideal".[27] The second Anglican document is chosen for its coverage of a different issue currently troubling Christians: cohabitation. In 1992 the Board for Social Responsibility of the Church of England set up a Working Party, chaired by the Bishop of Sherwood, whose terms of reference included "to perceive the will of God for the human family within contemporary English society, and in particular: to review the teaching and insights of Scripture and the Christian tradition about the nature of the family".[28] The 1992 General Synod had debated cohabitation, so the Working Party was asked to consider that issue as well. The Working Party advocated a positive acceptance of the practice and hinted at theological changes that might accommodate it. It was, of course, heavily criticised, and when the General Synod debated it in 1995, it was reluctant even to "take note" of it.[29] I have defended the report elsewhere, whilst acknowledging its theological weaknesses.[30] There was much public interest in what the report said about living together, and *The Sun*'s headline the day after publication was "Living in Sin No

Longer a Sin". The Archbishop of Canterbury publicly rejected its conclusions and it was quietly buried.

The 1998 Lambeth Conference Resolution 1.10 on "Human Sexuality", however, was not quietly buried. Indeed it has been described by the Anglican Primate as a "liberation" for most Anglicans. The Conference "believes that abstinence is right for those who are not called to marriage".[31] The resolution continued "We commit ourselves to listen to the experience of homosexual persons", but not apparently to hear about the blessing of God upon their partnerships because, yes, the Bible forbids them:

> while rejecting homosexual practice as incompatible with scripture, [the Conference] calls on all our people to minister pastorally and sensitively to all irrespective of sexual orientation and to condemn irrational fear of homosexuals, violence within marriage and any trivialisation and commercialisation of sex.

The Conference also "cannot advise the legitimising or blessing of same sex unions nor ordaining those involved in same gender unions".

Within 24 hours a group of bishops (eventually rising to 182, including 8 Archbishops), issued a pastoral statement to lesbian and gay Anglicans admitting that at the conference, "it has not been possible to hear adequately your voices", apologising "for any sense of rejection that has occurred because of this reality", pledging "that we will continue to reflect, pray and work for your full inclusion in the life of the Church", and "confessing that Communion-wide we are in great disagreement over what inclusion would mean". One bishop subsequently spoke of "the profound atmosphere of the sinister" at the Conference, and likened the plenary session to a Nuremberg rally.[32] Another spoke of his horror at the ignorance about sexuality within the group that had debated it. There were no conditions of membership for this group, such as, for example, recognised competence, knowledge of the burgeoning secular literature on sexuality, or grateful recognition by sexual minorities of ministry to them, etc. Homosexual people had once more been reduced to an object over whom [mainly] straight bishops could have a high-profile quarrel.

Authority in Protestant Traditions

Attention to the processes within Protestant denominations as they have dealt with matters of sexual ethics was intended to illuminate how Protestants handle authority in practice. I remain uncertain what conclusions we are entitled to draw. However, here are some tentative suggestions.

1. All Protestants accord authority to the Bible, but this can become a form of idolatry. The resolution used by the Presbyterians to extinguish the hope of

lesbian and gay people who had heard God's call to ministry spoke of obedience *to scripture*, not to Jesus Christ. The Church's confessional documents were treated as set in concrete, and no understanding of tradition as open to development was shown.

2. There is a commendable democratic ethos, at least to the American case studies. Both the Presbyterians and the Lutherans had structures available to them for consulting Churches and church members, and they used these. The same may be said for the Methodist and United Reformed Churches in England which both produced sexuality documents in the 1990s, and ensured widespread dissemination and study of them.[33]

3. Homosexuality appears to have become the single most important issue in sexual ethics among Protestants. This may require a *psychological*, not a theological explanation.

4. The mainline denominations appear to have given up any attempt to exert formal disciplinary control over lay-people (e.g., warning, interrogation, exclusion, excommunication, etc.). In one sense they don't need to, because informal sanctions against unwelcome members operate just as effectively without the need for formal enforcement. The ordination of lesbian and gay clergy is the problem which demonstrates the structure and outworking of authority. For the Presbyterians, homosexual practice is sinful. For the Lutherans, the church is not ready to take a decision. For the Anglican bishops, heterosexuality accords better with the order of creation, and celibacy accords better with the standards required of gay clergy than "practice". So practising gays are just about welcome, closet gays and celibate gays are very welcome, closeted gay clergy are just about welcome, but clergy who are out, proud, and in relationships, are bad news.

5. Sexuality has become a battleground among Christians, a "site of conflict" where much more than sexuality is at stake. Broader issues such as the authority and interpretation of the Bible, the role of experience as a possible source of theology, and the struggle for power between factions identifying as liberal, revisionist, or, progressive; or conservative, evangelical or traditional. Sexual minorities become objectified, treated as a problem, and then marginalized by majorities who often make no effort to understand them. The Church of England is especially good at doing this. While the 1998 Lambeth Conference committed itself "to listen to the experience of homosexual persons", the study group in fact refused to receive delegations from homosexual people at the time of their deliberations, and the subsequent pastoral statement to lesbian and gay Anglicans admitted that "it has not be possible to hear adequately your voices".

6. Some of the reports may have invited inadvertent controversy by inattention to theological detail or depth. The Presbyterian report scarcely mentioned marriage. It was not found in the table of contents. In fact only three

and a half pages (out of nearly 200) were devoted to it, and it did not feature at all among the "nine guiding principles" or the "four theological convictions" which, according to the Chair of the committee that produced the report, undergirded it.[34] This was always going to be a self-planted *lacuna* that would explode in the committee's faces. *Something to Celebrate* had innovative things to say about cohabitation before marriage, but the historical and theological issues which would have grounded its conclusions were not allowed to open up. Reactions to controversial positions could have been better anticipated and managed.

7. The documents can all be considered to be "heterosexist" and "homophobic": heterosexist because sexual practice is allowed for the heterosexual majority only, and homophobic because the treatment of lesbian and gay Christians has all the hallmarks of fear.. None of the churches appears to be able to admit that their teaching amounts to an infringement of human rights. In requiring celibacy of lesbian and gay persons, while allowing that only a tiny minority of heterosexual persons have the gift of celibacy, the churches treat a minority unequally. Rhetoric about listening to, welcoming and loving gay people is not only disingenuous, and often falsified by the refusal to do any of these things. It lets straight Christians avoid their share of responsibility for the fear of gay people which is expressed in particular formulations of Christian doctrines which themselves assume oppressive readings of scripture and tradition.

8. The positive response to the Lutheran report among women clergy deserves further research on the contribution of gender to responses to doctrinal and moral change. Did the women see themselves as beneficiaries of the revision of tradition, in having been ordained? Did the men find their masculinity further undermined by the suggestion that gay people are also made in the image of God? Are female Christians more responsive than men to carefully argued proposals for change? If so, the argument for the election of women at all levels of office in the Church is greatly strengthened.

9. I would like to think that the protracted debates about sexuality were necessary and produced gains for the churches. While there was pain and conflict (and sometimes ridicule from the secular media), many Christians learned to love their neighbours and themselves better as a result of it. Churches should not fear ridicule from media sources. However, the depths of heterosexism and homophobia within the churches was also manifested, and these disfigure the body of Christ.

10. While the democratic ethos of the debates is praiseworthy, there must be some doubt or ambiguity about the outcomes of the processes. Paradoxically the *openness* of the debates was itself perceived as a threat. Many Christians do not want to hear about sexuality, and especially homosexuality. Some are afraid of it and want to condemn it, while remaining in ignorance of it. One Presbyterian

complained of "a major impediment" to such dialog: "those in our denomination who themselves do not wish to talk about human sexuality, with all of its orientations and complexities, seek to be the conscience of others in the church by blocking and discouraging their dialog".[35] It should not be assumed that lengthy discussions are motivated by the desire to listen or to promote change. They can equally symbolise a lack of leadership and a determination to do nothing.

Sexuality, Authority and the Bible

We have already noted that, for Presbyterians, the Scriptures are "the unique and authoritative word of God, superior to all other authorities". This is a good example of the language generally used to describe the role of the Bible in Protestantism. Protestantism is in some parts overrun by Christians who would elevate the Bible to the status of divinity, so that its authority is allowed to supplant even the authority of Jesus Christ himself.

Let us first note some moderate views about biblical authority. Article 12 of the 39 Articles of Religion of the Church of England states:

> Holy Scripture containeth all things necessary to salvation: so that whatsoever is not read therein, nor may be proved thereby, is not be required of any man, that it should be believed as an article of the Faith, or be thought requisite or necessary to salvation.

The wording of the article is noteworthy for its inability to support later Protestant and evangelical "word of God" rhetoric which deliberately conflates the Word made flesh (*verbum*) with the words of scripture (*oratio*), the divine Person with the human proposition, and the self-manifestation of God in flesh with text. There is no dogma here about the Holy Spirit inspiring scripture, about its alleged inerrancy, or even directly about its authority. Its unstated authority lies in the ability of its content to provide salvation for its readers (the term "authority" is used not to describe the status of scripture in Article 12, but to distinguish (controversially) between canonical and non-canonical books).

This moderate view of scripture is found in the documents just discussed. *Keeping Body and Soul Together* courageously admitted "there is no single, consistent biblical ethic of sexuality. Diversity, not uniformity, is the character of the biblical witness". The "Jesus story" is placed above scripture:

> In Reformed theology, we affirm that the gospel at the center of Scripture is Jesus Christ and the reign of God in his life, ministry, death, and resurrection. We read Scripture in a discriminating fashion whenever we ask what is – and what is not – compatible with the Jesus story.[36]

Jesus and the gospel are placed above scripture, and scripture must be judged by compatibility with both. The Lutherans too, made the gospel, not the Bible, their "interpretive center".[37]

The House of Anglican Bishops was well aware that disagreement over "the issue of homosexuality" arises "from some of the sharpest controversies of faith in the Church at this time. They concern the way Scripture and Tradition are to be understood, and the authority which these are to have in matters of human living."[38] Their chapter "Scripture and Human Sexuality" evades the depth of conviction among conservative and evangelical Anglicans about the former. The bishops speak of "three distinct realities" which are involved in understanding the Bible: "the content of Scripture itself", "salvation history, that is, the overall shape of the biblical story as this has been perceived by Christian faith and interpreted and told in Christian tradition", and "our general view of the world and our experience of life". This "view of the world" includes a world-view absorbed from contemporary Christian culture and our awareness that we are "shaped by inheritance and nurture, cultural and economic forces, and biological and geophysical conditions".[39] However there is still such a thing as a unitary "scriptural view of human sexuality".[40] Scripture "provides its own criterion (*sic*) for judging its various contents". This includes the teaching and example of Jesus, "the guidance in the rest of the New Testament which came from reflection on the person and work of Christ by the leaders of the earliest church", and the light given by "God's own Spirit". This light is said to be available to Christians today: "The Spirit guides the Church in learning from the dialogue between Scripture and contemporary circumstance.... At any time we also feed into this spirit-led dialogue our own world view and our awareness of new circumstances."[41]

Many other examples could be provided of Protestant theologies driven by undoubted liberal sympathies and convictions, which consciously avoid authority-language, do not perpetuate the ambiguities of the term "Word of God", and which are aware of the relativising influences of history, culture, context, contemporaneity, etc. This is precisely what their conservative opponents look for and regard disingenuously, for however high the view of scripture commended in these documents, confirming code-phrases which are sought, e.g., "Word of God", "inspired", "full authority" "decisive in all matters of faith and doctrine", etc., will be found lacking and the documents declared "unsound", "soft on scripture", "unbiblical", and so on. For these Protestants, scripture is uniform ("Scripture teaches", "the Bible says") and the Holy Spirit helps them (but not apparently their opponents) to interpret it aright. There are sufficient numbers of Christians who believe the Bible is the inspired Word of God for them now to constitute majorities in the Protestant denominations. The Bible teaches that homosexuality is unnatural, and contrary to God's will and

Word. Any other view is seen to be challenging a view of the Bible on which everything has been staked.

The Protestant theologian Paul Tillich used the term "Protestant principle" to describe how "nothing finite can ever become identified with the infinite". The principle was thought to derive from the doctrine of justification by faith which Tillich understood to mean the courage to accept that one was accepted, in spite of oneself and one's just deserts.[42] The elevation of anything proximate to ultimacy, or of anything of great but finite worth to infinite worth was, for him "demonization" or "blasphemy". Yet, as Tillich thought, the Bible in parts of Protestantism had itself become a blasphemy, a usurpation of divine authority, an elevation of a gift of the divine to the status of being divine. Tillich thought it ironic that that part of the Church which was responsible for the Protestant principle was incapable of seeing that its own attitude to scripture stood in breach of it. There are important explanations for this which are well documented. So much disappears from the older Catholic world-view among the new reformed churches that the Bible is made to carry the weight of faith that was once more evenly distributed in Catholic doctrine, devotion and sacramental practice. The use of the Bible in Protestant devotion led to the expectation that God spoke to individuals directly through it, without the need either for ecclesial mediation or scholarly effort. The private use of the Bible contributes to the rise of individualism in Protestant countries. As its importance increased, so did its status. As the rise of science threatens literalism, more virulent forces of literalism appear (viz., fundamentalisms). As the world becomes more complex and uncertain, the craving for simplicity and certainty becomes overwhelming.

There is now a popular view or series of views about the Bible in Protestantism which are powerful, distressing and wrong. They create victims. A fairly literalist understanding of the Bible legitimises the condemnation of homosexuality (and so supports homophobia, just as the doctrine of the subjection of women to men subtly renders violence against women easier). But the injustice does not end there. The literalistic mind-set which reads "males behave indecently with males, and are paid in their own persons the fitting wage of such perversity" (Rom 1:28) is likely to see HIV and AIDS as divine retribution. But what is it to do with passages which permit polygamy (Dt 21:15-17), forbid sex during menstruation (Lev 18:19), forbid women to wear men's clothes (Dt 22:5), ostracise persons with deformed sexual organs (Dt 23:1), invent outrageous arguments for keeping women under the rule of men (1 Cor 11:2-15), keep women silent in the churches (1 Tim 2:12) and wives "subject to their husbands in everything" (Eph 5:24)? Slavery with its attendant violence is assumed in the New Testament, and can be amply justified by appeal to several texts.[43] In fact Protestant evangelicals have intense disagreements with each other about these matters.[44] Attempts to implement sound biblical teaching actually cause pastoral havoc and neurotic disorder, and provide positive proof of the dysfunctionality of the theology that drives them. Neither do the revisionists in these disagreements have consistency on their side. If the Bible is read as condemning homosexuality, then how can it *not* be read as also supporting polygamy, subordinationism, slavery, and so on?

Authority and ARCIC

Authority, says ARCIC II, "is about how the Church teaches, acts and reaches doctrinal decisions in faithfulness to the Gospel".[45] However, this document about authority disclaims any suggestion that it is authoritative.[46] That the document is explicitly *un*authoritative might embolden us to offer "loyal criticism"[47] of it without incurring the charge of disloyalty. At the heart of this document are two familiar models of the process of tradition which by themselves are sadly inadequate in their ability to grasp the complexity of the Church's historical being-in-the-world. In the realm of sexuality, these same models prejudice the Church's theologians against innovation of any kind. The two interlocking models are the *relay race* model and the *transmission* model. They have been around for a long time.

According to the relay race model, the Gospel is "continually handed on and received". Tradition is "a treasure to be received".[48] Indeed reception is the keyword in the relay race model, requiring grateful passivity. "Apostolic Tradition is a gift of God which must be constantly received." The "handing on" of Tradition is an act of communion. The Apostolic Tradition "is to be passed from one generation to another". There must be "constant and perpetual reception" of God's Word, indeed "re-reception" if it has been inadequately or misleadingly received "in a new context".[49] According to the transmission model, "Tradition" (suitably capitalised) is "The Gospel itself, *transmitted* from generation to generation in and by the Church".[50] The Word become flesh is "at the centre of what was transmitted from the beginning and what will be transmitted until the end".[51]

These familiar models allow serious theologians to mislead themselves that tradition is best conceived as a solid object which can be handled, passed on, unchanged, unaffected by the circumstances through which it passes. Everything else changes, but tradition doesn't. Tradition just passes through. Because it passes through time, it is not allowed to change *in* time or even contribute *to* time. Alternatively, tradition is transmitted. To "transmit" means to "send from one person, thing, or place to another", "pass on" (infections are also passed on), "send a signal, as by television or radio". The message received, given proper equipment and atmospheric conditions, is the message sent. It passes through space, unchanged and unchallenged, just as batons pass through time. There is a deliberate lack of diachronic sense in the transmission model. Signals can be transmitted and received in milli-seconds. Traditions form over millennia.

While these models have been proposed to advance the unity of Christ's Church, their imbalance is actually a threat to it. Where is the honest acknowledgement that the Christian tradition is deeply ambiguous, and that it has initiated untold violence, oppression, alienation and war? There is little sense that the Christian tradition, like all living traditions, *grows* or *develops*, or that the major impetus for development is interaction with rival views (e.g., of Jews, pagans, heretics) which change the tradition forever.[52] Transmission models can't register necessary interaction between past and present. They don't allow for innovation. That is why they are chosen by traditionalists who are opposed to change. Users of these models don't acknowledge the changes of the past, or admit that, if we are to be faithful to Jesus Christ, we may not know what we are doing (and for that very reason we need the Spirit's guidance). Once tradition is set up this way, many of the accidental historical accretions within the tradition can pass themselves off as essential elements of it when they may be simply the wilful perpetuation of past order. Androcentrism and sexism operate brilliantly in this milieu. They are enabled to pass themselves off as natural because, with rare exceptions, the tradition has always operated this way. These models make it easier for the church to say that women are subordinate, that contraception is an evil, that homosexuality is an objective disorder, that marriage is indissoluble, that celibacy is mandatory, that abortion is always wrong, and so on.

Protestants should not be signing up to a view of tradition that perpetuates these matters. It is scarcely conceivable that Anglicans will adopt this document with its deference to papal infallibility and ecclesial indefectibility, and its shrunken Spirit-less account of tradition. I can't think of *any* of the hundreds of Protestant denominations that could be attracted to it. If Protestant churches can contribute anything to discussions about authority it has to be their experience of breaking with the past, or discontinuity. Protestantism is a movement of *Protest* against controlling aspirations of hierarchies. Joseph Monti has proposed a model of tradition that emphasises continuity and discontinuity equally, and this is particularly apposite for handling questions about sexuality. He notes there is more required from fidelity to Christian tradition than the mere recapitulation of it. If faithful repetition only were required, there would be no need to construct a sexual ethic, only to hand one down hoping it would be received by grateful individuals and congregations, exactly as the authors of *The Gift of Authority* would like.

> The denominations are forgetting how the obligation of fidelity must be dialectically engaged with the equal obligation of contemporaneity – how Christian life must make sense in its own

> time, must be truthful and right-making, and promote the good in whatever world we find ourselves.[53]

Since the Church is a trans-historical body, it spans more than one "cosmological world",[54] and so cannot remain identified with any particular cosmological world, including of course our own. There is ample precedent for a positive estimation of non-Christian sexual morality in the tradition, as the historical appreciation and incorporation of Stoicism shows. Christian exegetes should beware the "geneticist residue" within the tradition, i.e., the damaging assumption that however different and novel are our questions, "we are called always to judge the present in terms of the past". Modernity has emphasised the particularity, the historicist and relativising character of all moral questions. So repetition of earlier answers prior to contemporary engagement with the questions is a Platonic evasion, a nostalgic abiding in mythical permanence.[55]

Christian self-understanding, continues Monti, is "always framed by the *external* stories of others – those different from us who challenge our penchant to claim that we have, so to speak, given birth to ourselves". It is claimed (following Richard Niebuhr) that the Church must tell two stories, which are dialectically related to each other, the internal and external stories. While the internal story is more obviously familiar and visible, it is often forgotten that this story cannot only be internal since it involved and involves critical conversation beyond the Church with the wider society and culture. "The cosmological and cultural environments of the Church are neither accidental nor only 'external', but foundational for what is commonly termed [Christian] 'self-identification'."[56] The dialectic has immediate relevance to the Church's theology of marriage. Just because Monti holds the *conservative* position that Christian sexual ethics are identified by marriage, the dialectic between the internal and external stories requires the Church, as an act of fidelity alike to tradition and to contemporaneity, to engage those who are marginalised by this aspect of the Church's internal story. So,

> if heterosexual marriage is to remain normatively identifying in the sexual morality of the Church, then it can only do so through critical conversations with those who are not married and not heterosexual. In this way heterosexual marriage as the Christian norm for sexual normality will find its identifying strengths as well as its limits – will have the "rest of its story" told.[57]

When Christians live the reign of God, anticipating God's future and exercising fidelity to Jesus Christ through fidelity to tradition and contemporaneity, they stand in the tradition and they also move it along. A model is needed for understanding this process, and the one Monti provides is that of an advancing spiral. Remembering, reading and affirming the Christian tradition is like belonging on an advancing spiral that constantly loops back as a precondition of advancement. This looping remembrance sets a continuity with the past that is internally necessary for the shape of the spiral and its advancement toward an anticipated future. However, when set in motion, such advancing spirals create new and discontinuous centers and radii. With this continuing recombination of the dimensions of continuity and discontinuity that mark historical experience, an historical foundation and model for critical discourse and argument is attained.[58]

The looping spiral is an excellent model for getting to grips with the continuity and discontinuity involved in growing traditions of faith (it is not suggested that there should be just a single model, or that any are fully adequate). It gives the continuities and discontinuities with past understandings something of a visual image. If the Church's understanding of marriage is also conceptualised as an advancing spiral, the exercise of "stedfast love", it is suggested, "is constant, but there are many different ways of expressing it across cultures".[59] Stedfast love gives the spiral of marriage its shape and direction: the different culturally conditioned ways of expressing it provide the "discontinuous centers".

Common Afflictions?

What then does Protestantism offer to those Roman Catholics who are urging further reforms in their Church, especially in the field of human sexuality? For one, there was a frankness about sexual matters in the denominational reports which Catholics may find surprising. The willingness to debate these issues at all levels of church life remains remarkable. Still, Protestant reformers involved in these debates might say that there were few real gains, and that they had underestimated the strength and depth of the conservative forces ranged against them. However, the question may be misplaced. Both traditions may be suffering from the same malaises, so reform may be better promoted by looking for common afflictions, rather than for differences of approach.

Foundationalism?

In philosophy, foundationalism is "the theory that knowledge of the world rests on a foundation of indubitable beliefs from which further propositions can be inferred to produce a superstructure of known truths". Anti-foundationalists are sceptical about exaggerated knowledge-claims, and sometimes speak in this connection of "the myth of the given".[60] There can be no doubt among Christians that the foundation of the Christian faith and Christian Church is Jesus Christ. Christ is the "corner-stone" (1 Pet 2:7). "There can be no other foundation than the one already laid: I mean Jesus Christ himself" (1 Cor 3:11). There can be no doubt that Jesus Christ is "given", and so revealed, a gift to the world, and so not controlled or invented by us in our wistful spiritual longings. But the attitudes to the Bible and to tradition which come tumbling out whenever sexuality issues are discussed in the churches cannot escape the charge of foundationalism. The strong pretence is urged that more is "given" than actually is. Is it not enough to know one is loved, affirmed, accepted, forgiven, set free and restored by God? Is it not enough to share the joy of Christian *koinònia*, to be spiritually nourished by the Eucharist, and to work for the reign of God in church and world? No it isn't. It is also necessary to know that one is right (or cannot be wrong) about one's religious convictions, and that one belongs to a Church that cannot be wrong either. The Presbyterians cannot be content to be obedient to Christ, using scripture, tradition, reason and experience appropriately in seeking what the mind of Christ might be. They have to be obedient to *scripture*, and that is a clear case of "serving two masters" (Matt 6:24). The Word made flesh is not enough for the Protestant biblicists. There are two Words of God, not one. Or perhaps there is just one – the scriptures. The Word of God is the Bible, not the Saviour of the world. Everything in the Bible comes to have the same authority as Jesus himself because it is all equally and conveniently "inspired" by the Holy Spirit. Indeed the teaching of Jesus in much Protestantism is not very important at all. A particular reading of the theology of St Paul is much more congenial.

The uncritical affirmation of "Tradition" is open to the same charge of foundationalism. This elevation of Bible and tradition to an uncritical ultimacy is open to the charge that it is a *failure* of faith, and not a vindication of it. Isn't it enough that God has given us Christ, and created an all-too-human community that derives its being from him, and tries to live "in the Spirit?" Why ask for more? Why the rush to affirm the Bible as the "Word of God" when a close reading of it reveals its androcentrism and flagrant immorality? Why affirm the glorious past of the churches, when an inclusive reading of the history of Christendom draws attention to the pain, violence, intolerance, slaughter and exclusion that went hand in hand with it? There is a deep spiritual malaise, perhaps, when the inability to stand being wrong becomes so strong that great edifices are built, not on the foundation which is Christ, but on the sand of human (male?) *hybris* which seeks escape from error and cannot tolerate being wrong. Anglicans are being asked by ARCIC to sign up to the idea of "the indefectibility of the Church" and to accept papal infallibility "at the service of the Church's indefectibility".[61] I would like to think that Protestants, aware of the "Protestant principle", would gently ask "Who wants to belong to an indefectible church?" Why do the churches persist in talking the language of absolutism and exclusion when they write documents about coseying up? How is this the gospel?

Zygmunt Bauman, among the postmodern theorists, has spoken of modernity as the age of conflict resolution – "Modernity is about conflict-*resolution*, and about admitting of no contradictions except conflicts amenable to, and awaiting resolution."[62] He identifies, as the single most obvious strand of modernity, the manufacture of discourse which avoids difference by skating over it. A language of absolutes and universals enables it to do this. Difference and otherness are thus unacknowledged, or papered over in the name of the dominant discourse. This, thinks Bauman, inevitably leads to conflict. A postmodern treatment is characterised by recognition of otherness, together with a determination to live in peace despite the *aporias* which are beyond human powers to resolve.[63] Is this not the way forward for *ecumenical* conversation? Are not ARCIC and other such documents unmistakeable products of late modernity which invent a special language in order to minimise or even deny the continuing rifts of Christendom?

Masculinism?

The second common scourge is *masculinism*, the promotion of the interests and rights of men, or the assumption that male experience is normative ("for us men and for our salvation"). The beginnings of Protestantism allowed married theologians and priests to write about marriage as practitioners, and while their frame of reference remained firmly patriarchal,[64] their experience of being loved by their wives added innovatively to the Christian understanding of marriage as a union of love. This began a reformation in theology that still has a long way to go. Until women eventually find an equal voice and influence in the church, the entire Christian tradition, and especially its teachings about sex, will appear skewed, starting with the way the names the first two Persons of the Trinity have been used by a male hierarchy, down to dogma about the meanings of sexual acts. Other chapters in this book have dealt with the debilitating and disastrous influence of patriarchy, not simply on women, but on some of the men who operate patriarchal systems, especially priests. It is commonplace for individuals to require professional help in understanding how they have come to be affected by it, and in overcoming it through treatment. What are we to make of the suggestion that the *Christian tradition itself is to be compared with a sick patient suffering from masculinism, acting sometimes bizarrely, and needing counselling and cure?*

Grace Jantzen makes this comparison (more precisely, between a disordered personality and something broader, "the western symbolic"). It is pointless, she says, giving reasons to patients with mental afflictions or personality disorder that they are behaving misguidedly.

> In a psychological context, the deep roots of the personality disorder can be allowed to come to the surface and be verbalized; and this bringing to consciousness of what had been repressed enables them to be less rigid and more open to suggestions – and

> indeed to reasons, evidence, and theory – than they were able to be before.

Applying these insights to the history of western language and thought she says:

> Now I suggest that it is fruitful to apply this pattern drawn from psychoanalytic procedure to the western symbolic itself: the western symbolic can be thought of as the patient, in the grip of a disorder called masculinism.[65]

Is there a case for applying her analogy more narrowly to that part of the western symbolic with which we are concerned, namely our Christian traditions and the authority they claim for themselves?

It is a genuine question, not an accusation. Neither is it a claim that one's theological opponents in the churches are mentally ill as well as wrong (where would the *hubris* lie then?)! It is a suggestion that where doctrinal decisions appear to reflect a fear of women or of lesbian and gay people, a possible explanation lies in the limited experience coupled with the deep anxieties of the doctrine-makers. The entire tradition, as it manifests itself in their anxious apprehensions of it, may appear to be unhealthy and discriminatory. Is it not hard to think that churches run exclusively by men, judged by their own rhetoric of the complementarity of the sexes, could possibly be balanced in their doctrines of sexuality, still less indefectible in their pronouncements? Is the inability to recognise this part of the condition of masculinism? And is resistance to dialogue a further symptom?

Heterosexism?

Is the preoccupation with homosexuality in the Protestant debates better understood clinically, i.e., as an *obsession*, or *compulsion*? Perhaps what is at stake is not even the authority of the Bible, but the place of the Bible in maintaining a fragile heterosexual identity which is frightened by the very existence of gay men? Men who have for centuries exercised "power over", whether over their wives, or slaves, or colonies, or congregations, have seen much of this power taken from them. Are gay men, now more visible than before, being made to bolster heterosexual identity by being all that straight men like to think they are not, effeminate, disgusting, corrupt, promiscuous, and so on? Straight men may find gay men a challenge to their masculinity; straights may project onto lesbians and gays their own dislike and disowning of their homosexual feelings; lesbians may unacceptably remind men that they are not required for validating the experience of at least some women; even envy may operate against the body-acceptance and ease of intimacy among lesbian and gay people as seen through heterosexual eyes.[66] On this view, ideologies are needed, and therefore manufactured, to show that heterosexism is divinely sanctioned, and the apparatus of overblown claims for scripture and tradition have enabled Protestants and Catholics alike to get away with it.

These are perhaps harsh thoughts, themselves open to the charge of polemics and further uncharity characteristic of the kind of debates just described. They are intended to show only that faith does not need foundationalism, the church does not need masculinism, and men don't need heterosexism. What we all need is more life in Christ.

Notes

1 *The Gift of Authority: Authority in the Church III: An Agreed Statement by the Second Anglican-Roman Catholic International Commission, ARCIC* (London: Catholic Truth Society; Toronto, Canada: Anglican Book Centre; New York: Church Publishing Incorporated, 1999).
2 General Assembly Special Committee on Human Sexuality, Presbyterian Church (USA), *Keeping Body and Soul Together: Sexuality, Spirituality and Social Justice* (1991) p. iii.
3 John J. Carey, "The Presbyterian Church (U.S.A.) and its Sexuality Report", in John J. Carey (ed.), *The Sexuality Debate in North American Churches, 1988-1995* (Lewiston, New York: Edwin Mellen Press, 1995) p. 5.
4 John J. Carey, "The Presbyterian Church", p. 10.
5 John J. Carey, "The Presbyterian General Assembly in Baltimore, June 1991", in John J. Carey, *The Sexuality Debate in North American Churches*, p. 42.
6 "The Church in its Own Life", *Church and Society* (July/August 1991) p. 45.
7 "The Church in its Own Life", *Church and Society* (September/October, 1996) p. 9.
8 *Ibid.*, p. 6.
9 *Ibid.*
10 Division for Church in Society, Department for Studies of the Evangelical Lutheran Church in America, *The Church and Human Sexuality: A Lutheran Perspective: First Draft of a Social Statement* (Chicago: 1993) p. v.
11 *The Church and Human Sexuality*, p. 17.
12 *Ibid.*, p. 7.
13 *Ibid.*, pp. 15-16.
14 "ELCA'S Top 1993 Headlines", *The Lutheran* (Jan. 94) pp. 30-1.
15 *Ibid.*, p.35.
16 "Checks and Balances Put in Place for Sexuality Draft", *The Lutheran* (Jan. 94) p. 36.
17 "Draft Draws Over 8,000 Responses", *The Lutheran* (June, 1994) p. 35.
18 *Human Sexuality Working Draft: A Possible Social Statement of the Evangelical Lutheran Church in America, with Accompanying Documents* (developed by the Division for Church in Society and its Writing Team, October, 1994).
19 *Ibid.*
20 Karen Bloomquist, "The Politics of Sex and Power in the Churches", in John J. Carey (ed.), *The Sexuality Debate in North American Churches, 1988-1995*, p. 149.
21 *Ibid.*, pp. 150, 157, 163, 164.
22 *Issues in Human Sexuality: A Statement by the House of Bishops of the General Synod of the Church of England, December 1991* (London: Church House Publishing, 1991) p. vii, citing Resolution 64 of the Lambeth Conference, 1988.
23 *Ibid.*, p. vii.
24 *Ibid.*, p. 41, para. 5.23.
25 *Ibid.*, p. 40, para. 5.2; p. 41, para. 5.4.
26 *Ibid.*, p. 41, para. 5.6.

27 Church of Scotland Panel on Doctrine, *Report on the Theology of Marriage*, p. 270.
28 Report of a Working Party of the Board for Social Responsibility, *Something to Celebrate: Valuing Families in Church and Society* (London: Church House Publishing, 1995) p. 3.
29 See, *The Church Times*, 8 December, 1995.
30 Adrian Thatcher, *Marriage After Modernity*, p. 107.
31 *The Church Times*, 21 August, 1998, p. 9.
32 *The Church Times*, 12 February, 1999, p. 3.
33 The Methodist Church, *Report of Commission on Human Sexuality – as presented to the Methodist Conference 1990* (Peterborough: Methodist Publishing House, 1990). In 1992 The United Reformed Church General Assembly passed a resolution welcoming "the willingness of the Church and Society Department to oversee publication of 'Homosexuality: A Christian view', and of further contributions to the continuing debate". An interim resolution was subsequently passed declaring that "the fact of a homosexual relationship shall not be the grounds for rejecting as candidate for [the] ministry". This is now reversed and a doctrinal statement sent for approval to the churches which "affirms and welcomes people of homosexual orientation within the life of the church and society, but does not believe that there is a sufficiently clear mind within the church at this time to affirm the acceptability of homosexual practice". This resolution will fall if more than one third of any of the local, district and provincial councils of the church reject it, and at the time of writing, it appears the resolution will not be accepted.
34 John J. Carey, "The Theological Foundations of the Presbyterian Report", in John J. Carey (ed.), *The Sexuality Debate in North American Churches, 1988-1995*, pp. 25-35.
35 John Sharick, "Dialog on Human Sexuality", *Church and Society* 81 (1995) p. 106.
36 *Keeping Body and Soul Together*, p. 25.
37 *The Church and Human Sexuality*, p. 2.
38 *Issues in Human Sexuality*, p. 1, para. 1.3.
39 *Ibid.*, pp. 5-6: para. 2.1, 2.2 and 2.3.
40 *Ibid.*, p. 9, para. 2.12.
41 *Ibid.*, p. 14, para. 2.21 and 2.22.
42 Adrian Thatcher, *The Ontology of Paul Tillich* (Oxford: Oxford University Press, 1978) pp. 144-146.
43 Adrian Thatcher, *Liberating Sex – A Christian Sexual Theology* (London: SPCK, 1993) p. 16.
44 See, for instance, John Piper and Wayne Grudem, *Recovering Biblical Manhood and Womanhood: A Response to Evangelical Feminism* (Illinois: Wheaton, 1991).
45 *The Gift of Authority*, pp. v-vi.
46 "The authorities who appointed the Commission have allowed the statement to be published so that it may be widely discussed. It is not an authoritative declaration by the Roman Catholic Church or by the Anglican Communion." *The Gift of Authority*, p. vii. Protestantism is thankfully broader than Anglicanism. I have chosen ARCIC because it involves a non-Roman church in dialogue with Rome, and it deals expressly with the theme of this consultation.
47 *The Gift of Authority*, para. 48.
48 *Ibid.*, para. 14, 15.
49 *Ibid.*, para. 16, 21, 25.
50 *Ibid.*, para. 14, note 1 (emphasis added).
51 *Ibid.*, para. 14, and see 15, 17, 21.
52 See Maurice Wiles, *The Development of Christian Doctrine* (London: SCM Press, 1974) pp. 4-5.
53 Joseph Monti, *Arguing About Sex: The Rhetoric of Christian Sexual Morality* (New York: State University of New York Press, 1995) pp. 3 and 6.
54 *Ibid.*, p. 21.
55 *Ibid.*, pp. 26-27, 34.
56 *Ibid.*, pp. 45, 47, and see 86-89.

57 *Ibid.*, p. 48, and see 90.
58 *Ibid.*, p. 61.
59 *Ibid.*, p. 65.
60 Ted Honderich (ed.), *The Oxford Companion to Philosophy* (Oxford, New York: Oxford University Press, 1995) p. 289.
61 *The Gift*, p. 30, para. 41; p. 31, para. 42.
62 Zygmunt Bauman, *Postmodern Ethics* (Oxford: Blackwell, 1993) p. 8.
63 An *aporia* is "in a nutshell, a contradiction that cannot be overcome, one that results in a conflict that cannot be resolved", *ibid.*, p. 8.
64 See, for instance, Derrick Sherwin Bailey, *The Man-Woman Relationship in Christian Thought* (London: Longmans, 1959) p. 202.
65 Grace M. Jantzen, *Becoming Divine: Towards a Feminist Philosophy of Religion* (Manchester: Manchester University Press, 1998) p. 97.
66 James B. Nelson, *Body Theology* (Louisville, Kentucky: Westminster/John Knox Press, 1992) chapter 4.

Chapter Nine

The Development of Catholic Tradition and Sexual Morality

Joseph Selling

Human sexuality represents a tremendous potential within the human community. It embodies the power to bond people together, to create new life and to influence the construction of kinship, community and the entire social structure. At the same time, however, it represents an extremely potent means to dominate, to manipulate and to oppress. In other words, the potential represented by human sexuality is not only great, it is fundamentally ambiguous. Like all human power and capacity, it can be used for good or evil. It will usually exhibit both positive and negative consequences. And regardless of the fact that most people today view human sexuality as a private affair, the potential ramifications of human sexual involvement are social, cultural and intergenerational.

It would be good if we could say that these observations are obvious or possibly even trite. Unfortunately, we all know that this is hardly the case. Individuals frequently engage in sexual behaviour, not to say exploits, in ways that appear arbitrary and short-sighted. While one might expect society and those who are responsible for social policy to exercise a much more circumspect attitude toward sexual behaviour, social history demonstrates a tremendous spectrum of over-regulation and under-regulation. Occasionally, one or another group may get it right in terms of regulating or guiding human sexual activity. However, human behaviour always takes place in history and within a myriad of changing circumstances, some predictable but most not, so that even when a particular group of people appears to have in place reasonable patterns of human sexual behaviour, the needs of the community may change so that the achieved patterns of behaviour become inappropriate. A case in point would be the mutual influence of hygiene, improved health care, levels of fecundity and population growth, all relating to the question of regulating fertility. Like every other moral issue we face, the maxim holds that as soon as we analyse, judge and act upon a given situation, our action simultaneously changes the content of that analysis, which can lead to an adjusted judgement and subsequently alternative action.

Be that as it may, the point here is that in approaching an area as vast and flexible as human sexuality, we can never be satisfied with a single pattern or model of behaviour. Perhaps the best example of the need for flexibility in our own time is the evolution that has taken place in Western society in respect to the status and role of women – in society, in marriage, in the family and even in the Church. Regardless of one's personal opinion about this evolution, it is undeniable that men can no longer presume to treat or relate to women in the same manner that may have been normative a generation ago. Some, shall we say of a more traditionalistic bent, will bemoan these changes and long for the "good old days", when women fulfilled a whole set of standard social, and especially masculine, expectations. Others, probably mostly women, will welcome these changes and look toward even further evolution in the future. Neither of these groups can deny the change itself. Neither of them can really stop or accelerate the process of change without doing some harm or even violence to themselves or others. Patterns of behaviour and the individual acts which make them up do not remain static over time. Those who believe or wish that they might, are fooling no one but themselves.

The Christian community, no less than the whole human community in general, is caught up in the evolution of sexual mores and in the process of trying to understand and cope with those evolutions. Probably not much different than society in general, sometimes we Christians do it well, and sometimes less well. Very occasionally we may be at the forefront of change and evolution, even improvement, of mores and morality. However, it is probably closer to the truth that we spend a great deal of time resisting change and proceeding by trial and error.

The Catholic Christian community, moreover, seems to suffer from a particular handicap in the business of sorting out sexual morality. For the universal or world-wide nature of the Catholic Church keeps it in constant contact with the widely varying rites and customs of a whole host of peoples. Needless to say, not all these peoples go through the same kinds of evolutions, nor do they change at the same pace. For instance, the status and role of women in marriage, in the workforce or in society in general differs widely between western Europe, Asia and Africa. On any one of these continents, it again differs widely from one region and one state to another. And even in one state it differs from one ethnic group, rural or urban setting, even one family to another.

This challenges us with the questions: how can we find our way clear to articulating a reasonable and comprehensible sexual, relational and marital ethic on the level of the universal Church? Perhaps a more pertinent question is whether such a thing is at all possible, or even desirable. We will, however, attempt to bracket the latter question by suggesting that whatever we might propose for approaching these areas of moral inquiry must remain on the fundamental or general level rather than address merely specific behaviours. In other words, we are concerned more with the kind of ethic we might propose, from a specifically Christian point of view, than with the details of that ethic as it might be lived out.

The Traditional Approach to Sexuality

This brings us to a central issue that confronts Catholic moral thinking at its most fundamental level. Since the period of the counter-reformation, the Church has been, shall we say, pro-active in its direction of moral behaviour. While many other Christian Churches have relied upon an ethics that is paradoxically founded upon scripture yet still reflecting contemporary cultural mores, the Catholic theological enterprise has built up an elaborate moral code based primarily upon what it referred to as "natural law". This largely philosophical system of moral thinking was enforced through the practice of the oral confession of sins in the sacrament of penance. Especially over the past 150 years, since the inception of the modern manuals of (moral) theology, Catholic moral practice and teaching has become extraordinarily specific, detailed and directive in the area of individual behaviour and decision-making. In short, Catholic morality has become largely act-centred, and subsequently sin-centred as well.

More specifically with respect to sexual morality, the handbooks of moral theology viewed this primarily from the point of view of an act the authors believed to be procreative in itself. Before sufficient biological knowledge about human fertility was achieved at the beginning of this century, every act of sexual intercourse was considered to be potentially procreative. Because this involved the coming into being of a human person who is a child of God and who deserves respect and response to all the needs they will exhibit in order to become a responsible adult, it was to be expected that this would be looked upon as extremely serious. However, the concern exhibited for the potential of creating new life led to a preoccupation with the achievement of sexual climax on the part of the male. This, in turn, led to a further preoccupation with anything whatsoever which would seem to put one on the virtually inevitable road to that outcome, namely any form of voluntary or accepted "venereal pleasure". Thus, any act whatsoever which would arouse or demonstrate acquiescence to venereal pleasure was considered to be a serious matter. If such an act were not directed or at least "open to" legitimate procreation, that is, taking place between a husband and wife within marriage, it was judged to be morally bad. And because it involved the life long well-being of a separate individual, the potential child, it was judged to be seriously, morally bad, no matter what the circumstances or intention of the acting person.

Without wishing to go into all the shortcomings of an act-centred morality, suffice it to say that it is the opinion of many that the positive aspects of this form of spiritual and moral guidance are far outweighed by the negative aspects of the inevitable sin-centred morality that accompanies it. The preoccupation with individual sin has crippled generations of faithful penitents, especially in the area of sexual morality, where each and every "offence" – even of the most trivial nature – was considered to be serious matter and thus grounds for mortal sin.

Act-centred morality has led us astray from the vital meaning of spiritual life by focusing attention on the single, frequently isolated act. It has also done tremendous damage to our understanding of human sexuality and any efforts to build a positive, human, integrated and community-building sexual ethics. The preoccupation with individual acts has blinded us to the big picture. It has reduced to mechanics what should be a vision of human and Christian integration.

That said, it is not my purpose or proposal here to dismiss the importance of individual human acts that perpetrate harm on oneself, other persons or social structures and institutions in the short or the long run. Individual (sinful) acts, whether perpetrated through ignorance or malice, will always need to be described for what they are and denounced. What I propose is that we go beyond such negative thinking and first attempt to correct the prejudices of the past.

Abandoning Act-centred Morality

In order to accomplish this, we must turn away from an act-centred and sin-centred morality and the ideological preconceptions that support it. Just as Jesus criticised the learned men of Israel for not being able to see beyond the literal meaning of the Law, so we must be critical of the philosophy that condemns individual behaviour without questioning its own presuppositions. That philosophy, of course, is natural law thinking and its primary presupposition, at least in regard to sexual morality, is a mechanistic image of the universe and of creation.

A natural law view of human sexuality is not so much wrong as it is extremely narrow. According to this view of the person and of creation, human sexual differentiation, male and female, is somehow connected with procreation, the propagation of the species. I write "somehow" because up until about 150 years ago and the development of the biological sciences, no one really knew how all this worked. Before then, one spoke of a man planting seeds in a woman. We even still use the word "semen" in our vocabulary. Women, on the other hand, provided fertile ground for the growth of these seeds. Thus it was the woman who was either fertile or infertile (barren), whereas the man might be sterile, without seed, or impotent, lacking the power to deliver the seed.

This natural law view of human sexuality became the prisoner of scientific rationalism. One could prove, demonstrate, and after the discovery of the cycle of female fertility in the 1920's, even predict the connection with procreation. As the so-called scientific data mounted up, many became more and more convinced of its "truth".

While Church teaching at the time of the codification of canon law in 1917/1918 had employed a clever euphemism to describe the sexual act in marriage as "*actus per se aptos ad prolis generationem*" (Can. 1081, § 2), by the time Pope Pius XI wrote his encyclical *Casti Connubii* in 1930, natural law thinking had become so overwhelmed by modern scientific rationalism that it could now pronounce about the "ends" or "purposes" of sexual behaviour. (Note that even canon law, as well as the teaching that predates it, was circumspect enough to propose that sexual acts were merely "apt" and not always specifically "destined" for procreation. Further, procreating and educating children was said to constitute the primary end of *marriage*, not sexual intercourse.)

All of this, of course, was correct. To accept this and defend it, one was not in error. To accept and defend in our day, as well, that there is a relationship between human sexual differentiation and procreation, one would still not be in error. To do so, however, would be tantamount to making a huge mistake. If one will pardon what I think is an American expression here, one's "take" on this idea had gone "amiss". The miss-take about this scientifically demonstrable observation is that in truly personal terms it very much misses the point.

To say that human sexual differentiation, and hence human sexuality, is about procreation, is analogous to observing that drinking a glass of wine is a way of quenching one's thirst. Of course, the observation is correct, and if we had nothing other than wine to drink we would not die of thirst. Indeed, if there were no other beverage available we would all be obliged to drink wine to preserve our lives. Anyone, however, who has tasted more than one variety of wine knows that there is a lot more here than merely quenching one's thirst and staying alive.

The same can and must be said for human sexuality. By the time of the Second Vatican Council (1965) most bishops of the Church had recognised this and they took an important step forward by merging their view of sexuality with an appreciation of its aesthetic values and its potential to embody love itself, the very core of the Gospel message. One could express love through sex in ways that are "noble and worthy" (*GS*, 49). In fact, the bishops could teach about love and sex without even mentioning procreation. In *Gaudium et Spes*, paragraph 49 does precisely this and describes marital love – explicitly stated to be expressed in a sexual way – as fully human, integrated and total, faithful and exclusive, and even virtuous. That said and established, the council devoted a separate paragraph (*GS*, 50) not to biological procreation but to "responsible parenthood".

It is clear that the conciliar teaching about human sexuality is filled with an aesthetic appreciation or what some would call a value-oriented approach. Through human sexuality, all sorts of goods may be achieved which might remain otherwise unattainable. Even celibacy is viewed not as a denial of one's sexual being but as a mode of living out one's human sexuality. One could rightly ask how this could ever be the case if the underlying presupposition is that the only way to fulfil the end or purpose of human sexuality is to achieve or to be "open to" procreation. Clearly it could not.

Before I attempt to elaborate this more aesthetic and appreciative view of human sexuality vis-à-vis the Christian community, it would seem appropriate at least in passing to lament the fact that when Pope Paul VI addressed the issues surrounding the delicate question of regulating human fertility in his 1968 encyclical, *Humanae Vitae*, all of this positive thinking about human sexuality was reduced to a single word and a single dimension. In place of the position of Pius XI that the primary, if not exclusive, end or purpose of human sexuality was its procreativity, Paul VI rephrased this idea with the expression "procreative meaning" (*significationem*) rather than end or purpose, and added to it a "unitive meaning" (*significationem*) that supposedly was to carry or express all the other things that sexuality could be. Unfortunately, this expression is not only extremely lean, it is also finally misleading. For, referring to human sexuality as "unitive" implies that the only persons involved are a couple of individuals, namely a husband and wife. One could rightly ask, where is the family in this image? Where are the generations, the kinship, the social structure? Indeed, on the assumption that human sexuality is about much more than achieving orgasm in an act of heterosexual intercourse, one could rightly query, where is celibacy and virginity in this view of things?

Clearly the answer to all these questions is that the view of human sexuality that lay behind *Humanae Vitae* was still act-centred. In fact, the attribution of these so-called procreative and unitive "meanings" is given (*HV*, 12) not to persons, relationships or even general sexual differentiation as a physiological phenomenon but rather specifically to the conjugal act, an act of heterosexual intercourse. So long as one operates with this view of human sexuality, it remains virtually impossible to escape an act-centred morality.

Moving Toward a Positive Approach

So let us now ask how we might proceed in approaching a broader, more positive view of human sexuality and subsequently human sexual relations. I would like to recall the reference to the appreciation of a glass of wine. While all persons are capable of uttering the "truth" that this is a beverage which can serve to protect individuals from dying of thirst, we immediately realise that it only takes a very small step to go beyond this simple, if not crude, observation.

I will presume that even if one is not a wine drinker, one has at one time or another been exposed to those who have educated themselves to appreciate this beverage. Perhaps you, as I, have occasionally even been amused by hearing the experts describe a glass of wine as containing a fruity bouquet and flavour. Not just the flavour of a grape, mind you, but that of apples, pears or gooseberries. Wine is said to exude the flavours of cinnamon, honey or even chocolate. It is said to be sharp, smooth, crisp, effervescent or flat. Indeed one could go on and on – and professional as well as amateur wine tasters frequently do!

My point here is that one could not describe a wine exhibiting the flavour of a pear or an apricot if one has no previous experience of tasting these fruits. One would not say that a particular wine is sharp or smooth if they had no previous sensation of these things. In other words, when we wish to describe or evaluate something within the realm of human experience, we inevitably draw upon other areas of our experience to provide us with a vocabulary and a framework for expression. The same can and must be said about human sexuality.

If we have nothing else to draw upon than scientific rationality, we would be forced to conclude, indeed we would be justified in uttering the "truth" that human sexuality has a procreative purpose or meaning. Given the scientific sociological observations about mating and kinship, one could also conclude that there is a unitive purpose or meaning as well. However, in the present state of affairs it appears that the interpretation of this unitive meaning is limited to *physiological coupling*. Furthermore, the unitive meaning is still treated as subordinate to the procreative one, at least as far as the teaching on contraception is concerned.

Let us then take the lesson that we have learned with our glass of wine and look to other areas of our experience in order to describe the meanings of human sexuality. One of the things that the Judeo-Christian faith has always drawn attention to is the *relational* character of human sexuality. This relational character has not been limited to a single man and a single woman, but has always been understood as familial, inter-generational and social. Thus, in order to find new ways to describe human sexuality, one should go beyond the areas treated by the usual virtue of chastity as a form of temperance. As relational in character, one could quite appropriately refer to the virtue of justice to describe human sexuality. As many contemporary feminist authors suggest, then, let us look toward the area of "sexual justice".

Probably one of the best representatives of this outlook is Lisa Cahill, professor of Christian Ethics at Boston College. In her book, *Sex, Gender and Christian Ethics* (1996), Cahill draws our attention to the New Testament's "concern to transform all human relations toward greater equality, compassion and solidarity" (p. 117). She goes on to describe what she calls a "Christian social ethic of sex" which has as its goal "to imbue sexual and reproductive behaviour with the qualities of respect, empathy, reciprocity, and mutual fidelity which would allow sexual and parental love to be transforming agents in society in general" (p. 119).

These sound like very nice words, but one could rightly ask whether they ever did or ever will have any impact. If we are looking for immediate and final impact here, we are bound to be disappointed, for as we mentioned above, the terrain covered by the field of (Christian) ethics is one of change, evolution, and cultural and historical particularity. Sometimes it takes a very long time for a community to understand or even permit the impact of the Gospel message to take hold. Sometimes that message breaks through at a crucial time. By the same token, sometimes even when it has been accepted and lived, it can be forgotten, at least for a time.

Let us take the example of St. Paul's preaching on slavery (among other places, in Eph 6:5-9). When slaves are told to obey their masters, they are urged to do it as we all are urged to obey the Lord. Masters are urged to treat their slaves as they know the Lord will treat all of us. Now the impact of this attitude on the part of slaves and masters would seem to militate against the very institution of slavery itself, and indeed it finally did. However, it took the Christian community at least a millennium and a half before this idea began to change social structures. We now wonder how we could have been blind for so long. Rather than look for some kind of justification or excuse to dismiss what we now see as an inconsistency, let us remember what was observed about the historicity and cultural specificity of morality in general. Christianity is a faith that is very much *in* the world, taking it seriously and suffering from its limitations as well as its opportunities. We do not have, nor can we readily see, moral solutions that are beyond the vision of the vast majority of persons of good will.

St. Paul also taught that wives should be subject to their husbands, but he immediately added "as to the Lord" (Eph 5:22). And three verses later he admonishes, "Husbands, love your wives, as Christ loved the Church and gave himself up for her" (5:25). Whereas the first part of this preaching was implemented, almost with a vengeance, without any reference to the relationship that one might have with Christ, the Lord himself, the second part was nearly totally forgotten, or at least grossly interpreted according to the local custom of the times.

Today, we look at the same phrases in Ephesians and invoke the liberating power of Christ over every form of oppression. We read this alongside 1 Cor 7:1-5, where wives and husbands are reminded that they are equal in their claims and their responsibilities. Exactly what changed the way in which we read these verses is matter for another discussion. The point that I wish to make here is that it is possible to achieve an entirely different reading and interpretation of classical texts, even scriptural texts, in light of new experience, new evidence and especially new sensitivity.

A Shift in Ethics Itself

It is on the last of these, human and moral sensitivity, that I wish to focus with respect to feminist theology's contribution to our understanding of human sexuality. For this has little to do directly with behavioural norms and much more to do with where we should be looking to inspire human relationships and the sexual dimensions of being human.

What has come to be known today as an "ethics of justice" is all too familiar to our textbook approach to morality in general. Rules, built on principles, trace their foundations to rational assessments about human possibilities and behaviours that may or may not fit into some kind of moral (read: "natural") order. On the other side of the spectrum, feminist ethics has come to be known as an "ethics of care" and traces its foundations to a heightened awareness of human needs and aspirations in oneself and in others and the kinds of behaviour that may or may not exhibit an appropriate response to those needs and aspirations. What is first and foremost is persons and relationships. On this basis, the response of moral sensitivity is almost always: how can I or we positively respond to this need, manifest in our fellow human being, our neighbour? We must ask ourselves, I believe, how much our contemporary view of human sexuality responds to the needs and aspirations of human persons and what are we doing to encourage those responses to be positive ones?

An ethics of care is other-oriented rather than self-oriented. In place of a preoccupation with acts and rules, it begins with human experience and a sensitivity to the needs of real, historically and culturally situated, persons. The minimum or bottom line, as it were, is respect for persons and an affirmation of their worth. Beyond that, Christians in particular are called to exercise empathy, both for the suffering of others and for their potentialities to grow and develop as persons within the context of meaningful relationships.

Sexual Ethics and Care

If we look first at some of the more basic needs of all human persons, we will readily recognise that every person experiences the need for safety, security, support, affirmation and belonging. To what extent does our sexual ethics respond to these real needs? To what extent does our teaching reflect a concern for meeting these needs? Unfortunately, I believe that current moral teaching perhaps suffers from the presumption that these essential components of any relational ethics are always implicit in sexual ethics and understood by everyone. Even a cursory observation of the world around us, however, would severely call this into question.

Notwithstanding the desire to uphold an ideal of loving, committed relationships (usually in a marital context) to embody sexual ethics, the fact is that we do not live in a world of ideals. What is worse is that the reality of the world that we do live in is usually not addressed directly. One thinks of several examples of sexual exploitation and coercion that take place even within marriage, not to mention marital and familial violence. One could draw attention to instances of child abuse and sexual intimidation, perpetrated by the clergy as well. And yet, these virtually common occurrences are generally ignored in the vast majority of teaching on sexual and relational ethics.

Rather than simply renouncing these things, we need to preach loudly and clearly that meeting the basic needs of human persons is a demand of a Christian way of living. In order to foster these basic needs, furthermore, it will be necessary to abandon our negative and restrictive attitudes toward human sexuality. Casting aside every form of sexual stereotyping and subordination, we need clearly to affirm the sexual identity of each and every person and to encourage an environment which will support the unfolding of that identity in a manner appropriate for each person's life situation. This is especially true for those persons who are usually the most exploited and abused.

Going beyond the basic needs, then, brings us to the level of human aspirations which are no less important in formulating a human and Christian sexual and relational ethics. This is the level of integration and wholeness, of experimentation and creativity that presupposes a secure response to the basic needs. On this level, human sexuality reaches toward aesthetic goods and celebrates the meaning of personhood embodied in a sexual existence. These goods are available to every mature person, whether celibate or physically and genitally active. They do not have to involve deeply engrossing physical experiences, but at the same time they can consist of profoundly involving physical expression and reception that envelopes all the senses. The pleasure that one experiences in these achievements should not be suspect or consciously avoided but rather accepted as a confirmation of doing something well.

Generativity is also usually counted as one among the higher aspirations of human persons which can also be applied to relational and sexual living. All too often this is minimised as a form of biological "procreation". Perhaps this is because much of contemporary sexual and relational morality has been formulated by men, who have not had the experience of conceiving, carrying, giving birth to and caring for a child from the moment of its virtually total helplessness. A mother's understanding of "having children" will obviously be much different from that of any man.

Generativity is about much more than having children. It refers to the very construction of social living with a view toward future generations. It implies creativity and a willingness to share with others the task of caring for all persons. It is not incompatible with the classic notion of parenting, but it is certainly not synonymous with it. One does not have to foster children to be generative in a truly human sense.

We must also ask ourselves the extent to which our sexual and relational ethics encompasses a call to realise these (and other) higher values and aspirations of the human person. For, insofar as these things are neglected, we are settling for a minimalist view of human sexual being that does not go much beyond the animal kingdom. Insofar as these fundamental ideas become an integral part of our understanding and teaching on sexual morality, they will transform what has been a largely negative and restrictive form of guidance to a positive and inspirational one.

Toward a Positive Sexual Ethics

When we compare this positive view of human sexual and relational needs and aspirations to the kind of sexual morality that appeared in the handbooks of moral theology, we can easily see the shortcomings of that traditional approach. It has been suggested that in light of this former negativity, and because even much contemporary teaching in this vital area of human experience continues to accentuate rules and restrictions rather than goals and encouragement, it would be better that the Church remain silent with regard to specific behaviour. Some have even suggested a moratorium be self-imposed on any pronouncements having to do with human sexuality for at least a generation.

While many can sympathise with this, I think that it is imperative not only to drastically reduce if not wholly abandon negative statements about specific human sexual behaviour, but also to somehow *let it be known* that we are maintaining silence on questions of sexual morality. One of the ways that this can be done is by a conscious effort to reaffirm some of the previous teaching that has been positive and open rather than to repeat statements and positions that have been negative and restrictive. One thinks immediately about the conciliar teaching on marriage and sexuality as well as its endorsement of responsible parenthood to deal with the issue of regulating fertility. There is a good deal of precedent for this kind of approach, especially in the area of social teaching.

Another way in which this can be done refers to the question raised earlier about whether it is possible or even desirable to articulate a comprehensive or universal sexual and relational ethic for all times and places. I suggested that we need to limit ourselves to the general or fundamental level and to work out *the kind of ethic* we might propose, even from a specifically Christian point of view. I would suggest that we might characterise that ethics in four ways; it would be positive, value-oriented, open and consistent.

It is hard to conceive of Catholic Christians developing anything other than a *positive* ethics when it is a question of remaining on the general or fundamental level. Since the time of the very early church, we have always taken a positive view of the *humanum* and developed an optimistic anthropology. While we have always recognised the presence of ignorance, immaturity, weakness, and even maliciousness or sin, we also believe that there is always offered grace, forgiveness, resiliency and growth, even through adversity. Our human nature may be wounded, but it is not corrupted beyond recognition and redemption. We firmly believe that persons of good will are capable of recognising and doing the good. Therefore, relational and sexual ethics would better be formulated in a way that is positive and optimistic.

This positive ethics would also be *value-oriented* rather than being negative and restrictive. Throughout our tradition we have learned to identify many things which are worthy of pursuit, especially in connection with an ethics of human relationships. We have learned that fidelity enhances human relationships and helps to carry them through adversity. Lastingness is a characteristic of not just sexual but all sorts of friendship relations. Faithful commitments in the sexual area are sometimes characterised as "monogamous" because this type of relationship has been found to protect our human vulnerability.

We have also learned many things about the multidimensionality of human sexuality. It is here that a more developed relational ethics is informed by what have come to be known as gender studies. Human sexuality pervades the whole person. It is not just physical but emotional and psychological as well. Sexuality is both formed and lived out in a social context, and the most personal and mature sexual relations demand developed skills in communication.

Human sexuality has often been characterised as life-giving, but too frequently this has been limited to the procreational dimension of physical sex. Without wishing to diminish our appreciation for this life-giving capacity, we should not forget that the generativity of all human relationships precedes and surrounds the task of having and raising children to be responsible members of society and of the Church. Our revised sexual and relational ethics should affirm the value of all life and all its dimensions, and not just be limited to acts which may or may not result in conception.

Thirdly, our ethic should be *open*. There is a great deal to learn about human sexuality and human relationships. The advance of our knowledge in these areas has been dramatic, particularly over the past two generations. What are commonly referred to as gender issues today pervade our entire understanding of human sexuality and have strong ramifications in society, in the workplace and even in the Church. Further, gender studies have taught us that many so-called sexual issues are really issues of power, of dominance and submission. They are about the use and abuse of power through the channel of one's sexuality.

Another significant learning to which we need to be open is the entire concept of sexual identity. Every human person is corporeal and lives out his or her multi-dimensional relations through their physical presence to groups and to other individuals. Being-a-man or being-a-woman in the world with others is not some kind of option or cloak that one can put on or pay attention to simply at will. Every human person must be recognised for exactly who they are, and this includes their sexuality, on every level and in every facet.

Perhaps the most difficult thing for many to accept is the fact that this sexual identity is not exclusively heterosexual. The relatively recent teaching of the Church, though remaining largely negative toward homosexuality in general, does in fact recognise that there are homosexual persons who have not chosen their sexual orientation. Regardless of our judgement about gay and lesbian behaviour, we find ourselves in the position where we are called to accept homosexual persons "with respect, compassion and sensitivity" (*Catechism of the Catholic Church*, 2358).

Finally, a positive and value-oriented openness to the importance of sexual identity is crucial for understanding and supporting those who have chosen to pursue a celibate lifestyle. Celibate persons do not cease to be sexual persons, and their gender remains an important component to all their human relationships. We must be careful not to treat or relate to celibate persons as if they were non-sexual.

Fourthly, sexual and relational ethics needs to be *consistent* with the whole of the Church's moral teaching. There are sometimes striking contrasts between different parts of this teaching, depending upon the subject matter under consideration. To use just one example, Pope Paul VI's encyclical *Populorum Progressio* (para. 39) in 1967 made explicit reference to the problem of uncontrolled population growth while his encyclical on regulating fertility one year later, *Humanae Vitae*, seemed to have been written as if the first observations were never made, or at least had no direct bearing on the subject of his second letter. In general, social teaching has tended to treat natural events as morally neutral and to understand human behaviour as statistically rather than "naturally" normative. In sexual issues, the opposite is more the case and human behaviour is judged on the basis of whether or not it is falls into line with what is considered to be "natural" and presented as morally normative. The methodological differences between the way the Church takes on social issues and how human sexuality and sexual behaviour are ethically evaluated has been the object of many, serious theological studies. It has also not escaped the notice of a growing number of the faithful who are acutely aware of these inconsistencies.

The development of a sexual and relational ethics that is positive, value-oriented, open, and consistent with the whole of the Church's moral teaching would go a long way to strengthening credibility in the areas of authority and governance in the Church in general. Further, it would open the way to better understanding what is really Christian in our approach to human sexuality and relational morality in general by setting us free from the narrow, act-centred, natural law ethics that has dominated this field in the past.

Having set ourselves free from a preoccupation with individual acts, we should be able to go even beyond the fundamental demand of responding to the needs and aspirations of persons and seek the meaning of genuine reciprocity in our ethical teaching. We will be able to transcend simple, behavioural rules and look to the larger issues and the long term development of human relations in all their individual, familial and social dimensions. Recognising that the Sabbath has been created for humankind and not the opposite way around, we can respect and deepen our appreciation for the function of rules and expectations rather than being enslaved by them.

Finally, we may come closer to recognising and realising our vocation to practice empathy and mutuality in all our human relationships, both intimately with other human persons and socially in our relations to all other human persons who are corporeal and therefore sexual beings. We are all children of God, whether male or female, whether sexually active or celibate, whether enjoying fruitful and meaningful relationships or suffering loneliness and brokenness. We believe that all human persons are created in the image and likeness of God and that our existence in this world, though temporary, is purposeful and significant in the eyes of God. It is therefore our calling not to reject human sexuality but to embrace it and to celebrate it for the gift that it is.

Selected References

Cahill, Lisa Sowle. *Sex, Gender & Christian Ethics* (Cambridge: Univ. Pr., 1996).

Dominion, Jack. *Proposals for a New Sexual Ethic* (London: DLT, 1977).

Guindon, André. *The Sexual Creators: An Ethical Proposal for Concerned Christians* (N.Y./London: Univ. Pr. of America, 1986).

Kosnik, Anthony, et al., *Human Sexuality: New Directions in Catholic Thought* (London: Search Press, 1977).

Selling, Joseph, "The 'Meanings' of Human Sexuality", *Louvain Studies* 23 (1998) 22-37.

PART IV

EMBRACING SEXUALITY

Chapter Ten

Sexuality: Personal, Communal, Responsible

Lisa Sowle Cahill

The essays in this volume are unusual and commendable in that they offer a nuanced treatment of sexuality that both celebrates its power and warns of its destructiveness; that both deconstructs traditional Christian strictures on sex, and retrieves values like commitment and parenthood needed to channel sex in positive directions. The contributors testify to the intrinsic ambivalence of sexuality. It is private and public, good and bad, psycho-spiritual and intensely physical. While a modern view of sex is likely to define it as private, good, and spiritual, it is not entirely a provocative overstatement to say that Christian tradition judged sex a public danger, more often evil than virtuous, and more a sign of the corruption of the body than of the transcendence of the soul. Such a generalisation calls for nuance, of course. While the influential sex theorist, Augustine, saw sex primarily as an unruly physical passion needing to be rigorously disciplined through the institution of marriage and the justifying purpose of procreation, it is also true that authors from Saint Paul to Thomas Aquinas saw sex as something that unites spouses in a relation of reciprocity coloured by love, leading their relationship toward children, a social as well as personal gift.

Present and Past

Today we might think that the biggest distinction between pre-modern Christian views of sex and our own is that the former emphasised the dangers of sex, with an eye to social control, while we celebrate sexual pleasures, with an interest in sexual opportunity. There is much truth in such an idea, but it rests on an even more important underlying distinction. While modern-day people (at least in Europe and North America) see "sexuality" as primarily a personal capacity, experience, or activity, for most people in other cultures and eras, sex is primarily a social phenomenon that expresses or creates the individual's social roles and defines the person in his or her social space. This is why "procreation" is so prominent a feature of ancient definitions of sexual morality, whereas our term "sexuality" refers to an individual's experience of sex, rather than to her or his partner or social context.

Michel Foucault explains that "sexuality" is a modern term, one that is part of and helps constitute a discourse of sex in which it is in the "truth" of sex that we hope to find the truth of ourselves and to live with authenticity.[1] Since Freud, not only is our sexuality our key to meaning, but that meaning is found through the introspective re-appropriation of our own sexual impulses. St. Augustine, in contrast, had so much difficulty separating sexuality from the social roles and obligations of parenthood and marriage, that he could portray individual sexual experience only in negative terms, as lustful, self-indulgent passion too often sundered from its justifying connection to procreation, the common good, and the divine creative purpose.[2] In reality, sex or sexuality is both personal and communal (beginning with the interpersonal). Responsible sexual behaviour must take into account both sides of this reality.

Similarly, sexuality is both physical and psychological. Physical sex gives us an opening to transcendence, not only through the quasi-ecstatic state of union some may experience in sexual acts, but also through the ongoing personal relationships with partner and family that sex anchors in the relationship of the committed sexual couple. While earlier authors like Augustine manifested appreciation for this transcendent possibility of sex by linking *sacramentality* with commitment, fidelity and offspring, current Christians see sex itself and sexual pleasure as key dimensions of a personal, sexual relationship that has spiritual potential.

In sum, Christian tradition past and present identifies several values related to sexuality that define its positive aspects and help us to understand the nature and causes of its distortions. The goods of sexuality include the sex act itself as physically unitive, pleasurable, and possibly reproductive; the fact of reproduction, continued and socialised in a relationship of parent and child; the co-operation of sexual partners forming a domestic partnership for mutual aid and in raising their child; and the affective relationship of sexual partners, hopefully a positive one, enhancing their sexual, domestic, parental, and social partnership.

These values have been recognised and prioritised differently over time, within a broad range of the cultural contexts. Various assumptions, values, and institutions have had a significant impact on the Christian or Catholic approach to sexuality. In recent times, Catholic teaching about sexual morality has been defined by *Humanae Vitae*[3] which, while forbidding artificial means of birth control and advancing traditional procreation-centred norms for sex, describes sex as both procreative and unitive. This encyclical defines sex in interpersonal terms as the "mutual self-gift" of the couple, a gift in which sexual pleasure as well as physical union and procreation play at least an implicit part. This transition reflects modern cultural values, including the equality of the sexes, the importance of personal fulfilment and love in human relationships, and the idea that personal psychosexual experience is as important in defining marital love as are the domestic, economic, and social relationships that the couple may share. Greatly diminished if not gone entirely is the emphasis on controlling and restraining sexual passion lest it easily devolve into "lust".

A Christian Perspective

The current Catholic appreciation of sexual love as both bodily and spiritual, personal and communal, good or even sacred (within limits) has taken a long time to evolve. For example, it is a cultural and historical fact that marriage and family can be conservative institutions that organise material goods and social benefits to the advantage of social elites and their relatives, and in which women and children are often controlled by patriarchal interests. This is one important reason why early Christianity hesitated to endorse marriage unequivocally as a structure of discipleship and instead held up the counter-cultural practice of celibacy as a Christian ideal. Even so, marriage and parenthood could be paths to holiness for both men and women (1 Cor 7), and churches formed in and around the homes of Christian families.

Although marriage did not come to be officially defined as a sacrament until the Council of Trent (1545-63), there was a "sacramentalising" tendency regarding marriage as early as Ephesians 5:23, with its comparison of the love of Christ for the church to that of a husband for a wife (gender unequal though the implications of that analogy may be). Sexuality took on value within this context, even though St. Paul held up no special duty of Christians to procreate. Procreation was a duty generally imposed on married couples in the ancient world, one geared not to their own satisfaction, but to the welfare of family and state. Serving these traditional authorities was, however, not key to Christian identity, or at least not to its radical call to give up possessions and embrace the stranger, the needy, and the outcast. Christian authors like Augustine realised that conceiving and rearing children can be a form of service to society and church. Yet they did not think parenthood equal in importance to celibacy, which had the dual function of resisting cultural norms and of taming dangerous sexual drives. The gradual development of a sacramental theology and practical norms for marriage may seem in some ways to constrain and even repress sexual love through the requirements that spouses make an indissoluble commitment and try to produce offspring. However, indissolubility as grounded in personal consent (defined at Trent) was also a way to ensure that marriages were entered upon by the free will of the couple, that they could not be ordered or ended by families for political and economic reasons, and that fertility would not be a test or precondition of the formation of permanent marriage.

Positive sexual ideals yielded by Catholic tradition are commitment and parenthood (the familiar "unitive and procreative" meanings of sex), informed increasingly today by the values of gender equality and affective reciprocity and depth. Fortunately, we are witnessing in many cultures an increase in gender equality: rights for women in sex, marriage, and family, and legal prosecution of sexual and domestic abusers. We see people entering marriage because of personal attraction and commitment, and not only due to social necessity. Sex today is seen more as an expression of personal fulfilment and of interpersonal relationship, and less as a means of producing heirs (at least in "modern" societies). Nonetheless, manipulative sex, uncommitted sex, transitory sex, sexual abuse, infidelity, and lack of responsibility are still around.

An Outdated View?

The fact is that most theologians currently writing about Catholic sexual morality remember Vatican II as a formative experience in their moral, religious and theological outlook. We tend to react to contemporary debates about sex on the basis of mental, emotional, and moral frameworks formed at that time. We often define the important questions largely in terms of *Humanae Vitae* and its more or less immediate aftermath. These effects are, of course, still felt today, especially in inner-ecclesial debates about "orthodoxy" in moral theology.

But young people whose sexual identities and behaviour are being formed now have grown up in quite a different culture, both ecclesially and socially. Many of our concerns may seem outmoded to them. They may face new and different problems. Not least among these is the fact, that, unlike the repressive culture of the 1950's (in Europe and North America), their culture is extremely permissive, even to the point of being nihilistic. "Embracing sexuality" may sound less like a liberating new Catholic agenda, and more like the blare of MTV. The answer, of course, is not to invent new sexual repression. Yet we need to recover and, where necessary, reinvent the positive ideals and even norms of the tradition. Can we interpret Catholic tradition in such a way that positive sexual ideals are attractive in their own right, and actually make sense of the world as we (and our children or students) experience it?

Many of today's young people, at least in post-industrial societies, are growing up in a sexual culture that is directionless and trivial at best, nihilistic and exploitative at worst. As Richard Bernstein wrote in a review of a new novel by Amy Sohn, a young "sex columnist" for a "conservative" New York weekly, we are witnessing "a sort of spiritual inversion in which sex, for example, along with a cynical, solipsistic self-satisfaction replaces the outward-looking idealism that was once characteristic of youth".[4] Younger Catholics are completely alien to the cultural space of the 1950's that immediately preceded and was partly responsible for the Council and its reforms. If sexually repressive and gender unequal, it was at least a culture with a sense of purpose in which sex was controlled for a reason. Young Catholics today are unlike "our" generation in that they are not striking out against this culture, nor can they rely on whatever safety went along with it.

As Anna Roper comments in her essay for the present collection, the younger generation of Catholics is facing a culture in which television productions like *Ally McBeal*, *Friends*, or even *Sex in the City* influence behavioural norms and expectations. On the one hand, the Church seems to respond slowly, not at all, or counterproductively to pervasive cultural trends. On the other hand, many young people realise from their own experience that sexual aimlessness and experimentation can be empty, frustrating, or painful. Moreover, it disguises gender inequities in prevalent sexual customs (including female responsibility for pregnancy) that seem hardly less acute than in previous generations. The Church – not only its "official" authorities but all of the members who are aware of these problems – need to speak out against distorted, trivialising, and exploitative sexualities. But how? And what precisely is the message that is needed, can be heard, and will be effective?

Non-traditional Attitudes

There is a significant minority of young adult Catholics, at least in the U.S., who embrace papal teaching about sex and gender, including the limitation of birth control to "natural" methods, because they are looking for ideals, inspiration and discipline in a chaotic sexual world. It is important to realise that such young adults are not necessarily reconsidering traditional practices because they are afraid of hell, a confessor, or the ire of their parents. In the spirit of their generation, they adopt these views as a free choice and as embodying a more meaningful sexual life than the alternatives they think are available.[5] Most are firm believers in gender equality and in equal access for women to education and employment, whether or not they own the name "feminist". They often subscribe to the current papal view that equality does not preclude a special nurturing role for women, though they would recoil from the subordination recommended as recently as 1930, by Pius XI, in *Casti Connubii*. Such ethical commitments cannot be easily dismissed as "out of touch" or "reactionary". On the contrary, they are responsive to ingredients in our current cultural mix that we, in their parents' generation, ignore at the peril of a truly contemporary Catholic ethics. We need to move past a 1970's framing of the issues, and shape a coherent Christian answer to sexual relativism.

This is essential if we want to be heard by other young Catholics (the majority?) who are caught somewhere between the culture's sexual "do everything" and the Church's "do virtually nothing". They know that committed love and the rewards of parenthood are valuable long-term aspirations, though they do not permit themselves to be defined exclusively by such goals. In the meantime, they want a sense of sexual and personal integrity that can sustain them through times of confusion, social pressure, loneliness, and disappointment. To these young women and men, Catholicism can and should speak a word of encouragement and inspiration, calling them to high ideals of commitment and service without focusing on prohibitions or being unduly condemnatory of the need for discernment and growth.

Recent developments in our moral tradition (yes, including parts of *Humanae Vitae*) can offer groundwork for this task. Several positive developments have emerged as a result of Vatican II. First, even *Humane Vitae* comes out of and represents a more "personalist" approach to sexuality, in which the "intersubjective" relationship of the couple is the ground of all else, including their long-term commitment, their sexual expression, and their endeavour of shared parenthood. Secondly, within this general rethinking of sex as expressing a personal commitment and relationship, a much higher priority is given to that relationship in defining the morality of sex. However imperfect it may be, the current pontiff's repeated insistence that procreation is a necessary aspect of sex, because without it, the "self-giving" relationship itself would be defective, is an illustration of this trend. (I would affirm that the relationship is the condition of possibility of moral sex and moral parenthood, but would not then go so far as to say that any sex act that "artificially" avoids conception is a violation of this interpersonal relationship. The final analysis may be wrong, but the line of thinking is correct.) Now it is rightly understood that procreation is not just "a physical function", much less one properly attributed to individual sex acts. Parenthood is an entire personal and social relationship, that must be undertaken with responsibility and commitment (developing the theme of "responsible parenthood").

Thirdly, gender equality has begun to emerge, even in Catholic sexual morality, reflecting wider cultural trends toward the expansion of social roles for women. On the topic of sexual morality, one might well ask whether the limitation of birth control to what are often unreliable means really is consistent with sexual and parental equality for women and men. Many Catholic feminists (myself included) take exception to the proposal that motherhood is the highest vocation of women in a way that is not true of fatherhood for men, or that women's "special genius" is nurturing, or that "true femininity" is easily threatened by women's public roles (these ideas are all suggested in *Familiaris Consortio*). Still, it is quite a change to hear John Paul II proclaiming that women should have equal access to all social roles and functions (as he does in *Familiaris Consortio*), or that the Church bears responsibility for complicity in sexism (as he does in his 1995 *Letter to Women*), compared with what was emanating from Rome a generation or two ago.[6]

Re-reading Tradition

In summary, the sexual morality that has surfaced in recent tradition holds sex to be an expression of mutual, reciprocal love and commitment between two equal partners, with children and parenthood as expressing and fulfilling *this relationship*, rather than as required components of individual sex acts. This broader understanding, developing even within the magisterium, has resulted in a loosening of norms on contraception, divorce, premarital sex, and homosexuality. This is true of institutional teaching and practice, to an extent (e.g., the "pastoral" approach to birth control and annulments, the pastoral acceptance of candidates for marriage who are already living together, and outreach to those of homosexual "orientation"). But it is certainly much more true of "unofficial" moral theology, some grassroots pastoral practice, and the practice and viewpoints of lay Catholics. This discrepancy is, obviously, what has constituted sexual morality as an area of crisis of authority and governance within the Catholic Church.

While more flexibility in sexual morality is in general a good development, we should not neglect attention to some undeniably negative aspects. What seems like appreciation and integration of sex as "just another part of life" can mask pressures, especially on young women, to be sexually active outside of committed relationships, and that can be quite exploitative of women and children. A similar evaluation can be made of readily accessible divorce. The ability to end a marriage can represent a possibility of escape for maltreated partners, and this is important. Yet a completely non-judgmental attitude increases the possibility of abandonment for those whose partners seek greener pastures. Divorce today, as well as the refusal of some men to make commitments to sexual partners in the first place, have contributed to what some U.S. authors (including the bishops) have termed "the feminisation of poverty".

For all its faults, Catholic moral tradition has been marked by a positive commitment to moral truth and to concrete moral guidance. The role of conscience needs to be more respected in determining what individual moral responsibility requires, and the social determinants of sexual behaviour need to be taken explicitly into account. In these ways, past teaching was inadequate and harmful. Even more importantly today, the voices of those previously excluded from defining "normative" sexual morality need to be taken into a conversation about good or virtuous sexual behaviour that will always be open-ended and never finally complete. A multicultural and intergenerational conversation might, indeed, generate some critical insights about values held by both the defenders of orthodoxy and its typical "revisionist" adversaries. We might learn that sexual freedom is not the burning issue that it was in the 1960's and 1970's, and that parenthood, family and community are much more important and valuable parameters for defining sexual identity and conduct in Asian, African, and Latin American traditions than they are in the minds of the "liberal" Catholic academy. I think (or hope) that greater participation by women of all cultures in defining sexuality in relation to personal fulfilment, family, and social roles would lead to a morality of more mutual and equal sexual relationships for Catholics (and others) everywhere.

The crisis of authority concerning Catholic sexual morality is not primarily caused by the teaching Church's continuing insistence on certain norms of the past, especially since people who do not find them to make sense are not following them in any event. Younger Catholics follow Church teaching if they find it congenial to their own experience and needs, not simply because it is passed down from an authority or couched in threats and sanctions. The real crisis in Catholic sexual morality is to provide credible moral leadership in defining the parameters of a responsible, satisfying, and authentic sexual life. Such leadership cannot just emanate from the hierarchy, but depends as well on the co-operative efforts of theologians, laity, religious educators, teachers, pastors, parents, and young people just discovering what sexuality is about.

A genuinely traditional sexual morality should be formed by the values of embodied sexual pleasure and union, affective unity, commitment and fidelity, shared parenthood, and partnership of life. If today's Catholic sexual morality is also to be genuinely contemporary it must incorporate newer values of gender equality; relational, familial, and social justice; some flexibility in accommodating ideals to concrete situations; and a sense of moral perspective in which sexuality is accorded the respect it deserves, without disproportionate emphasis, as one element in a coherent moral life.

Notes

1 Michel Foucault, *The History of Sexuality, Volume I: An Introduction* (trans. Robert Hurley; New York: Random House, 1978) pp. 68-70.
2 Augustine, *City of God*, XIV. 24, 26.
3 Paul VI, *Humanae Vitae* (Boston: St. Paul Editions, 1968).
4 Richard Bernsten, "Generational profile? No, It's the Sex, Stupid", *New York Times*, August 20, 1999.
5 See Jennifer J. Popiel, "Necessary Connections? Catholicism, Feminism and Contraception", *America* 181 (1999) 22-25.
6 See John Paul II, *Familiaris Consortio* (Washington D.C.: United States Catholic Conference, 1981) nr. 23; and John Paul II, "Letter to Women", *Origins* 25 (1995) 138, 139-143.

Chapter Eleven

Dialogue and Institution

Marcella Sires

The Art of Dialogue is a difficult one for many people to master. Dialogue does not only imply two people talking with each other, but more pointedly, it describes the process of two different voices being expressed and being heard clearly. Paying attention to clear self-expression and taking the responsibility for and ownership of one's thoughts, feelings and beliefs is but one movement within the entire process of dialoguing. Another of these moments, beautiful in its simplicity and equally as difficult to accomplish, is the Art of Listening. Active listening is listening with an open mind and an open heart and with the great hope of actually trying to come to an adequate understanding of the point of view of the other. Dialogue involves an openness to change.

The Art of Listening

The Art of Dialogue is not the same thing as the Art of Persuasion, although very often the latter is misrepresented as dialogue. True dialogue is not an attempt to convince the "opponent" to abandon the error of their beliefs and then to insert the truth of one's own conviction in its place. Points are not scored or tallied, it is not a winner-take-all scenario. Dialogue is not a debate nor a verbal competition. In true dialogue there are no losers, as both sides win. When describing dialogue as an openness to change, one is not alluding to an attempt to change the other party but rather to an openness to allow change to happen within oneself. Dialogue entails the possibility of coming to a new understanding, gaining a new perspective. It is the possibility that an idea or insight that was not previously there may come into being precisely through direct interaction with the other. Dialogue has the potential to move participants beyond their initial starting points. It is, in a sense, a mutual journey of discovery and creation and as such, in addition to the fatigue of hard work and focused attention, can be accompanied by a sense of satisfaction, joy and wonderment. Understanding and change does not necessarily lead to agreement but it is the process of developing the necessary foundational steps for any type of possible agreement to be built upon.

It will come as no surprise that at the very essence of this process of dialoguing is the exercise of focused, active listening. Often through inattentiveness and the inability to stay focused in the immediacy of the moment, active listening degenerates to passive listening and finally a simple monitoring of words and sentences. To maintain active listening one must pay close attention to the words and ideas of the other in a very mindful and focused fashion, periodically checking to see if the message heard was indeed the message sent, if the idea interpreted was indeed the idea intended. Unfortunately, many people are sloppy listeners. Having heard a bit of the message they often jump to the assumption that they know exactly what the other means and where the other is leading them in their conclusions. This can lead to confusion in so far as the listener is often busy formulating their responses to the assumed stance of the other while simultaneously monitoring the words of the other, thereby splitting their attention to the moment ever farther. Rather than listening in a focused fashion they actively fill in the rest of the message themselves thereby taking on the roles of both sides of the dialogue and negating the need for the presence of the other altogether.

Active listening entails the listener taking responsibility for checking and clarifying those ideas and messages that are unclear. There is a genuine interest in this asking for clarification of details. It is an honest attempt for the listener to try to stay with the thoughts of the other in order to facilitate understanding. This genuineness is a very different attitude from one of constant interruption. It is not the use of questioning to try to trip up the other or to outwit them or even to insert editorial comments of one's own. It is an attempt to clarify discrepancies that may be causing real confusion or misunderstandings rather than simply the pointing out of inconsistencies to the other in an attempt to discredit the message or even dismiss the messenger.

Trust and Respect

One of the obvious obstacles to active listening and openness is a lack of trust in the other. How well do I know this person? How safe is it to speak from the heart and leave myself vulnerable? Will my own words be used as a weapon against me? Is the other truly open to dialogue? If I listen to them with an openness to change, can I reasonably expect that there will be a mutual openness on their part to the hearing of my message as well? Will I really get a chance to express myself at all? Does the other realise that change does not mean assimilation into the belief system of the other? Will they play by the rules?

Respect for the other, precisely as other than self, is a crucial attitude throughout the entire dialogue process. Oftentimes an interpretation of the history of the relationship between the dialoguing parties will inhibit the attitudes of openness, trust and respect necessary for change to take place. Monologues are engaged in utilising such tools as holding fast to pre-suppositions, second-guessing the strategy of the other, or even attempts at "mind reading". The other begins to take on stereotypical status, encouraging the development of relational myths replacing the here and now reality. Listening becomes distorted and only that which validates the caricature of the other that is being built in the listener's mind will register or be heard. That which does not fit the image will be conveniently ignored. The "otherness" of the other becomes a self-fulfilling prophecy and a limiting, impoverishing definition of who they are and what they believe. The other is labelled as hostile and/or dangerous. The conservative, the liberal, the authoritarian, the rebel, the gay, the straight, the youth of today, the righteous, all are born in this movement. The richness of a real person is lost and replaced by the poverty of a stereotype. All information and behaviour will be suspect and interpreted within the frame of reference that we ourselves have built up as a projection of our own deepest fears and anxieties. Defensive and pre-emptive tactics are employed to ensure our safety and survival. Fear has become an obstacle to openness to change. There is no trust and little or no respect for the other as other. Fear is now an obstacle to dialogue.

Trust is not naïveté. Trust as it is used here is not only seen as a thing in itself, as a foundation of the dialogue, it is also the description of a relational attitude. It is part of an ongoing process and as such it is being checked and tested continuously. A certain amount of caution is realistically called for when proceeding in a dialogue. Trust builds upon itself in progressively increasing layers of intimacy, verifying, testing, proceeding and sometimes retracing itself. Trust is both a condition for and a consequence of good dialogue. While already noting that fear can be a paralysing obstacle to dialogue, a certain amount of healthy respect and awareness of the other as other can be a highly motivating factor. It urges us cautiously on to engage in the mutual exploration of thoughts, feelings, ideas and beliefs through dialogue. This moves us beyond the realm of simple conversation into the realm of dialogue.

Dialogue with(in) Institutions

Dialoguing with another individual can be a difficult art to master. Dialoguing with an institution is actually impossible. One can only dialogue with people, with the other. One cannot dialogue with "the Church" as such. There can be ongoing dialogue within the Church, among its members, but the parts cannot dialogue with the whole of which the parts are a constitutive member. How, then, does one dialogue within an institution?

If one can only dialogue with individuals, then identifying the parties or the partners within the institutions with whom to dialogue becomes the issue. Within the institution there may be individuals who are recognised as official representatives of the ideas, beliefs and values held and affirmed by the members of the institution and as such may be granted the authority to speak on behalf of the other members. There may be people who through their insight, wisdom, or specific expertise are recognised as authorities in their field and have become recognised spokesperson for other members. There may even be those speaking to remind us that there are many who, for what ever reason, remain or are forced to remain silent and should not be simply overlooked or discarded.

Hopefully the partner who will give a face to the other will be someone who has the ability to listen, show respect, and enter into true dialogue with others with a willingness to change. Too often those who are most enthusiastic and emotionally committed to one extreme belief or are dedicated and committed to defending one specific position put themselves forth in the role of spokesperson. While recognising the sincerity of their belief and their loyalty to their positions, it is not always evident that the people who are the most visible, vocal or committed to a particular cause are the ones most skilled at handling the situation. How well can they listen? How trusting are they of the sincerity of the other? How respectful of the other partner are they when faced with a different voice? How open are they to change?

One must also be cautious that the person who functions as spokesperson in a dialogue is not put into a position where there may be a conflict of roles, creating a conflict of interest. Ideally someone who simultaneously functions to judge, sanction, censure or grant or withdraw rights and privileges should not be caught up in this situation. Threats of sanctions and censure and the fear that they instil have no place in dialogue. That is coercion.

Stasis and Homeostasis

Unfortunately, it sometimes happens that the participants in a dialogue forget about listening to the perspective of the other and become preoccupied with the outcome of the entire process instead. In such a case, patience, trust, and respect for the other as other are put aside and the dialogue takes on the proportions of an argument. The content of the argument and the end conclusion become the motivating factors for interpersonal engagement. A power struggle, often based on the claim of the exclusive ownership of objective truth or the correct insight into reality ensues. These attitudes, especially when dealing with individuals claiming to represent an institution, are usually in function of maintaining homeostasis and the identity of the institution, as they envision it. Change is perceived as a threat to the continuity of the institution itself and perhaps to the position of the individual within the institution. The argument from this position can be seen as an attempt to protect both themselves and the institution from attack. The argument is motivated by a sense of self-defence in function of survival. The other is viewed as a danger and becomes the identified enemy. Again dialogue is not possible if there is no trust in the partner and the very process of dialogue itself.

On the other hand, other members of the same institution may be attempting to incorporate new ideas and experiences and initiate movement and growth to guarantee the survival of the same institution precisely through change. Those cautioning conservation or even a return to older ways are seen as a hindrance to progress and renewal. Those maintaining the status quo are viewed with suspicion for having lost touch with the real world and the real problems confronting many of the institution's members. The fear of stasis leading to obsolescence and extinction is as real and important to them as the need for homeostasis is for the other.

Both arguments are motivated by the desire to maintain the survival of the institution of which both are members. Both parties in their own way are very loyal, even loving members of the same institution. Finding or creating a balance that allows enough change for growth and enough conservation for continuity is a very difficult task. A distrust in the ability of the other to listen and understand and even a very deep-seated distrust of the motivation and behaviour of the other create an atmosphere non-conducive to dialogue and openness.

Getting the balance between stasis and homeostasis, conservation and renewal should be an ongoing process whose positive tension should help to ensure the continuation of the institution as well as dialogue among its individual members. A recognition of the mutual dependency of the institution and the members who constitute it should motivate if not mandate continuous dialogue among those loyal and loving members who may have very different, individual life experiences. It is only when there is a recognition of this loyalty to the institution that trust can begin to be established. Recognition and respect for the other as other, as a unique individual, and simultaneously as same, as a loving, loyal and concerned member of the same institution as myself, is an essential element in fostering that trust. Together we need to identify the purpose and good of our institution and decide together what behaviours, changes and constants will best promote those ends.

If the individual members walk away from each other in frustration and disillusionment the institution will eventually disappear. If the institution cannot grow in a changing world it will become dysfunctional and obsolete and will not be able to meet the needs of its members. If members refuse or cannot maintain a certain level of coherency and belief in the essential tenets necessary for the recognition of the identity of the institution and their own membership in it, they threaten the very existence of the institution. If certain members of the institution fail to recognise the membership of other members of the institution or claim to be able to unilaterally judge what tenets are essential for membership in the institution they doom the institution to become a relic of itself.

Dialoguing is an act of trust. Dialoguing within the institution is an act of generosity. Dialoguing among the members of the institution is an act of sharing based on Faith. Dialoguing within the Church is a sign of Hope and an act of Love.

Chapter Twelve

Marriage and Sexuality in the Catholic Church

Mary Grey and Joseph Selling

In 1997, a working group was put together by The Research Centre of The Queen's Foundation for Ecumenical Theological Education, in Birmingham, to study what was perceived to be a deepening breakdown in communication between the hierarchy of a number of Christian Churches and significant portions of the ordinary faithful. This project had as its goal to convert what was perceived by many to be a "confrontation" into a "conversation" in which both parties would make an effort clearly to express what they wished to say and to listen to what the other party was putting forward.

The project, which came to be known as the conversation about "Authority and Governance in the Church", and which ultimately was concerned with points of tension within the Roman Catholic Church in particular, was subdivided into a number of themes and subprojects. Perhaps the most elaborate subproject of this endeavour, which culminated (but hopefully has not ended) in Robinson College, Cambridge in June 2000, was that dedicated to issues of marriage and sexuality. Two seminars were held at Sarum College, in Salisbury, in December 1999 and March 2000 in order to bring these issues into "conversation". Every member of the hierarchy in Great Britain was invited to participate in these seminars, but no bishop was able to attend. Apart from the Abbot of Ampleforth, no representative or participant of the governing structures of the Catholic Church took part in the seminars.

Sarum College was chosen as the venue for these seminars because of its emphasis on developing theological programmes that focus upon the lived experience of the believing community. Across the scope of issues that appeared to beg for more elaborate "conversation" within the Catholic Church, marriage and sexuality seemed to merit particular attention. Traditionally, issues in sexual and marital morality are decided upon and judged by members of the (male) hierarchy, none of whom have a direct, personal experience in the questions that frequently surface in these fields. While no one who took part in the seminars even suggested that ethical issues should be decided on the basis of majority opinion, or exclusively by those who have personal experience of and interest in the matters under discussion, there was a strong feeling that the experience of the faithful in these matters was not being reflected in many of the pronouncements of the magisterium. Many fail to "find themselves" in the teaching of the Church about marriage and sexuality.

The Sarum seminars consisted in the presentation of nine papers, a workshop on communication and two reports on the experience of priests and religious in regard to sexuality.[1] Each of the papers was presented and responded to by persons with theoretical knowledge and/or years of practical experience in the topic they were asked to address. Each presentation was followed by a discussion, and the two seminars concluded with an overall evaluation in two parts. At the end of the second seminar an attempt was made to summarise the ground that was covered, the points made and those that were missed, as well as the principal issues that the group wished to be brought forth at Cambridge. In a second stage, all the participants were invited to respond in written form within the weeks following the conclusion of the seminars. The use of electronic mail available to the majority of participants greatly aided this process.

The evaluation and commentaries on the seminars were compiled by the authors of this essay and presented to the parent project in June 2000. The following represents a synthesis of those written and verbal presentations. Two general comments should be made before we present the synthesis. First, the participants at Sarum were convinced that young persons were severely underrepresented not only in the seminars but also and especially in most public and private, social and ecclesiastical discussions on sexuality and relationships. Perhaps too few young persons are invited to such participation; perhaps few young persons feel that anything can come from their participation. Whatever the cause, the effect remains that most discussion that takes place in (Roman Catholic) Church environments is basically carried on by an older generation, frequently one that is still concerned about questions that have little to do with the experience, concerns and priorities of young persons.

Secondly, the participants at Sarum were virtually unanimous in reporting their appreciation for the practical learning that comes about through a process of active and engaged listening. On the one hand, we recognised that most of the participants were "ideologically similar", sharing the same problems with the current moral statements of the Church and expecting the solutions to those problems to move in a certain direction. We realised that there were few "dissenting voices" participant in the seminars, and in retrospect, some suggestions were made about the need to redress that imbalance. On the other hand, the participants deeply felt that although a genuine effort had been made on the part of the faithful to listen to the teaching and advice of the magisterium in these matters, precious little listening has been done on the part of the representatives of authority and governance in the Church to the experience, the witness and the advice of the faithful. We fear that if this situation does not change, the gulf that exists between official teaching and the experience of the faithful will continue to widen.

Attention to the Traditional Teaching

A curious element in a minority of the responses to the seminars was the observation that there was no forum provided for airing, explaining and possibly even defending the traditional teaching of the Roman Catholic Church in the areas of marriage and sexuality. This came as something of a surprise, for a major presumption in organising the seminars in the first place was that there was a certain problem of credibility about that teaching which was well known. Although the Church's teaching and practice in the areas associated with human sexuality continues to function for some members of the Church, it is no longer considered helpful or even meaningful by other members. The problems being faced by this teaching are either widespread, as with respect to the issue of contraception, or experienced by more particular groups, as with respect to the issue of homosexuality. There are any number of issues that lie between these two poles, including questions involving human fertility in general (the enhancement as well as the limitation of fecundity), the pre-marital practices of a growing number of persons in the developed countries of the world (including cohabitation), and the entire area of women's experience in the Church.

Furthermore, one of the stated purposes of these seminars was not simply to air the points of disagreement or lack of credibility but to communicate these issues to members of the governing hierarchy of the Church. With the intended audience of the seminars to be the members of the governing bodies, the aim was twofold. First, and relatively superficially, it was intended to name the areas of difficulty as experienced both by the general populace of the Church and by specific groups within the Church. Secondly, the intention was to investigate what is being experienced by many as an impasse between the hierarchy and the laity by exposing the underlying causes and dynamics of the issues. Thus, the majority of the presentations for the seminars were geared to expose and explore the issues in depth, offering an alternative manner of understanding the points of disagreement. Conversation, and not confrontation, was the hope.

Nevertheless, it is a valid observation that if one wishes to present an "alternative" view of things that departs from a so-called traditional or "received" teaching, it is fair that such teaching be clearly known and understood. It was assumed by the organisers that those called upon to give presentations as well as the members of the hierarchy who were invited to participate would be familiar with these teachings and be aware of the points of disagreement. This, however, did not prove to be the case. For a small number of participants felt that the actual teaching and practice of the church in these areas was not given sufficient exposure. In order to address this, we believe that we must outline the contours of that teaching for the sake of continued discussion.

The Teaching of the Hierarchical Magisterium

The first problem in delineating this subject area is the meaning of the term "magisterium". Up until roughly the first Vatican Council (1870) this term was used primarily to refer to those who had developed a specific competence in teaching and explaining the content of the faith of the Church. The term "magister" was (and still is) used as a title for the highest degree conferred upon a theologian, usually on the basis of work already accomplished, especially on the basis of publications which were deemed worthy by professional colleagues. At the time of Vatican I, with the promulgation of the concept of infallibility, the teaching function in the Catholic Church began to become more centralised in Rome. The juridical power of the hierarchy to intervene in order to settle disputes of a theological nature began to be extended to the actual practice of teaching itself.

At first, this presumption into the area of teaching remained dependent upon the "recognised authorities". However, as the Vatican began to expand its notion of what constituted its teaching prerogative, it also began to assemble its own group of "in house" theologians who had a tendency to think along the same lines, being as they were chosen not only by the same authority but also on the advice of those who were already in place. Eventually, members of this teaching corps became promoted to the ranks of the hierarchy, and the appointments that were made to the positions of the new "teaching authority" came more from the ranks of the hierarchy than from the theological community.

Still, in the nineteenth century, classical authors were considered the primary source of theological wisdom. Leo XIII's elevation of St. Thomas and his theology to the ranks of semi-official teaching had a tremendous influence upon what was considered acceptable teaching. Leo XIII also took the step of assuming the role of universal teacher by expanding the encyclical tradition and using this medium to disseminate his ideas on a world wide scale. *Rerum Novarum* (1891) is considered by most observers to constitute the modern "origin" of the social teaching of the church. One could suggest that this same pope's encyclical *Arcanum Divinae Sapientiae* (1880) constitutes the beginning of papal teaching on issues of conjugal morality, although the content of this text is largely restricted to the juridical status of the sacrament.

Previous to the papacy of Pius XI (1922-1939) *Arcanum* was the sole document from Rome that touched upon issues connected with the marital state. There were, of course, countless statements which came from the Roman

Penitentiary and which ruled upon specific questions of a moral nature. These were aimed primarily, if not exclusively, at confessional practice and were not intended to be a source of teaching.

When Pius XI promulgated his famous encyclical, *Casti Connubii* (1930) in reaction to the Lambeth Conference of the Anglican Community in that same year, he formulated the first systematic approach to conjugal and sexual morality that was ever issued by a Roman pontiff. In doing so, Pius XI chose the teaching of St. Augustine as his primary inspiration. Thus, the first modern, centralised magisterial teaching on marriage issued by Vatican authority was essentially an interpretation of the teaching of a fifth century, North African bishop. We must stress that this teaching represented an interpretation, for a comparison with the original texts reveals significant differences between Augustine and the representation of his teaching in the encyclical.

On the one hand, Augustine taught that each and every act of sexual intercourse between married persons which was not aimed explicitly toward procreation constituted an at least venial sin. This doctrine is summed up in Augustine's classical phrase *concubitus propter solam procreationem*. Augustine also believed that it was through the act of sexual intercourse that original sin was passed on to children. Thus, there was an assumed, direct connection between an act of sexual congress and the coming into being of a human person – the bearer of original sin – even though there was completely no understanding of how the biological processes of conception took place.

On the other hand, the teaching of Augustine had already gone through centuries of interpretation at the hands of the theological community. Even Thomas dared not neglect his teaching, although he himself drastically mitigated the dualism present in Augustine's works and played down the pessimism of his attitude toward sexuality. In the time following the council of Trent (1545-1563), theologians, who were primarily teachers in seminaries, used Thomas more than they did Augustine and became heavily reliant upon the dictates of canon law rather than upon schools of theological and philosophical speculation. The result of this trend was a heavy emphasis upon the appeal to something called "natural law" to deal with issues of a moral nature that were not explicitly enunciated by biblical injunctions.

The Argument from Natural Law

To make a long story short, the approach to sexual and conjugal morality that began to be formulated and promulgated by the hierarchical magisterium in the first half of the twentieth century was dependent upon a certain interpretation of classical authors and based primarily upon a particular interpretation of the so-called natural law. According to this interpretation, human sexuality was and is a biological phenomenon which was created for the express and sole purpose of propagating the species. Any deviation from this norm was considered to be immediately gravely sinful. There was no such thing as "light" or non-serious matter in sexual sins. Simply giving consent to any thoughts or actions which might, however remote, lead to any form of erotic awakening or stimulation was considered gravely sinful. Between a husband and wife, any erotic awakening must ultimately culminate in an act of "natural" sexual intercourse in which nothing was done to impede the possibility of fertilisation taking place.

When the knowledge became available that fertility might be predictable (circa 1925), the married couple could know with relative certainty when their sexual encounter would in all likelihood not lead to procreation. This phenomenon was first addressed by Pius XI in his encyclical of 1930 and his teaching was that such an act remained free from sin, so long as the structure of sexual intercourse remained intact, with semen being deposited in such a way that, were the women fertile, this would result in procreation. Pius XI justified this with the argument that sexual intercourse "also" could be used to satisfy the "secondary ends of marriage" (as laid down by canon law in 1917)[2] provided that nothing is done to interfere with the physical structure of the act. This teaching represented the first time that the Catholic Church allowed for the moral justification of a sexual act that was known to be infertile. Even in such circumstances, however, it was still considered necessary that such an act remain, to use the words formulated by Paul VI, "open to procreation", even though procreation was impossible.

The teaching of the magisterium on this issue, however, was far from complete. For more than twenty years the Church struggled with the question whether it was morally licit for a married couple to *intentionally* limit their sexual activities to the period of infertility for the purpose of avoiding procreation (so-called "periodic continence"). This issue was finally resolved by Pius XII in 1951 who ruled that this practice could be tolerated as long as there were "serious reasons" (medical, eugenic, economic or social) to avoid the realisation of the "primary purpose of marriage".

Ironically, the manner in which Pius XII changed the traditional teaching on the regulation of fertility was more juridical than theological or moral. The argument he used was that the "obligation" to procreate, and hence propagate the species, is a positive obligation that rests on the shoulders of the entire human race. Therefore, the individual couple could be "excused" from participating in this communal obligation if they had a sufficient, "serious" reason.

What relatively few people noticed, however, was that the teachings of Pius XI and Pius XII set up a paradox for sexual morality in the Church. On the one hand, both popes admitted that (at least marital) sexual activity did not have to be explicitly procreative in order to be morally upright. According to Pius XII, and later Paul VI, a couple could even go to great lengths to be absolutely certain that procreation would not take place. On the other hand, the teaching of the hierarchical magisterium insisted that every explicitly sexual (i.e., genital) encounter must culminate in an unhindered act of intercourse, so that semen is deposited in the proximity of the cervix. This is the act which is so-called "open to procreation", even though the couple may have gone to considerable trouble to insure that procreation would not happen.

This paradox manifests itself on many levels, the most obvious of which are physical (do something that exposes you to a result you wish to avoid) and verbal (an infertile event is "open to procreation"). More significant is the theological paradox: God, who is the "author" of natural law, created sexuality exclusively to bring about procreation, but the Church has ruled that a couple may avoid procreation while still remaining sexually active. Yet the Church upholds its position on the evil of contraception, as well as any other sexual activity, on the basis of its interpretation of the natural law, namely, that God created sexuality for the purpose of achieving procreation. Although it has never been admitted by the magisterium, with the teaching on periodic continence the natural law approach to sexual morality had reached a cul-de-sac.

A Brief Attempt at Theological Revision

When 2500 bishops gathered for the Second Vatican Council addressed the topic of "fostering the nobility of marriage and the family" in the first chapter of the second part of the Pastoral Constitution, *Gaudium et Spes* (1965), they were aware of the fact that however the reigning pope, Paul VI, might later choose to deal with the question of contraception (see footnote 14 in *GS*, Part II, Ch. I), something had to be said about the Church's understanding of human sexuality. The Church could no longer describe sexuality simply as a biological, procreative mechanism, especially since the two previous popes had admitted that the marital sexual encounter was capable of realising other ends or purposes without any possibility for procreation being present. Pius XI had cited the secondary ends of marriage as a valid, while Pius XII had even accepted moderate pleasure as a worthy goal.

In the text that passed through many drafts and that finally achieved the overwhelming approval of the vast majority of bishops, it was clearly stated that, "The sexual characteristics of humankind and the human faculty of reproduction wonderfully exceed the dispositions of lower forms of life" (*GS*, 51). And in explicit connection with specific sexual activity, the council fathers wrote: "[Conjugal] love is uniquely expressed and perfected through the marital act. The actions within marriage by which the couple are united intimately and chastely are noble and worthy ones" (*GS*, 49). Note that this observation occurs in a section of the Pastoral Constitution that does not even mention procreation.

From such observations, many theologians and pastors took the cue that human sexuality should no longer be thought of or written about only in terms of its procreative potential. That is why so many had expected that the "traditional" position regarding contraception would change and why so many were disappointed with the promulgation of *Humanae Vitae* in 1968. That papal letter not only repeated the teaching that any form of artificial contraception is "*intrinsece inhonestum*", it introduced a new teaching that had never been seen before, namely that there were in fact two, inseparable "meanings [*significationes*] of sexual intercourse", namely the procreative meaning and the unitive meaning.[3] This had never been taught before.

What is more, the encyclical returned to a biological understanding of the sexual encounter by emphasising that "each and every conjugal act must remain open to the transmission of life".[4] Since the practice of periodic continence had been accepted since 1951, the only meaning that the phrase "open to the transmission of life" could carry would be the deposit of semen through an act of sexual intercourse. It is the "generative faculties as such" which exhibit an "intrinsic ordination towards the raising up of new life" (*HV*, 13). Some attempts to explain and defend the encyclical after its promulgation emphasised that there was not just one (procreative and therefore physical or biological) meaning to be protected but in fact two (the unitive meaning as well). Nevertheless, the Vatican's own "Declaration on Certain Questions concerning Sexual Ethics", (*Persona Humana*, 1975) based its entire teaching upon what it referred to as "the finality of the specific function of sexuality" (*PH*, 5). No mention is made in this document to the so-called "unitive meaning" or the need to realise two meanings simultaneously in the same act. The only thing that is invoked to establish a moral norm is the integrity of the physical act of heterosexual intercourse – a purely biological phenomenon.

From 1968 until the present time, the Vatican has continued to defend its teaching on the whole of sexual morality based upon its interpretation of the "natural law" which dictates that human sexual activity must always be aimed at achieving its finality, its "openness to the transmission of life". This is especially true with respect to the Vatican's evaluation and condemnation of homosexuality which is said to be "intrinsically disordered", precisely because it cannot achieve the essential "finality" of the sexual function, namely being "open to procreation".

Developments Outside of the Magisterium's Teaching

While the magisterium's teaching about human sexuality returned to a natural law paradigm after 1968, the human sciences exploded with new studies and insights into the meaning and potential of human sexuality, particularly the importance of sexuality in personality formation and individual expression. It became clear at first to the researchers and, with the parallel explosion in the communications media, shortly thereafter to the general public, that human sexuality was an extremely flexible and multidimensional phenomenon.

Not all the news, of course, was good. For we simultaneously became aware of how human sexuality and sexual gestures not only could but frequently were being used as expressions of aggression, domination and manipulation, even within marriage.

By the third quarter of the twentieth century, the woman's movement had gained not only momentum but credibility across a widening spectrum of contexts. Not the least important item on the agenda of this movement was a revaluation of human sexuality with a particular emphasis upon something that had been almost completely neglected in Western culture, namely the female experience of sexuality. Until the groundbreaking studies of Masters and Johnson,[5] few had even bothered to consider the physiology of female sexual pleasure. Even the Church had for the most part neglected the so-called "sexual sins" that could be committed by women. Masturbation, for instance, was looked upon largely as a male issue.

Against this background, it began to appear that the magisterium's position on sexual morality was disproportionately focused upon male eroticism and ejaculation. Much too little attention had been given to the fact that sexuality itself, whether or not male ejaculation takes place, is fundamentally an interpersonal and communicative phenomenon. Yet, the primary norm that continued to be invoked was that of the "procreative finality of the faculty".

In stark contrast to this, many people were encountering another set of values which were tied up with human sexuality: intimacy, mutuality, affection, affirmation, a sense of self and of other. They were discovering that a sexual encounter doesn't just say "I want to have a child with you". It also says: I love you, I enjoy being with you, I wish to be close to you, I want you to enjoy our being close as much as I do, I appreciate you, I respect you, I wish to give you pleasure and to receive pleasure myself, and I wish to care for you and to be cared for by you.

At the same time, we must not blind ourselves to the negative and destructive things that the sexual encounter could be saying. Our moral sensitivity leads us to reject such messages and the manner in which they occur. Therefore, there develops a heightened awareness of the evils of child and spousal abuse. Indeed, the proclamation of "family values" which ignores injustice within the family has weakened the Church's credibility. Sexual exploitation and harassment form an integral and morally significant part of contemporary consciousness. Yet, it was not the mainstream Churches or the magisterium that led the way in denouncing these evils. In many cases, unfortunately, quite the opposite occurred and ecclesiastical structures were discovered to be denying and covering up cases of known sexual abuse.

Whatever has occurred during the past few decades in regard to our experience and understanding of human sexuality will simply not go away. For better or for worse, the genie will not go back into the bottle. One can refer to it as one wills, sexual revolution, sexual liberation or sexual degradation. The one thing that one cannot do, without utterly destroying credibility, is to remain blind to the fact that these changes have taken place.

The Need for Change

Before we highlight some of the issues that the participants at Sarum believed needed to be reassessed, it is good to point out that we did wish to express an appreciation for the positive aspects of the traditional teaching and the valuable contributions that the Church continues to make in this area. The Church has always taught, for instance, that human sexuality is deeply personal and not to be equated with mere animal sexual differentiation. Regardless of some deviations in the past, most of which it must be pointed out were frequently made anathema, mainstream teaching has always upheld that being-a-woman and being-a-man, in relation to others, is a God-given vocation that should be lived out in love and respect.

Human sexuality has always been characterised as something good. It constitutes a very special part of what it means to be a person in relationship. It involves intimacy and vulnerability. Therefore, the circumstances within which sexual encounter takes place are very important. Social structures, such as pre-marital customs and prohibitions, function to protect persons and to help create the best possible situations within which personal relationships can grow and mature.

Human sexual relationships have always been described in the context of familial and social ties that go beyond the individual couple. Sex is not a private thing, simply reducible to the narrow criterion of "two consenting adults". Because of the intimate connection with procreativity, human sexuality has always been understood in an intergenerational context. It is not just "babies" that are important here but families, relations, kinship, and future generations. Even without procreativity, however, human sexual relations always have an impact upon all of our "other" relationships. The relation that takes place through a sexual encounter, if not typified as a form of bonding, still creates and alters ties with entire clusters of persons. We neglect this at our peril.

There are a number of aspects of traditional Church teaching on marriage and sexuality that merit close attention and repetition. These, however, were not the focus of the seminars. For there are other aspects of that teaching that no longer function in a credible manner, particularly in light of the new knowledge that has been gained about human sexuality and relationships and the validation of the experience of countless persons who see their sexuality not as something dangerous and in need of control but rather as a gift of God to be celebrated.

Many believe that it is time for the mainstream Christian Churches to change. We should strive to go beyond a natural law conception of human sexuality and embrace everything that we have learned about this wonderful gift from God. We need to investigate further how it can be used and misused. We will not accomplish this by holding on to "old ways" and defending valid but radically partial perspectives (such as the absolute good of fertility). We need to go beyond the expanding but still too narrow idea of the so-called "procreative and unitive meanings". For in the final analysis, everyone knows that these are merely code words for an obsolete view of a very complex and fascinating human phenomenon.

The teaching of the past, coming as it has from the top down, has not sufficiently responded to the issues that trouble us most. Some of that teaching, in fact, has been experienced as dysfunctional. Families who suffer from material deprivation or who have already given birth to and raised several children are told that if they use contraception they are acting in a manner that is "anti-life". Victims of broken marriages who have been trying to rebuild their lives and even provide some kind of care and stability for their children have been told that they must remain single or live like brother and sister with someone who truly cares for them. Parents and families of homosexual persons are told that their children and relatives have a condition that is "intrinsically disordered" and an offence to the God who created them. Homosexual persons themselves are told that they are incapable of leading normal lives, that they cannot express love and affection in any way other than through acts which are selfish and depraved, and that they should not expect to enjoy the same civil rights as heterosexual persons. Young persons are still being told that sex is dangerous, cheap and a serious source of moral guilt, unless one is married, which somehow makes the very same acts legitimate (although not really all that nice).

Most of the participants at Sarum felt that, whether or not the leadership in the Church chooses to recognise it, and whether or not one accepts the argument that the admission of periodic continence signalled an end to the necessity of a procreative "end" (*Casti Connubii*), "meaning" (*Humanae Vitae*) or "finality" (*Persona Humana*) for human sexual relations, a huge proportion of women and men in our society, especially young persons, no longer accept the idea that sex is always about, or must always include, an "openness to procreation". This is not enough. We need a wider, less naturalistic and more personalistic concept of human sexuality upon which to build a credible and communicative sexual morality. We need a broader understanding of human relationships in order to sketch out how human and Christian values can be realised and protected in the world in which we live.

Furthermore, we need to go beyond the relatively narrow, private view of human sexuality that has dominated moral teaching in the past. Appreciating the connection between intimacy and sexuality is one thing, ignoring it in just about every single discussion about human sexuality is quite another. Like a growing number of (especially young) people in our society, we should exhibit a willingness to discuss sexual matters without fear or embarrassment. We need to face the fact that sex and sexual relations are no longer a taboo in Western society. If anything, the media exhibit a view of sex that is omnipresent and demanding, and few would disagree that the commercialisation of sex borders on the absurd. However, we will not deal with this adequately by accepting the role of passive submission, hiding from the very conversations in which we should be outspoken participants.

From Sexuality to Gender Issues

There is a new awareness that all sexual experience is gendered experience. We cannot separate sexual issues and gender issues and expect to achieve any kind of a reasonable hearing. Being-a-woman and being-a-man in the world in which we live is not simply about assuming roles which have been pre-determined and passed on from generation to generation. Every generation redefines itself and prioritises its values in response, not necessarily in imitation, to previous generations. The strides that women have made in society, in the workplace and in the family over the past two generations have not been reflected in official Church teaching in any meaningful way. While "gender-equality" falls from the lips of those who preach social justice, little or none of this is reflected in Church practices.

It cannot be denied that the dominant model of understanding sexuality has been based upon the male experience. This most often focuses upon penetrative sexual intercourse in which men are characterised as active perpetrators and women as passive recipients. This model in itself forms an apt basis for a wide range of abuse, but its more subtle reflection in social relationships has also resulted in a parallel social model of domination and submission in general. In contrast to this, the female model of sexuality tends to be focused on relationality, mutuality, affectivity and tenderness. One could make a good case for such a model to reflect gospel values more closely.

Another aspect of a male dominated view of sexuality is that women are inevitably held up to a biological, essentialist ideal of "motherhood" as their supreme, if not exclusive, vocation. While men are almost never judged upon their success in playing out the role of "fatherhood", women are expected to be models of self-giving and self-sacrifice. While appreciating that we live in times when the family is fragile and vulnerable, we believe that the way to strengthen the family unit and build stronger relationships is not through insisting that women seek their fulfilment solely through motherhood, but rather that men be expected to adopt and live out the values that women have symbolised for time immemorial.

Toward New Generations

There can be little doubt that Pope John Paul II has been one of the most charismatic figures of our day. Most everywhere he goes, he attracts crowds of people, some onlookers, many devout. At the same time, few will disagree that the kinds of devotion practised by those who admire this extraordinary Bishop of Rome are not all the same. Some may indeed share John Paul's visions of women as mothers, of sex as always open to procreation and of alternative lifestyles as contrary to God's wishes.

Others, however, may admire the charisma but have a much more selective attitude toward relational and sexual mores. There are several studies that demonstrate that the behaviour of Catholics does not differ significantly from that of the general population. The size of Catholic families is not significantly different (larger) than those of non-Catholics. Catholics divorce at about the same rate as the general population. And many young Catholics appear to share the same anxiety about marriage as their non-Catholic contemporaries and take the option of cohabitation at least prior to if not as a substitute for sacramental marriage.

We do not intend to suggest that the entire Catholic populace lives in a manner that is no different from the so-called secular society. We only wish to point out that there is a pluralism of lifestyles and moral expectations among Catholics that reflects the cultures within which they find themselves. As is to be expected, this manifests itself most clearly among the younger members of our communities who are either more adaptable or more easily influenced by the forces around them.

Nor do we wish to suggest that our goal should be simply to accommodate ourselves to the current patterns of behaviour. For we know that there is both good and bad in most cultural phenomena which needs to be carefully discerned.

What we would like to plead for is an open attitude that is not blinded to the good because of its zealousness to find and denounce what at first appears to be bad.

We believe that many young persons are looking for leadership to help them deal with the uncertainties of a world that seems to make everything possible but appears to promise little and guarantee nothing. Against the background of egoism, commercialism, and what might justifiably be called hedonism, sincere persons are looking for alternative visions of how to live, how to build relationships and how to come to terms with their sexuality. We believe that if we embrace human sexuality for the gift that it is, we can come to accept it into our lives and teach our children to accept it with responsibility and love for themselves and for others.

So how shall we go about such a task? The first thing that needs to be done is that those who teach and preach on the subject should be fully informed on its history and development through time. What is being taught today is significantly different from what was being taught at the time of the council, during the pontificate of Pius XII, during the earlier pontificate of Pius XI, and certainly very, very different from the classical textbook tradition. In the name of intellectual honesty, we should abandon misleading phrases such as "constant teaching".

Next, we should review the sources that we use to present a specifically Christian view of human relationships and human sexuality. Besides admitting that textbook theology was primarily based upon a very particular, narrow school of philosophical thought, we should also face the fact that very little classical moral thinking made any attempt to draw its inspiration from Sacred Scripture. This is certainly true in respect to sexual morality. The Old Testament is referred to in a highly selective manner. Some passages are presented uncritically and with little or no recognition of context, such as the stories of Onan and Sodom. Other passages are conveniently ignored, such as the purity stipulations of Leviticus that forbid sexual relations during menstruation; while others never seem to have any influence, such as the sexual imagery of the Song of Songs.

When it comes to the New Testament, virtually no attention is given to Jesus' teaching on the commandment to love in sexual ethics, and St. Paul emerges as the primary if not exclusive source for moral teaching, although the process of selective reading is once again used here as well. All of Paul's writing is deeply immersed in specific contexts, and it is necessary to interpret each of his letters in that light. Further, it is now common knowledge that St. Paul drew upon Stoic philosophy in his moralising and wrote with the expectation that the Lord would be returning before his own death. These influences had a profound effect on his understanding of marriage and sexuality.

That said, we should be able to take a leaf out of Paul's own journals and seek out the best available information and understanding of moral matters before we begin to make our own pronouncements upon specific items. Paul turned to the Stoics and the classical philosophy of his day. In our own time, we can turn to the human sciences to provide information and to alternative (to the natural law) moral methodologies to point in the direction of responsible and loving behaviour.

Integrating New Information into the Church

There is a tremendous amount of information available about human sexuality and human relationships that is hardly ever tapped into by Church teaching. Anthropology, sociology, psychology and sexology are valuable starting points for understanding how human persons relate to each other within various social and historical contexts. This is the data of experience within which people live. It describes the material of ethical discussion in ways in which people will be able to understand.

The "Pastoral Constitution on the Church in the Modern World" states,

> If by the autonomy of earthly affairs we mean that created things and societies themselves enjoy their own laws and values which must be gradually deciphered, put to use, and regulated by the human community, then it is entirely right to demand that autonomy. Such is not merely required, but harmonises also with the will of the Creator. For by the very circumstance of their having been created, all things are endowed with their own stability, truth, goodness, proper laws and order. We need to respect these as we isolate them by the appropriate methods of the individual sciences or arts. Therefore if methodical investigation within every branch of learning is carried out in a genuinely scientific manner and in accord with moral norms, it never truly conflicts with faith. For earthly matters and the concerns of faith derive from the same God. Indeed whoever labours to penetrate the secrets of reality with a humble and steady mind, even though unaware of the fact, is nevertheless being led by the hand of God, who holds all things in existence, and gives them their identity. Consequently, we cannot but deplore certain habits of mind, which are sometimes also found among Christians which do not sufficiently attend to the rightful independence of science and which, from the arguments and controversies they spark, lead many minds to conclude that faith and science are mutually opposed. (*GS*, 36)

In light of this, how can we continue to ignore the insights of the human sciences when it comes to this area of moral discourse? This is not to suggest that "science has the (ethical) answers", only that whatever ethics has to say about a given area of human endeavour should reflect the actual situations being addressed and not simply present an abstract model of human behaviour. In other words, we need to pay more attention to human experience.

How can the Church continue to ignore the experience of the faithful in an area of human life that they are living day by day? Without wishing to disparage the good will and the sincere dedication of the clergy and religious, it has become difficult for the overwhelming majority of the faithful to understand and accept official teaching in matters of marriage and sexuality that is being formulated and taught by a celibate minority. Many, if not most, of the faithful do not recognise themselves or their lives being reflected in at least some of that teaching. In their experience, (openness to) procreation does not constitute the most important, and especially not a primary and absolutely necessary element, of sexual relations. What is essential to understanding and living sexuality is love, respect, mutuality, trust and joy. Discovering one's partner and oneself is a journey of many years, thousands of encounters and uncountable details, many of which are unique to this person, this relationship and this historical and cultural setting.

Marriage and the forms of sexual expression and encounter that are an intimate part of that relationship are not something that magically come about with the public pronouncement of vows. Marriage, at least in the operative model in the Western world, is a relationship that grows from first meeting through various stages of friendship and intimacy, into different levels of commitment, through the trial and error of building a working relationship, into the complex reality of sharing the same home, resources, limitations and opportunities, along with the possible arrival and presence of children, into a maturity of years and the growth of their own offspring, past the thresholds and crises of partnership, parenthood, and, for a steadily increasing portion of the population, into the beginning of yet another form of commitment that can span several decades into old age and a completely different kind of relationship.

Teaching about the "primary and secondary ends of marriage" pales in comparison with this rich diversity of human experience. The same can and must be said about the tragedy of marital breakdown and the subsequent, real termination of a relationship which has exposed the individuals involved to a pain and grief that will never be fathomed by a person who has never married. When the Christian community that defines itself as living in the love of God and neighbour refuses to recognise that pain and offer solace, it clouds the ordinary person's ability to recognise the message of the gospel that must be lived as well as spoken. When the Church that claims to possess the keys to bind and loose on earth cannot find a way to offer reconciliation to the victims of this tragedy, it throws into question its ability to represent its very founder who could forgive anything, "seventy times seven" (Mt 18:21-35).

To turn once more to the young persons in our community, it would be an equally tragic mistake to ignore the experience of precisely those persons who are searching for an authentic, and at the same time realistic, vision of human sexuality and relationships. They live in a world where sex is commercialised and trivialised but, curiously enough, also in which sex is dealt with much more openly and honestly than it was in previous generations. While older people may say that sex is neither wicked nor dirty nor something to be ashamed of, many younger people are simply living that out to its logical conclusion.

These young persons live in a world where individual relationships are no longer understood as the single, defining factor of personal identity. Marriage is no longer seen as an "end point" in one's life: the end of being single and independent, the end of experimentation and creativity, the end of mobility, change and development. What is more striking is that marriage is not understood as a guarantee of permanency. Like all human relationships, it is fragile and vulnerable. It is not a haven from the world but, like the Barque of Peter itself, it is a vessel that must weather the storms and calms of life. It needs fuel, supplies and constant maintenance. And although all loving relationships may be headed for the same ultimate goal in the Reign of God, the route by which they make their way is far more diverse than all the shipping lanes in all the seas of the earth.

Regardless of what we might like to think, this is the experience of young persons and it is precisely this experience which needs to be addressed. It does not respond to clichés and platitudes. It cannot be fit into a single mould. Nor is it about to be submissive and obedient to some voice of authority that presents unrecognised, abstract models of human behaviour and relationships.

In fact, the entire project of listening to, rather than speaking at, the experience of the faithful, including the younger generations, in the Church can present an opening for the enrichment of our understanding of Christian living and even the sacraments. For too long, Church teaching has been preoccupied with the dangers of sexuality and its abuse. Sexual activity involves pleasure which, in turn, could easily become a substitute for the entire range of goods and values that such activity might serve. Preoccupation with that pleasure has bred fear and suspicion. So far has this gone, that many consider sexual desire to be synonymous with the "pursuit of pleasure".

Suppose, however, we began to think of sexual activity as a means for giving pleasure rather than simply receiving it. Could it not function literally to em-body a loving relationship, by giving pleasure to a beloved? And what, then, of the receiving of pleasure as a gift from someone you love, respect, and – obviously because of our vulnerability – someone you trust? To allow oneself to be loved, to open oneself to receiving the signs and symbols of love, to expose oneself to the touch of another, to let oneself discover the joy, the pleasure, the ecstasy that is only available at the hands of another, could there be any better preparation for opening ourselves to the gratuitous, overwhelming and blinding pleasure that we (will) experience in the presence of God?

If the whole Church listens to the experience of the whole Church, there is much to be gained. The people who gathered at the Sarum seminars and those who took part in the entire "Authority and Governance" project are loyal, faithful believers who are convinced that change is not only necessary but possible. Despite some feelings of frustration and even alienation, we remain within the structures that give human form to the people of God because we have confidence that the Church is capable of responding to the need for change and recovering lost credibility.

What gives us that confidence is the fact that the call for change is coming from within, from believers who retain the inspiration of Vatican II and the call to co-responsibility and collaboration. We believe in a theology for a "Pilgrim Church" that, although it may not have it "just right" at the moment, will move on to something else in the never ending search for truth under the guidance of the Spirit. We hope and we anticipate that the Church as the people of God will learn to embrace sexuality for the wonderful gift that it is.

Notes

1 Elizabeth Mann, "Psychosexual Problems of Male Priests and Religious", and Michael Doyle, "The Psychological Difficulties of Contemporary Priesthood: Problems and Solutions". These two reports were presented by Elizabeth Mann and were followed by questions, clarifications and discussion. There was no direct response to the reports as such. The material gathered in these two studies will be published elsewhere.

2 Canon 1013 § 1: "The primary purpose of marriage is the procreation and education of offspring; the secondary purpose is mutual assistance and the remedy of concupiscence."

3 *Humanae Vitae*, 12: "That teaching, often set forth by the magisterium, is founded upon the inseparable connection, willed by God and unable to be broken by man on his own initiative, between the two meanings of the conjugal act: the unitive meaning and the procreative meaning."

4 *Humanae Vitae*, 11: "*...quilibet matrimonii usus* ad vitam humanam procreandam per se distinatus permaneat."

5 William H. Masters and Virginia E. Johnson, *Human Sexual Response* (Boston: Little Brown, 1966).